Women, Poetry and the Voice of a Nation

For Joe and Caitlin

Women, Poetry and the Voice of a Nation

Anne Varty

EDINBURGH
University Press

Edinburgh University Press is one of the leading university presses in the UK. We publish academic books and journals in our selected subject areas across the humanities and social sciences, combining cutting-edge scholarship with high editorial and production values to produce academic works of lasting importance. For more information visit our website: edinburghuniversitypress.com

© Anne Varty, 2022, 2023

Grateful acknowledgement is made to the sources listed for permission to reproduce material previously published elsewhere. Every effort has been made to trace the copyright holders, but if any have been inadvertently overlooked, the publisher will be pleased to make the necessary arrangements at the first opportunity.

Edinburgh University Press Ltd
The Tun – Holyrood Road
12(2f) Jackson's Entry
Edinburgh EH8 8PJ

First published in hardback by Edinburgh University Press 2022

Typeset in Typeset in 10.5/13 Bembo by
IDSUK (DataConnection) Ltd

A CIP record for this book is available from the British Library

ISBN 978 1 4744 8984 3 (hardback)
ISBN 978 1 4744 8985 0 (paperback)
ISBN 978 1 4744 8986 7 (webready PDF)
ISBN 978 1 4744 8987 4 (epub)

The right of Anne Varty to be identified as the author of this work has been asserted in accordance with the Copyright, Designs and Patents Act 1988, and the Copyright and Related Rights Regulations 2003 (SI No. 2498).

Contents

Acknowledgements	vi
Introduction	1
1. Women, Poetry and the Voice of a Nation	3
2. The Laureate Roles: Three Poets and a Professor	15
3. Gillian Clarke: From Woman Poet to National Poet	35
4. Paula Meehan: Poetry across Boundaries	71
5. Liz Lochhead: Performing Scotland	100
6. Carol Ann Duffy: 'The edge has become the centre'	121
7. Answering Back: Poetry in Conversation with Wordsworth, Burns and Yeats	144
8. National Poets and the National Curriculum	167
9. Brexit and Britannia	194
10. Postscript for the Future	208
Works Cited	212
Index	229

Acknowledgements

Gillian Clarke, for permission to quote from her National Poet of Wales reports to the Academi/Literature Wales.

Warmest thanks to my friends and colleagues in the English Department at Royal Holloway for keeping momentum up during the pandemic, especially to Judith Hawley and all the members of Write Club.

Introduction

It's an extraordinary time for poetry. All three top posts in England, Scotland and Wales are held by women at present. As Duffy says: 'Yeah, you wait 400 years for a woman Poet Laureate and three come along at once.'[1] (*The Times*, 2011)

The appointment of Carol Ann Duffy to the role of Poet Laureate for the United Kingdom in 2009 was groundbreaking. It was the first time in the 400-year history of the laureateship that a woman had been appointed to this office. As a result, poetry by women became publicly validated as never before. In taking on public office for poetry, Duffy joined the serving National Poet of Wales, Gillian Clarke, who occupied that role from 2008 until 2016. Duffy and Clarke were soon in the company of Liz Lochhead, who was appointed Scots Makar for a five-year term in 2011. The Ireland Chair of Poetry, a laureate rather than a national role, serving the citizens of the whole island of Ireland, was held from 2013 to 2016 by Paula Meehan. For a three-year period, then, from 2013 to 2016, all laureate roles in the four kingdoms of the UK were held by women. While this fact did not escape the attention of festival organisers, it has received no critical scrutiny. This unique constellation of women in public office represents a watershed for poetry. It sets new horizons for the authority of who speaks in public, what subject matters can be addressed there and how nationhood is articulated. Their tenures have also presided over a unique era of growing self-assertion amongst the nations of the UK as well as growing political engagement with the relationship between human activity and the environment, subjects to which they all attend.

In the last decade of the twentieth century it was unthinkable that poetry by a woman could carry sufficient authority to be accepted as a public voice. But there was no shortage of ambition. Liz Lochhead exhorted her peers, '[w]e've just got to burst their bloody canon by the sheer volume and quality of what we say. That's my big hope for women and women's writing as we approach 2000.'[2] Nor was there a shortage of perseverance. Kathleen Jamie, for example, asserted at the millennium that 'much of writing is about permission. I mean here the long process of becoming a poet of any authority.'[3] Within just a few years of the new century, the tenacity and energy of such enterprises had been so successful that the effort itself seemed to have been forgotten. In 2008, for example, the North Wales *Daily Post* announced Gillian Clarke's appointment as National Poet of Wales with the headline, 'Poet to take on tenure as voice of Wales; Gillian to become ambassador for nation's verse.'[4] Almost overnight it seemed that women were stepping into the canon and assuming unquestioned authority, not just as isolated exceptions, but across all four nations of the UK.

What changed? This study sets out to understand how Clarke, Duffy, Lochhead and Meehan reached their laureate roles, what disabilities they encountered on the way, and what innovations for the articulation of national belonging are augured by their appointments. It begins with an exploration of critical attitudes to the legitimacy of women as spokespersons, yoking these with women's historical position as a second sex in relation to citizenship and therefore national identity. It moves on to present the formation of the National Poet and laureate roles within the UK, all of which except the Poet Laureateship arose as expressions of national or cultural identity emerging during the late 1990s in the context of political devolution.

Four central chapters scrutinise the work of each poet, with a particular focus on how they gained access to the business of publishing poetry in an environment dominated by men, on how each has critiqued prevailing representations of her home nation, and on poetic strategies by which each has moved from positions of liminality into the very heart of cultural institution. Three individually themed chapters follow. 'Answering Back' probes their appropriation of work by the nationally iconic poets Wordsworth, Burns and Yeats. 'National Poets and the National Curriculum' examines the sometimes fraught relationship between their work and school curricula which themselves convey nation-building politics. The study closes by tracing the way these poets and their peers responded to the polarising national politics of the Brexit referendum.

Notes

1. Dougary, 'Poetry is the music of being human'.
2. Quoted in Galloway, 'Introduction', in *Meantime*; cited in McCulloch, 'Women and Scottish Poetry, 1972–1999', p. 58.
3. Jamie, 'Holding Fast', p. 277.
4. Powell, 'Poet to take on tenure as voice of Wales'.

1
Women, Poetry and the Voice of a Nation

Gillian Clarke, Carol Ann Duffy, Liz Lochhead and Paula Meehan, as National Poets and as Ireland Professor of Poetry, stood together at the intersection of two historically conflicted relationships: between women and poetry, between women and nation. The tensions of these relationships, by turns creative and obstructive, have conditioned their careers and have been palpable throughout them. While the simultaneous appointment of women to all four leadership roles may suggest that frictions between women, poetry and nation have been largely resolved, this assumption cannot go unscrutinised. The critic Vicki Bertram asserted in 1999 that 'in terms of poetry's reception . . . many . . . are instinctively resistant to the idea of accepting a woman speaking on their behalf, as their spokesperson'.[1] Jane Dowson, writing in the same issue of the *Feminist Review*, stated 'as we approach the millennium, there is little foundation in literary criticism to believe that women's poetry will accrue an authority which it has failed to do in the last three centuries'.[2] This chapter sets the scene of the triangulated tension between women, poetry and nation, in order to see a context from which these poets emerged to assume the authority of public voice.

Outside History: Women and Nation from Virginia Woolf to Eavan Boland

In 1928 all adult women in Britain were enfranchised to vote for representation in parliament, granting them full citizenship on an equal footing with their fathers, husbands, sons and brothers. The political campaign for women's suffrage had lasted for approximately seventy years (if we take it from 1866, when J. S. Mill petitioned the House of Commons for women's suffrage), during which women's civic disabilities as well as their sexual and gender stereotyping had been placed under severe and contentious scrutiny. The bitter divisions of the campaign now belong to archives, but its final outcome has just departed from the living memory of the oldest generation in the UK. The names of campaigners are alive in cultural memory, proclaimed afresh in Eavan Boland's centennial poem, 'Our Future Will Become the Past of Other Women'.[3] In other words, the legitimation of British and Irish women by their nation is a recent and hardly historical change, while the terms on which women are included, or include themselves, in the state are still divisive. By any socio-economic measure, for example, women have remained, since the Victorian period, of lesser value than men; there is a gender pay gap and, two Queens and two women prime ministers notwithstanding, women occupy fewer and lesser positions of social, cultural and economic power than men. Andrew Parker has gone so far as to claim that '[n]o nationalism in the world has ever granted women and men the same privileged access to the resources of the nation state.'[4]

Not all women have wanted the same privileged access to the nation state. Virginia Woolf, writing in 1938, famously rejected the idea of nation altogether: '[a]s a woman I have no country. As a woman I want no country. As a woman my country is the whole world.'[5] Why did Woolf make these assertions? Do they express an aftershock of the centuries of women's internal exile, or a literary posture? Was her rejection of country the positive embrace of new territory? Or was it, rather, more rooted in contemporary politics, a reaction against the threat of National Socialism gathering on the Continent? Was it, rather, backward-looking, a rejection of patriotism and Empire following the First World War? Woolf's reasons for using one essentialist form of self-definition to counter another (woman versus country) may have entailed a combination of many factors, from which the only certainty is that she regarded a 'country' as a source of confinement.

In side-stepping the patriarchal structures of nationhood, putting aside the homogenising or normative identity of 'my country', Woolf was at least claiming some kind of liberty, for her politics as for her aesthetic choices. But as the feminist movement developed, particularly from the 1970s onwards, women, as writers and critics, increasingly viewed Woolf's opt-out as inadequate. Nina Auerbach, in an editorial for a collection of essays on *Woman and Nation* in 1987, is wary of Woolf's siren call: 'Do I or any of us want to relinquish our citizenship, nominal though it may be, in our countries or in any institutions, those of our profession, our religion, our cities or towns, on behalf of a mystic freemasonry of gender that says it will give us "the whole world"?'[6] Eavan Boland also identifies the danger: 'it is easy, and intellectually seductive, for a woman artist to walk away from the idea of a nation'.[7] Tension between being a woman and being a citizen is still evident amongst writers twelve years later: the poet Sarah Maguire asserted, 'I think of myself as a gendered, historical subject and I hope I have a nuanced, subtle, complex enough understanding of what that means for me not to be pressurized into writing "correct" poetry.' At the same time, Maguire concedes, 'although many of us are enormously privileged in ways our mothers could not even have dreamt of, we still inhabit a patriarchal society. We are not yet fully human.'[8]

Boland's work must be central to any discussion of the relationship between women poets and national belonging, as she has so clearly articulated the case of their historical exclusion and explored its consequences in the present. Her 2014 collection is named as a deliberate echo of Virginia Woolf's mantra, *A Woman Without a Country*,[9] a title which asserts that feminist acts of revision and recuperation are not restricted to the investigation of precursor texts by male writers. Boland's proposition is simple, and grows out of her experience as a poet. Women, she argues, have been silent and invisible in the written records of history and literature. Women have therefore lived their lives, she states, 'outside history'. Boland's phrase, 'outside history', to describe the historical erasure of women's lives, is the name of a chapter in her volume of autobiographical and critical essays, *Object Lessons: The Life of the Woman and the Poet in Our Time* (1995), and it is also the title of her *Selected Poems*, published in 1990.[10] The phrase surfaces again in Boland's 'Lesson 1' of her 2014 poem 'A Woman without a Country': 'My grandmother lived outside history. And she died there ... Did she find her nation? And does it matter?'[11] Here Boland reaches into the era of the campaign for women's suffrage, when activists were already articulating these issues.

Elizabeth Robins, for example, suffragist and playwright, anticipated Boland's argument in an essay entitled *Woman's Secret* (1905), in which she asserted, 'Schliemann may uncover one Troy after another, six separate cities deep, and never come the nearer to what Helen thought. All that is not silence is the voice of man.'[12] For Boland, it is not simply that women's voices have not previously been heard in public, but, as Robins' example of Helen of Troy suggests, women have been particularly co-opted to represent the nation in 'passive, decorative, emblematic' forms.[13] Marina Warner, in her 1995 study of the allegory of the female form, concurs:

> On to the female body have been projected the fantasies and longings and terrors of generations of men and through them of women, in order to conjure them into reality or exorcize them into oblivion. The iconography appears chiefly in public commissions and in the edifices where authority resides because the language of female allegory suits those in command.[14]

The historical subjectivity of real women has thereby been distorted, and their release from images made in the service of maintaining the status quo of political power has been made all the more difficult.

Boland considers the objectification of women and their exclusion from citizenship to be intimately connected through the feminine personification of the Irish nation, whether as Hibernia or, for example, '[t]he Cathleen ni Houlihan of Yeats's play and a hundred more subtle, understated feminizations of the national and nationalizations of the feminine'.[15] She devotes her critical work to identifying this situation, and her creativity as a poet to changing it. Engaging herself in a 'politic . . . where the previously passive objects of a work of art . . . become the authors of it' releases tremendous energy for her own poetic practice.[16] It facilitates, or coincides with, a similar liberation amongst other writers, vitality arising from resistance, subversion and opposition. Kathryn Kirkpatrick contends that, 'for women everywhere, the very act of writing challenges patriarchal practices of the state by representing national identity . . . as other than male'.[17] The transition from object to subject, image made to image makers, is primary in the relationship between women and poetry during the latter decades of the twentieth century. The process encompasses not simply the act of writing poetry at all, but also the representation of topics and revaluations expressed within it: negotiation with images imposed on women by patriarchy, changing aesthetic sensibility and criteria, repossession of roles previously used to contain women, transformation of the spaces they had traditionally inhabited, recovery of lost stories and reframing of history, new subject matters to include women's perspective and experience; ultimately a move from silence to voice, invisibility to visibility, individuation, an emergence into the public sphere and thereby a reconfiguration of the public sphere itself.

That these challenges have not been merely theoretical considerations but real lived experiences articulated by the poets considered here is evident throughout their careers and can be read off the most cursory glance at early titles of their work. Liz Lochhead's *Dreaming Frankenstein* (1984) trades in the supposed monstrosity of women's imagination; Carol Ann Duffy's *Standing Female Nude* (1985) defies traditional power relationships between artist and model; Gillian Clarke's *The King of Britain's Daughter* (1993) brings women into genealogy and inheritance; Paula Meehan's *Mysteries of the Home* (1996) foregrounds and amplifies the traditionally hidden, feminised space of the domestic.[18] Yet the release of such energy also entails risk. 'To be a creative woman in a gender-polarised culture is to be a divided self,' asserted the poet and critic Alicia Ostriker.[19] Writing as a divided subject, the hazard centres once again most specifically on the topic of authority. Without internal cohesion, can a woman speak with a single voice? How seriously are women prepared to take their own voices, newly audible to themselves?

For both Gillian Clarke and Carol Ann Duffy, the sense that women poets could hear each other's voices was vital for the development of their writing selves. There needed to be a tradition of women's poetry into which they could write, and there needed to be a professional audience. Instrumental in the creation of both of these conditions was the work of Sylvia Plath. Clarke wrote to Duffy that, 'in speaking when she did, Plath fired the wild hearts of the last silenced generation of poets in Britain. We all began to speak in our own way, because suddenly someone was listening.'[20] Of this pivotal moment in the 1960s, Duffy affirms, '[w]omen writers were listening to one another' as she acknowledges with gratitude her inheritance in the 1980s from the 'older sisters in poetry who had already cleared so much ground for my generation'.[21] The question remains, how seriously will others take them, their voices heard in public for the first time?

Women and Poetry: A Question of Authority

Since Boland uses her poetry as an instrument to redress women's exclusion from the historiography of national identity, this discussion has already tilted into a consideration of the second of the conflicted relationships: the friction between women and poetry. Germaine Greer summarises the problem in terms which link the patriarchal structures of national identity with those of poetic tradition: '[t]he more we know about the women who wrote poetry in English before 1900, the more we must realise that it is not a question of women poets having been ignored or obscured but of women's poetry remaining unwritten because women were disabled and deflected by the great tradition itself.'[22] Boland is an astute articulator of these deflections. She begins her 1994 lecture by stating 'I am an Irish poet. A woman poet. In the first category I enter the tradition of the English language at an angle. In the second, I enter my own tradition at an even more steep angle.'[23] Starting out in her career and wishing to locate herself within the Irish poetic tradition, Boland outlines her frustrations with the aesthetic practices of her predominantly male predecessors and the modes in which they represented women (if at all). She saw too that Irish Gaelic poetry had been suppressed by British rule since the eighteenth century, and that the Irish Anglophone poetry of the nineteenth century was compromised by colonial expectations of how a subordinate nation should express itself. She views representations of women during this period as projections of male imagination. The way in which she has tuned her poetry to these disadvantages and dispossessions is the story of her career.

For the purposes of this discussion, two critical responses to Boland's work help to advance understanding of the way poetry by women achieves, or fails to achieve, authority on a national stage. The first is an article by Alison Light, published in 1994, 'Outside History? Stevie Smith, Women Poets and the National Voice', taking Boland to task for her assertion that women ever lived 'outside history'. The second is the chapter 'Eavan Boland' by Justin Quinn, published in the 2017 *Cambridge Companion to Irish Poets*, edited by Gerald Dawe, a brutal and efficient demolition of every aspect of Boland's struggle to find her place as a woman poet within a national tradition.

To take each of these in turn, Light begins her inquiry by asking, '[is] there any particularly different relationship to nation and to its invention that could be traced amongst women writers?'[24] She follows this with another question. If women experience and express their sense of nation and their national belonging in ways which differ from men, 'how might this change (perhaps even revolutionise) our concepts of both nation and its history?' She proposes that women in the past have articulated their sense of psychic and bodily identity, and taken ownership of their domestic spaces, perfectly successfully; she posits that from the woman writer's point of view there has been no severing of a national sensibility, nor – and here she directly counters Boland – has she positioned herself, or been positioned, 'outside history'. It is rather the heroic narrative of nation which excludes her and diminishes her value. It is historiography, with its masculine measures of ambition and success, its sense of which actions matter for the sustaining or furthering of a nation's status, that has failed to take account of women and which has not aligned with women's experience of themselves within their communities and country. Traditional conceptions of nationhood, Light argues, have been deaf, for example, to the potential for nursery rhyme and fairy tale to express collective identity, blind to actions of domestic labour and the patriotic sources of its energy, unable to connect the private life of the home with the public life of the battlefield or debating chamber.

Crucially, Light does not argue for a breakdown of barriers between male and female experience, but instead celebrates variety and difference in ways of being English: 'it is precisely in . . . the setting up of internal as well as external boundaries to what the nation means and where it lives its sense of itself, that are central to what gives Englishness its resonances'.[25] She concludes with a plea to recognise the artificiality and contingency of nation itself, finally suggesting: '[u]ntil such time that women and the concerns which they have represented are recognised as having always been inside history, I don't think we can afford to keep our songs to ourselves.'[26] For all Light's resistance to the notion that anyone can be 'outside' history, and her persuasion that the exclusion of women from the national voice is due only to the patriarchal traditions which have determined it, what is fundamentally at stake for Light writing about the expression of being English is the same as for Boland writing about the expression of being Irish. The issue for both is 'the centrality of gender to the claiming of literary authority and to literary value itself.'²⁷

The questions of literary authority and literary value are at the forefront of the second response to Boland's work as a poet and as a critic to consider here, Quinn's chapter, 'Eavan Boland'. She is inaccurate, Quinn explains, to suggest that Irish Gaelic poetry was stamped out by English colonial rule in the eighteenth and nineteenth centuries; she is mistaken in her belief that Anglophone Irish writers of the nineteenth century appropriated indigenous folklore and poetry only to shore up a sentimental, colonised sense of Irish identity; she is arrogant and self-serving in her use of feminist ideology to foreground her own work as the single-handed saviour of Irish women, past and present. In sum, 'she has simplified many of the contours of Irish literary history, of gender issues and of politics'.²⁸ Quinn marshals many critics in support of these views. Amongst them is Brian Henry on Boland's poem 'The Achill Woman': 'it is an excellent example of Boland using the power of poetry to objectify other women while empowering herself'.²⁹ Alternatively, he cites the critic Ní Fhrighil's evidence that 'Boland was able to portray herself as a pioneer of Irish women's poetry only by erasing the significant achievements of her female forebears.'³⁰ He refers to Edna Longley's complaint that Boland overlooks the claims of Northern Ireland on fashioning and complicating what it is to be Irish. Concluding, he asks rhetorically, '[d]o a particular writer's inaccurate accounts of literary history, national history and gender, mean that we must take their work less seriously?' Quinn ends his essay with one claim for the positive value of Boland's poetry: he allows that she may be a poet of 'suburbia ... less compelling ... but still valuable as part of the anglophone poetry of the period'.³¹

If Quinn's objections to Boland's account of her enterprise are so self-evidently true, we might ask why it is that the volume in which his claims appear contains only one chapter on an Irish poet who wrote in Gaelic before the twentieth century (Aogán Ó'Raithille, c.1670–1729) and why the two further chapters devoted to Irish-language poets are about twentieth-century women, both of whom are near contemporaries of Eavan Boland (born in 1944): Eiléan Ní Chuilleanáin, b. 1942, and Nuala Ní Dhomhnaill, b. 1952. Finally, why, out of the thirty chapters in the book, are twenty-five about men while only four are about women, all of whom were born in the twentieth century? *The Cambridge Companion to Irish Poets* is published by an esteemed university press, edited by a distinguished poet and scholar, and takes its place in a highly regarded series of critical works, the Cambridge Companions. All these features give the publication an authoritative position in literary studies. This crudest numerical survey of its contents suggests that Boland's characterisation of Irish poetic tradition is not so easy to dismiss as Quinn contends, but that once again we are witnessing a destabilisation of the woman's voice by claims of ignorance, prejudice and arrogance. It can also be mooted that, by focusing on the detail of Boland's view of the fate of Gaelic poetry and the tenor of nineteenth-century Irish Anglophone poetry, Quinn misses Boland's larger point. At the heart of her historical observations is her claim that Irish poetry since the eighteenth century has been a colonised poetry, that the British occupied not just the land but also the language of Ireland, and that the emergence into post-colonial identity involves confrontation of lacunae and misrepresentation that is not unlike the difficulties encountered by the emergence of women into full citizenship and subjectivity.

And how are we to assess Quinn's evaluation of 'suburbia'? To present Boland's ambition to take her place in a national tradition of Irish poetry, and then to conclude that she should, at best, be considered as a poet of suburbia, is to offer a picture of failure. Yet even to accept Quinn's judgement at face value is to concur with certain assumptions. It is to presume that suburbia, with its aura of routine and repression, its eccentricities and fantasies, above all its littleness, its lack of defined location, the apparent smallness of its ambition, is not part of national life. Does the representation of ordinary life have no part in a nation's understanding of itself? Alison Light, comparing the relative standing of Philip Larkin and Stevie Smith on precisely the topic of their representation of suburbia, questions why it is that 'a bloke in his bicycle clips wandering into Church can represent the nation, but not the spinster or the schoolmistress'.[32] Light makes a persuasive case for the national importance of the suburban and its interiors both spatial and psychic. They are worthy of literary representation, she argues, and flow into the configuration of a nation, disruptive for traditional narratives of citizenship and public life though that might be.

However we wish to weigh its value today, suburbia is a liminal place, a threshold between city and pasture, a zone of change and exchange. This is exactly where Boland, in 'Anna Liffey', her narrative of national self-understanding, has placed '[a] woman in a doorway' as a medium to facilitate exchange, enlargement and enrichment.[33] The contrasting ways in which these two essays respond to Eavan Boland's work suggests that the argument about how much authority is accorded to women's voices is far from settled. It also suggests that, amongst critics at least, the shape of a nation, what a nation can or should include, is also still open to debate. Finally, and perhaps most disturbingly, given the quarter of a century that separates Light's work from that of Quinn, it suggests that literary criticism itself may be much more reactionary than the material it purports to interpret. While Quinn's parting shot is a statement of the pusillanimous quality of Boland's imagination, Light ends with an invocation: '[p]erhaps we must first have a woman Poet Laureate before we can be rid of Laureates altogether.'[34]

Light's imaginary woman laureate would, we assume from her argument, represent alternative pictures of national belonging, illuminate off-centre ways of living, self-understanding and social positioning that are conventionally unimportant to masculine narratives of nation. Her poetry would use forms such as fairy tale and nursery rhyme, cliché and common speech to interrogate the ordinary, suburban and liminal, forms as removed from the court and the debating chamber as their subject matter. The investing of such material with the authority of the laureateship would be, for Light, an achievement both literary and political. The resulting dispersal of central and centralising vision would, Light predicts, precipitate the abandonment of the laureate role itself.

The simultaneous tenure by four women in laureate roles within the UK and Ireland was not the decentralising solution she envisaged. Devolved government of the four nations was not at that time on the political agenda; women were economically and therefore socially less powerful than their male contemporaries, as evidenced by the need for the Equality Act 2010; and women poets were still far from achieving the respect and wide readership that would sustain a leading position. Yet the unforeseen appointments of Clarke, Duffy, Lochhead and Meehan legitimate a radical shift in the perspective of nation-building narratives, and sanction what Paula Meehan describes as 'the margins moving to the centre'.[35] Their appointments keep step with the devolution of political power following the referenda of 1997 and represent a realignment of cultural authority within the union in terms of both national and gender politics. Their embodiment of inherited and new boundaries, whether psychic or geopolitical, guarantees a remapping of territory.

'"Englishness"', Robert Hampson contends, 'is a text constantly being written, rewritten, interpreted and reinterpreted within a long history of the migrations of peoples and cultures.'[36] As women, these poets occupy the slant territory of the migrant, newly arrived in their home place where they are at once insiders and outsiders. They have assumed representative roles against the tide of tradition, which a chorus of critical voices in the 1990s predicted would be impossible. Not only by gender, but also by social class and family heritage, do they embody complex, hybrid identities by which 'English' (middle-class, white, male and English) is no longer the normative national identity within the UK. Duffy, for example, of Irish and Scottish parentage, has stated: 'when I go to Scotland I feel Scottish and when I go to Ireland I feel Irish. I suppose the one thing I don't feel is English.'[37] Set within a politics of nationhood, their appointments demand not only a recalibration of the historical relationship between women and poetry, but also a reconfiguration of national self-understanding. This chimes with Robert McCrum's question, as Andrew Motion's tenure of the laureateship was drawing to a close, 'can any single writer – poet, playwright or novelist – fully apprehend the British mood and give it lyrical expression?'[38]

It may be that only by writing from a position of former exclusion can such apprehension be approached, and that the previously oppositional perspective of the 'woman poet' is actually an advantage in demonstrating at least an ambition for change, diversity and inclusion at the heart of cultural institution. Gillian Clarke stated in 1985 that '[b]eing a woman and Welsh and therefore in two senses not wholly ready to count myself as one of the grown-ups, not easily able to feel I was permitted to be myself, to be a writer, an artist . . . I didn't begin writing properly until I was thirty.'[39] Just twenty years later, in 2005, Gwyneth Lewis was appointed as the first National Poet of Wales, marking the shift in according authority to a previously marginalised gender and nation. In the context of a four-nations United Kingdom, the position of UK Poet Laureate is relieved of some of the responsibility to 'fully apprehend the British mood' in being flanked by the National Poets of Scotland and Wales, and by the Ireland Professor. Together these roles assert a degree of heterogeneity within the idea of 'British' identity in the post-devolution United Kingdom.

Confirming her acceptance of the laureateship on Radio 4 during an interview on *Woman's Hour* on 1 May 2009, Duffy stated that being a woman was the deciding factor: 'I think my decision was purely because there has not been a woman. I see this as being a recognition of the great women poets we now have . . . and I decided to accept it for that reason.'[40] Neither her poetry, nor poetry by any other woman, changed overnight. Yet its status and authority changed at a stroke. Women's poetry claimed media space and public attention as never before. The very next day the *Guardian* published thirteen new poems by women, curated by Duffy, showcasing 'great women poets we now have' of many ethnicities from across the UK.[41]

Clarke, Duffy, Lochhead and Meehan have, then, entered the stage at a point of multiple transitions in gender politics, post-devolution politics and new briefs for the roles themselves. The appointments of women to these roles represent an unusual convergence of what Kirkpatrick has called the 'administrative practices of the State' which have been typically patriarchal, with 'the cultural processes of nation' in which women have previously included themselves as a means of effecting change in the former.[42] Individually and collectively these appointments are more significant than a 'first' for women, and more culturally enriching than a welcome opportunity for 'festival organisers' to '[programme] them together'.[43] The study which follows explores how these poets have helped to bring about the momentous changes in the literary authority of poetry by women which their appointments signal. It also considers how their journeys from woman poet to laureate poet have altered how a nation thinks of itself, who and what is included within a poetics of national identity, and how national belonging may be a struggle as much as a given.

Notes

1. Bertram, 'Editorial: Contemporary Women Poets', p. 3.
2. Dowson, '"Older Sisters"', p. 16.
3. Boland, 'Our Future Will Become the Past of Other Women', in *The Historians*, pp. 63–7.
4. Parker et al. (ed.), *Nationalisms and Sexualities*, p. 6; cited in Kirkpatrick (ed.), *Border Crossings*, p. 11.
5. Woolf, *Three Guineas*, p. 197.
6. Auerbach, 'Introduction: Women and Nations', p. 182.
7. Boland, 'Outside History', in *Object Lessons*, p. 145.
8. Maguire, 'Dilemmas and Developments', p. 63; p. 65.
9. Boland, *A Woman Without a Country*.
10. Boland, *Outside History*.
11. Boland, 'A Woman Without a Country', *PN Review*.
12. Robins, *Woman's Secret*, p. 4.
13. Boland, 'Outside History', p. 134.
14. Warner, *Monuments and Maidens*, p. 96.
15. Boland, '"Gods make their own importance"', p. 12.
16. Boland, 'Outside History', p. 127.
17. Kirkpatrick, *Border Crossings*, p. 7.
18. Lochhead, *Dreaming Frankenstein*; Duffy, *Standing Female Nude*; Clarke, *The King of Britain's Daughter*; Meehan, *The Mysteries of the Home*.
19. Ostriker, *Stealing the Language*, p. 60.
20. Duffy, 'Poetry: Permission not to be nice'.
21. Ibid.
22. Greer, *Slip-Shod Sibyls*, p. xxiii.
23. Boland, '"Gods make their own importance"', p. 10.
24. Light, 'Outside History?', p. 237.
25. Ibid. p. 255.
26. Ibid. p. 258.
27. Ibid. p. 253.
28. Quinn, 'Eavan Boland', p. 340.

29. Ibid. p. 341.
30. Ibid. p. 342.
31. Ibid. p. 343.
32. Light, 'Outside History?', p. 246.
33. Boland, 'Anna Liffey' (1994), in *Collected Poems*, p. 199.
34. Light, 'Outside History?', p. 258.
35. Meehan, 'Imaginary Bonnets with Real Bees in Them', in *Imaginary Bonnets*, p. 19.
36. Hampson, 'Custodians and Active Citizens', p. 72.
37. Dowson, *Carol Ann Duffy*, p. 171, citation of Ross, 'Interview with Carol Ann Duffy'.
38. McCrum, 'The royal family doesn't need a poet'.
39. Butler (ed.), *Common Ground*, p. 196.
40. Moore, 'Carol Ann Duffy is first woman Poet Laureate'.
41. Duffy, 'New work from Carol Ann Duffy's favourite women poets'.
42. Kirkpatrick, *Border Crossings*, p. 5.
43. Marsack, 'On the National Poet's First Year', p. 11.

2
The Laureate Roles: Three Poets and a Professor

The roles of Poet Laureate, the Ireland Chair of Poetry, the Scots Makar and the National Poet of Wales are at once bureaucratic and honorary, offices which confer status on both poet and country, while, as institutions, they also make powerful statements of nation-building ambition. Simply by existing, these roles create cultural space, projected as geographical territory. They speak of overlapping and sometimes competing political aspirations within and between the four nations of the United Kingdom. They are vessels in which community identities can be configured, and from which they can be broadcast. They can be instruments of national cohesion as well as a means to articulate internal division. What follows is an overview of the offices themselves, given in the chronological sequence of their formation, together with an account of how Clarke, Duffy, Lochhead and Meehan approached their tenures.

Poet Laureate

'Poetry for the Palace' was an exhibition held from August to November 2014 at the Palace of Holyroodhouse, Edinburgh, to mark the midpoint of Carol Ann Duffy's tenure as Poet Laureate.[1] Its theme was introduced as follows:

> The office of Poet Laureate is a special honour awarded by the Sovereign to a poet whose work is of national significance.
>
> This exhibition celebrates the work of the current Poet Laureate, Carol Ann Duffy, at the half-way point in her laureateship.
>
> It explores the role of the Poet Laureate, and the close relationship between poet and monarch over the last three and a half centuries.[2]

The exhibition presented the conventional historical starting point of the role as the appointment of John Dryden by Charles II in 1668.³ There are alternative historiographies. For example, it has been argued that Elizabeth I appointed Edmund Spenser as her court poet in 1590, and that *The Faerie Queene* is an offering by the laureate to the monarch, fulfilling the dual functions of aggrandising monarchy and nation. The nineteenth-century journalist John Timbs, editor of *The Mirror of Literature, Amusement and Instruction*, found a still earlier origin, announcing that 'the first regular Poet-Laureate of England we read of, was in the reign of Edward IV. His name was John Kave', which would date the tradition to between 1461 and 1483.⁴ The Poetry Society, on its 'Poet Laureate' webpages, notes that Geoffrey Chaucer is also an early contender, having been paid ten shillings a year by Henry I.⁵ Apart from establishing the length of the line of male incumbents to precede Carol Ann Duffy, the antiquity of the role is relatively unimportant for the present discussion, but there is one aspect of its history which continues to bring tension into its function. This is the relationship between the Poet Laureate and the four nations of the United Kingdom.

If we accept 1668 as the starting point of the modern laureateship, this was after the 1536 Act of Union between England and Wales, and after the 1603 Union of the Crowns which anointed James VI of Scotland as King of England, Scotland and Ireland, but before the 1707 Act of Union between England and Scotland from which came 'the United Kingdom of Great Britain', and well before the 1801 Act of Union between England and Ireland, let alone the secession of Northern Ireland from the Dominion of the Irish Free State in 1922. The complexity of these royal and political unions may explain the customary shorthand of referring to post-holders as the 'English Poet Laureate', though the time-honoured linguistic slippage between 'English' and 'British' is a more likely explanation.

Artists, journalists and critics have all been prone to this. Examples abound. Amongst critics, an early study by Edmund Kemper Broadus was called *The Laureateship. A study of the office of poet laureate in England, with some account of the poets.*⁶ More recently, and more casually, Peter Hoffenberg refers to 'John Masefield (1868–1967), the English Poet Laureate who visited Gallipoli in summer 1915'.⁷ Journalists since the nineteenth century have used the same term. An 1873 article about Tennyson was called 'The English Poet Laureate and his love of retirement'.⁸ The appointment of his successor was announced in 1896: 'Alfred Austin has secured the position of English poet-laureate and entered upon his duties with the beginning of the new year.'⁹ In 1926 it was stated that 'Robert Bridges, the English Poet Laureate, believes that [the radio] will be a purifying influence [on speech].'¹⁰ In 2013 readers of the *Wall*

Street Journal were told that 'Daniel Day-Lewis, the son of an English poet laureate and a member of the Royal Shakespeare Company, just won his third Academy Award.'[11] In the visual arts, Erich Hartmann's 1966 photograph of John Betjeman is called 'English Poet Laureate'. In 1999, the Northern Irish poet, Paul Muldoon, reflected that a sense of Englishness was a necessary qualification for the role of Poet Laureate:

> Andrew [Motion] . . . has a great, deep-rooted sense of Englishness, which is, let's face it, what that job's all about. I was somewhat astonished when Ted Hughes took the job; I'd always thought of him as being an outsider, a renegade, a loner. But then as I thought about it, I realised how right it was. He was so deeply engaged in ideas of what England and Englishness meant. As I think is Andrew. Certainly as it's constituted, it's a job for an English poet.[12]

The men in this line of succession are all English by birth, and Carol Ann Duffy was the first non-English poet in the role. No doubt the staging of the 'Poetry for the Palace' exhibition in Edinburgh rather than London was designed to convey something of that departure, as well as to embed Duffy within the tradition. But the appellation 'English Poet Laureate' was never meant so literally, and its inaccuracy is exposed, in the post-devolution United Kingdom, as a blatant assertion of cultural and political domination. The monarch reigns over all four nations, and if the Laureate serves the monarch, he or she writes not just for the English.

Ironically, at the historical moment when Duffy's national identity foregrounds the British rather than the English honour and service of the laureateship, this very aspect of the role becomes almost redundant since it coincides with the period when the Scots, the Welsh and the Irish have all consolidated their own laureate roles. The last of these to be created was that of the National Poet of Wales, inaugurated in 2005, midway through Andrew Motion's tenure, making Duffy the first Poet Laureate to work with peers across all partner nations throughout her tenure. These new roles contribute to a reshaping of the laureateship, in ways which may have been unforeseen and have not yet been clarified. Edwin Morgan saw this potential at the outset of his tenure as the first Scots Makar, stating in 2004, '[Mr Motion's] post is officially for the United Kingdom but essentially it's an English post. It has never been held by any Welsh, Irish or Scottish poet, so this is a good thing. It will possibly make the English think about their own poet laureate and their relation to Scotland and other parts of the UK.'[13] These new National Poet roles shift the laureateship away from an expectation of speaking to or for the United Kingdom as a whole; they therefore make the Poet Laureate's association with the monarchy more rather than less important. This is for the very reason that, unlike Westminster or the devolved administrations, the sovereign reigns equally in all four nations, and it is only by serving the Crown that the Laureate's voice reaches beyond England without competing with its sibling roles. Alternatively, if it is argued that no closer link between monarch and laureate is compelled, then the laureateship is, for the first time in its history, overtly an instrument of Englishness rather than Britishness.

Both sides of the partnership, court and poet, have, in fact, adjusted their positions in light of the post-devolution configuration of nations and their poets. The website for the Royal Family announced during Duffy's tenure: '[r]ecent holders of the post have sought to champion the reading and writing of poetry as well as addressing whichever public issues have seemed of importance to them, not simply Royal events.'[14] This statement draws attention to the fact that the post carries no explicit job description, and what the Poet Laureate chooses to write is determined more by precedent than by requirement. Duffy's view of the role and its relationship with the monarchy has also undergone considerable change. Her 1999 position, reported again in the *Guardian* on her appointment in 2009, was that 'the role needed to be "much more democratic", more people's poet than monarch's bard, and that she would "not write a poem for Edward and Sophie – no self-respecting poet should have to."'[15] She moderated this in 2009 by seeking to refocus the public aspect of the role, emphasising instead a common ground: 'I am a poet of the family, and the symbol of the Royal Family is entwined with the history of Britain. I don't see why that can't make a good poem. On the other hand, no one would thank me for writing bad poems to order.'[16] From there she embarked on a sustained effort to build on the modernising and democratising potential of the role introduced by Andrew Motion in 1999 when he fixed the term of office to ten years and gave the authority of his laureate voice to organisations, causes and charities outside royalty, so creating a more dispersed or democratic view of what was deserving of institutionalised poetic attention.

Duffy's approach towards royal occasions such as weddings and jubilees has been to provide a platform from which many poets could be heard. So, for example, to celebrate the wedding between Prince William and Catherine Middleton in April 2011, Duffy assembled seventeen poets, each to write a 'poem for a wedding', published in the *Guardian* on 23 April 2011 as a 'feast of new poems which can be uttered as vows or read as epithalamiums' to be 'spoken in future years at partnerships and weddings'.[17] Duffy's commissioning of *Jubilee Lines* to celebrate the Queen's Diamond Jubilee in 2012 follows the same pattern. The gender balance of contributing poets was carefully balanced: twenty-eight women and thirty-two men; their ethnic origins or national belongings ranged from Guyana to India. Introducing the collection, she writes that 'the poems offer a fascinating mix of the personal and the public, the political and the poetic'.[18] She thereby disperses the responsibility of the laureateship, gives a platform to her fellow poets, and seeks to deliver poetry for a wide spectrum of tastes and needs amongst British readers: 'the individual voices of the poets are always personal and particular, and variously accessible or complex, free or formal – a truly democratic mix'.[19] Duffy's own contribution is the culminating poem, 'The Thames, London 2012'. A dramatic monologue spoken by the river, it deftly avoids confrontation with contemporary politics, reaching instead to a pre-modern Empire, 'Caesar named me'. The poem's non-human speaker observes the occasion of the Jubilee flotilla while placing it within a picture of transience, using the indefinite article 'a', rather than 'the', to introduce its subject, 'A Queen sails now into the sun'.[20]

Duffy has favoured the dramatic monologue form since the start of her career. Her first-person speakers, human, non-human, living or legendary, the 'thrown voice' of the ventriloquist, as she has described them,[21] enable her to explore the widest range of subject positions and perspectives and have focused the attention of much critical commentary. When she adopts the lyric mode, however, and deploys a public-facing voice which speaks for 'us' and 'we', expressing 'our' views or feelings, the question of who is represented by these pronouns remains unresolved. For example, the sonnet commissioned by the National Trust in 2012 to celebrate its purchase of a stretch of the Dover coastline, 'White Cliffs', concludes, 'something fair and strong implied in chalk,/ what we might wish ourselves'.[22] The metaphor works in obvious, if disputable, ways for England or the Crown, but the white cliffs of Dover are of far lesser iconic significance for the Scots or the Welsh, and can have little bearing on Northern Ireland. An alternative example is the sonnet written for the outcome of the Scottish independence referendum, published in the *Guardian* but not reprinted in her *Collected Poems* (2016), nor in *Sincerity* (2018). The headline 'Britain's poet laureate wrote this poem for the *Guardian* on the morning after the Scottish Independence Referendum', heralds 'September 2014'. The poem concludes, 'the thistle jags our hearts,/take these roses/from our bloodied hands'.[23] Whose hearts? Whose hands? Since the thistle is the flower of Scotland, and the rose symbolises both England and the Crown, it would seem that 'our bloodied hands' could belong to either. But what is not included in 'our' is the four-nations Britain announced by the *Guardian* headline, and Scotland is explicitly beyond the pale. Jane Dowson concurs that the poem articulates an English perspective, '[a]cknowledging the indelible scars of English colonialism, she expresses the shame and love that sympathetic English onlookers to the referendum could barely put into words.'[24] The predominantly English perspective of Duffy's public laureate poetry is not problematic in itself, but does indicate either a lack of clarity about how the Poet Laureate role is positioned in relation to the four nations of the United Kingdom, or a continuing slippage between the British and English aspects of the role which was conventional prior to devolution.

The Ireland Chair of Poetry

The Ireland Chair of Poetry was established in 1998.[25] It was set up to celebrate the award of the Nobel Prize for Literature to Seamus Heaney in 1995, and is forged from a unique collaboration between the Arts Councils of Northern Ireland and the Republic of Ireland/An Chomhairle Ealaíon together with three universities: Queen's University Belfast, Trinity College Dublin and University College Dublin. Pioneered by Sir Donnell Deeny, Chairman of the Arts Council of Northern Ireland, the cross-border partnership recognises Seamus Heaney's dual identity: 'a distinguished northerner, resident in Dublin'.[26] The role is governed by a charitable trust administered by a Board of Trustees drawn from members of all five sponsoring bodies, together with one poet.[27] In its first year the Chair's annual honorarium of £20,000 was funded by charitable donation and the first incumbent was selected by the Board after nominations were sought from the public through press advertisements:

> Universities and arts councils north and south of the Irish border are collaborating to set up the first Ireland Chair of Poetry. The poet who wins the three-year professorship, worth £20,000 a year, will be attached to each of the three participating universities (Trinity Dublin, Queen's Belfast and University College Dublin) in turn, and be required to be in residence at each for approximately an academic term each year.
>
> The chair has been established to celebrate the awarding of the 1995 Nobel Prize for Literature to Seamus Heaney, and Heaney will be on the panel judging applications.
>
> Suggestions for suitable candidates should be sent to Donnell Deeny, QC, 77 Malone Road, Belfast BT9 6AQ, by March 6.[28]

This public consultation took place only for the first appointment, to be replaced by a selection process overseen by the Board of Trustees. On 14 May 1998 Ulster poet John Montague was pronounced the first Ireland Chair of Poetry at a ceremony in the Belfast headquarters of the Arts Council of Northern Ireland, the *Belfast Telegraph* reporting, 'Seamus Heaney said it was an "epoch-making occasion", as being made Irish Professor of Poetry was intended to be an honour as well as an office.'[29] The celebratory aspect to the role intensified in 2011 when all five of Meehan's predecessors, John Montague, Nuala Ní Dhomhnaill, Paul Durcan, Michael Longley and Harry Clifton, as well as Seamus Heaney himself, were awarded honorary degrees at a single ceremony by one of the sponsoring bodies, University College Dublin.[30]

The 'epoch-making' achievement of the award lies in the way it inscribes partnership between Northern Ireland and the Republic, using the poet and poetry as a means of cultural diplomacy. The governance of the role by the three universities and the two Arts Councils indicates that the Chair was designed to be as independent of political influence as possible, configured as an academic rather than a national role. Nevertheless, the use of poetry to cross borders and further dialogue is itself a political intent, and the establishment of the Chair took place in the immediate context of the signing of the Good Friday Agreement (10 April 1998) which promoted accord for an all-island and cross-border pursuit of the common good. Also political is the name, 'The Ireland Chair' or 'The Ireland Professor of Poetry' ('IPoP' for short),[31] which affirms the artistic integrity of the island of Ireland, whole in itself and separate from Britain. Heaney himself had famously quipped, on finding his poetry included in an anthology of British poetry in 1982, 'Be advised my passport's green./No glass of ours was ever raised/to toast the Queen.'[32] An oppositional perspective seems to be embedded in the role. Meehan's immediate predecessor, Harry Clifton, stated before her inauguration, 'I think it's very important that this appointment is not just a lap of honour, but that the person comes into it with a bit of anger. It's a chance to really say something.'[33]

The Chair's brief is outlined by the Arts Council of the Republic of Ireland:

During their tenure the holder spends a year attached to each of the three universities and resides for a period of approximately eight weeks at each. While in residence, the poet gives informal workshops or readings, spends time working with students and performing outreach work and makes one formal presentation a year, usually in the form of a lecture.[34]

Paula Meehan is the sixth poet and the fourth Irish national to hold the three-year appointment. The President of Ireland, Michael Higgins, announced Meehan's selection on 13 September 2013 in Trinity College, Dublin. She was greeted by Bob Collins, Chair of the Board of Trustees, with the aspirational declaration, '[t]he relevance of poetry, the prophetic voice of the poet, the potential of the arts in general are celebrated in this appointment.'[35] Seamus Heaney had died unexpectedly just a fortnight earlier, on 30 August 2013;

his death was the major context in which Meehan began her tenure. Collins' speech continued, '[t]hese same values were reflected in a very particular way in the outpouring of affection and the manifest sense of loss at the death two weeks ago of Seamus Heaney. He enriched the lives of the people and shaped our communities in ways that we do not yet fully appreciate.' Meehan herself, reporting to the Trustees after her first year of tenure which was held in Belfast at Queens University, observed that Heaney's death shaped her experience: 'this first year of the Professorship has had a particular emotional freight for all concerned. Everywhere I went the grief was palpable and there was a particular sense of loss in the north of Ireland.'[36]

In accepting the Chair, the *Irish Times* reported that Meehan said she felt 'privileged to live in a country that is represented by a poet. Not only a poet but also someone who puts their eloquence at the service of justice and sanity in civic affairs . . . I think my natural place is somewhere where the energies of the academy meet the energies of the street, and I think there is great potential for the inter-animation of both places.'[37] The *Irish Independent* reported that Meehan said, '[t]he Greeks say it takes a village to raise a child, the same could be said of a poet – it takes a community . . . One of the great draws of this for me is that I get to work with the different students in the different universities. I'll be continuing the work I've always done, teaching the craft of poetry . . . and standing up for poetry.'[38] The editorial in the *Irish Times* on 14 September 2013 reflected on what Meehan brought to the role:

> If Yeats and Heaney are the standard bearers, raising poetry into public consciousness, Meehan is among the pivotal poets whose grace notes enhance an art that is our jewel in the crown. In a time of so much loss, to the soul of the nation and to Irish poetry, she is a powerful public advocate to speak on behalf of both. In true bardic tradition, she listens to others to speak on their behalf. In that decade of bewildering headlines when Ireland needed the serenity of poetry, she delivered it in 'The Statue of the Virgin at Granard Speaks'.[39]

These are qualities which had previously earned Meehan the title of 'Dublin's informal poet laureate',[40] and they are reiterated by Bob Collins in his 'Foreword' to the publication of the three lectures which she delivered in her capacity as Ireland Chair of Poetry, *Imaginary Bonnets with Real Bees in Them*, '[t]hese lectures . . . are a living out of the commitment to poetry's place in the public realm.'[41]

Meehan's annual reports to the Trustees of the Ireland Chair record in detail the activities which she undertook during her tenure. They evidence an extraordinarily demanding schedule of events, some of which would have taken place had she not been in post, but, she states, 'I believe the title [Ireland Professor] upped the ante in terms of both expectation and enthusiasm.'[42] During her first year alone she took part in more than sixty-four engagements, some of which were workshops and readings that lasted over a period of days and some of which took her away from Ireland to New Jersey, Maryland, New York, Washington, Greece, France and England. In addition to formal readings, weekly master classes with students at the Seamus Heaney Centre at Queens University, Meehan made a point of visiting creative writing groups situated in remoter parts of Northern Ireland. These were documented by Joan and Kate Newmann, included in Meehan's first submission to the Trustees. Of her visit to the Burnavon Writers in Cookstown, they noted that '[t]here was a residual feeling that they never expected the Chair of Poetry to visit them. It raised the self-esteem of the entire group.'[43] Her workshop with the Fermanagh Women's Aid Group was interrupted by an unscheduled visit by two Members of the Northern Ireland Assembly, 'Tom Elliott (UUP) and Phil Flanagan (Sinn Fein) and Paula gave a most eloquent, unprepared, five-minute address, as to why government needed to fund groups like this, and the importance of an arts input, especially writing. It was an unlikely evening with a very positive outcome.'[44] Joan and Kate Newmann conclude that Meehan's residency in Northern Ireland, through her inclusive approach and wide range of activities, 'had a momentous and enduring effect on the Arts scene in Belfast and throughout the province'.[45]

Meehan maintained this intense pace of activity and international range throughout the remaining two years of her tenure. She recorded eighty-four separate engagements during her second year in office (2014–15), based at Trinity College, Dublin, and over sixty during her last year (2015–16), based at University College, Dublin. In December 2014 Meehan represented Irish arts for the President of Ireland, Michael D. Higgins and Sabina Higgins, on a state visit to the People's Republic of China, and gave a poetry reading in Beijing. This was an unusual engagement for the Ireland Professor of Poetry, which, as can be seen from the rest of Meehan's diary, is a role more concerned with the promotion of reading and writing poetry in communities than it is with the ceremonials of state. The role's academic base as well as its dual national belonging (including funding) means that it is not easily aligned with the interests of either one of its sponsoring administrations.

Scots Makar and National Poet of Wales

'What does it mean', asks Robyn Marsack, then both Chair of the Literature Forum for Scotland and Director of the Scottish Poetry Library, 'for a modern nation to have a poet laureate? What does it say about tradition, language, ambition? Or indeed, politics?'[46] With obvious nation-building agendas, the National Poet roles in Scotland and Wales were created as a direct consequence of devolved government which followed the referenda about devolution held in Scotland and Wales in 1997. The Scottish Government and the National Assembly of Wales were both established in 1999, after which the office of Scots Makar was inaugurated in 2004 and the National Poet of Wales followed just a year later, in 2005.[47]

The incumbents are appointed by government ministers or officials, and the roles, like those for the Poet Laureate and the Ireland Chair of Poetry, are funded (very modestly) by public money. While there are agreements and minimally specified obligations for each role, both have been broadly shaped by what the poets in post choose to undertake, rather than by rules or contracts, transferring the artistic freedoms associated with the Poet Laureateship to the roles as they are held in the newly formed administrations. Yet as Marsack implies, the very creation of these positions makes strong claims on ambition for the articulation of national identity, which follow through to the poets' practice, commissions and engagement calendars.

While in Scotland the selection of individual poets took place 'above party lines',[48] and the role of Makar is conceived as a 'non-political appointment',[49] the simple fact of the establishment of both Makar and National Poet of Wales is a political act which subjects the roles to political spin. This became immediately evident when Alex Salmond announced Lochhead's selection in a government press release and at a ceremony in the National Library of Scotland on 19 January 2011. He credited, falsely, 'the communities of Scotland' for creating the role of national poet, and asserted that this was a demonstration of the importance of 'the many aspects of culture which lie at the heart of our identity'.[50] In Scotland, the office of Makar was created, without consultation and without competition, in 2004 by the First Minister of the Scottish Parliament, Jack McConnell, to honour Scotland's undisputedly most distinguished poet, Edwin Morgan. The unstated purpose was to commission from him a poem for the opening of the new Scottish Parliament Building in the same year. Morgan's poem, 'Open the Doors', was read at the inauguration of the building on 9 October 2004 by Liz Lochhead, his close friend, her performance having been rehearsed by Morgan as he was too ill to attend in person.

When Edwin Morgan died at the age of ninety in August 2010 the post fell vacant and speculation arose about whether and how the role of Makar would be continued. In January 2011 key questions were raised by Robyn Marsack. Interviewed in the *Guardian* she stated, 'I feel . . . strongly about the process. I think that . . . people shouldn't be suggesting names before they know what the government thinks a poet laureate is or what the poet laureate is expected to do hasn't been clearly defined.' Marsack continued, 'Nobody has given me any timetable, so I don't know how they're thinking of doing it or when they're thinking of releasing it.'[51] While Marsack, and those working with her in the Literature Forum for Scotland, were clear that opportunity lay even in the uncertainty about how to shape the brief for Scotland's poet laureate, these opportunities were not fully acted upon by the Scottish government in 2011. Some potential parameters of the brief which, in Marsack's view, needed to be clarified, were reported in the same *Guardian* article:

> The definition of what the laureate would do, how long the post would last and how he or she would be judged as the best for the post could have a significant impact on who would want the role or be most suitable for it.

There had been no public discussion about whether it would be a 'working' role or purely honorary. Marsack said some poets would relish a time-limited appointment; others would be ideal if it involved visiting schools and promoting poetry to new audiences; while some very popular poets could be great ambassadors even if they were not technically the best.

Speculation about Morgan's successor was printed on the same page of the *Guardian*, 'The Contenders'. This named several poets: Robin Robertson, Don Patterson, John Burnside, Jackie Kay, Kathleen Jamie and 'the reigning mother and father of Scottish poetry, Douglas Dunn . . . – and Liz Lochhead, who has spent nearly half a century investigating politics, gender and place in lubricious, lyrical verse.'[52] The identity of the new Makar was revealed just sixteen days later, when the *Guardian* reported that a private meeting had been held between Scotland's three successive First Ministers, the SNP leader 'Alex Salmond and his two Labour predecessors Jack McConnell and Henry McLeish', in which they selected Liz Lochhead from 'a list of suggestions supplied by the Scottish Poetry Library and the government's arts advisers' from Creative Scotland.[53] The report further stated that she had been appointed for a fixed term of five years, that she would be paid an annual honorarium of £10,000 and that 'at the end of her term the government will also publish a volume of Lochhead's poetry – mirroring a similar tradition for New Zealand's national poet'.[54]

The role therefore evolved significantly between the tenures of the first and second Makars. Edwin Morgan was appointed by fiat, for a 'three year' term which extended from 2004 to his death in 2010, and with a very general brief, 'to represent poetry in the public consciousness, promote poetic creativity in Scotland, and to be an ambassador for Scottish Poetry'.[55] Lochhead was appointed by an eventually transparent process of consultation, for a fixed term of five years (observed this time) and with a more delineated brief.[56] The Scottish Government outlined the role on its website during Liz Lochhead's tenure, but subsequently removed it:

> The responsibilities of the National Poet are:
> In the course of their tenure to produce a poem or poems commenting on significant national events
> To read his/her poems publicly and to be free to comment publicly on poetry, the arts and any and all related matters in Scotland and internationally
> To give public lectures/readings through Literary Festivals/organisations in Scotland
> To encourage the reading and writing of poetry, particularly by young people[57]

Lochhead's response? 'Poets have never been ower fond/of politicians.' Precedent merges into tradition quickly: these lines are from the poem she wrote for the opening of the Fourth Session of the Scottish Parliament. 'Opening the doors again' was read by Lochhead to the overwhelmingly SNP members of the newly elected parliament, as well as the Queen, on 1 July 2011. The poem responds to Edwin Morgan's 'Open the doors', reiterating his stated ambitions for the parliament, reminding members of their responsibilities and holding them to account. Unlike Carol Ann Duffy, Lochhead can speak on behalf of a defined nation, using the pronoun 'our' in a straightforward manner: 'When Burns vented his scorn for/thon "Parcel of Rogues"/they were oor ain rogues, mind, in/oor ain nation./Morgan wisnae blate either aboot/dishin oot a flytin – in advance –/to you, our brand new parliamentarians.'[58] She writes in Scots thereby legitimating its use in this arena, rallies identity around poets who are icons of national pride, and situates herself firmly on the side of the people in potential opposition to their politicians. This position of 'people's poet' is one which Duffy too has frequently adopted, both before and during her laureateship; ironically, Duffy's authority in this mode is more compelling when she is not writing to ceremonial order than when she is. The Makar's address to the new parliament is a tradition continued by Lochhead's successor, Jackie Kay, who composed 'Thresholds' for the opening of the Fifth Session on 2 July 2016.[59]

Lochhead often attended more than one engagement a week throughout her five years in post. Her readings took place across Scotland, from the Borders to Shetland, as well as on the international stage in China, Canada, Europe and the Middle East. She wrote for numerous organisations, helped to raise funds for charities such as food banks,[60] supported the Scottish Poetry Library 'Living Voices' project for Scotland's older population.[61] Despite not being 'ower fond of politicians', Lochhead served on the Scottish Studies Working Group in the Scottish Parliament (from January 2012), gave her authority to curriculum reform, campaigned for Scottish independence and supported the Scottish Whisky Industry with a commissioned poem, 'Lines for the centenary of the Scotch Whisky Association'.[62] Although Lochhead was the second poet in the post of Makar, hers was the first actively engaged tenure. She has been enormously influential in transforming the role from imagined potential to a delivered reality, shaping it for her successor, Jackie Kay.

The post of National Poet of Wales is the most recently founded of the four roles. It was heralded on the day that Edwin Morgan's appointment as Scots Makar was announced:

> Peter Finch, chief executive of the Welsh Academi, the Welsh literary promotion agency, said that he was in discussion with Alan Pugh, the Welsh Arts Minister, over a national poet. 'Wales is moving towards a Welsh poet laureate,' he said. 'We are just sorry Scotland got there first.'[63]

Finch is reported as saying that 'he was very pleased with the work Mr Motion had done to promote poetry in Wales, but that the Principality needed its own poet who could write in both languages'.[64] The need for the poet to speak to the nation in its own languages is as primary for Wales as for Scotland and provides a powerful underpinning argument against the viability of an 'English' laureate. The National Poet of Wales was established in 2005 by the Arts Council of Wales and funded by an annual £5,000 lottery grant. Carrying defined responsibilities since its inception, the role was initially administered by the Welsh Academi, transferring to Literature Wales in 2011. Finch, whose campaign for the post began shortly after devolution,[65] stated in 2005, 'England was first with its Poet Laureate, then Scotland with its Maker [sic] and now Wales – ample evidence of our growing cultural nationhood.'[66] The role was designed to promote the cultural visibility of Wales, to be an ambassador on the international stage, while at home articulating matters of national significance and composing works for official occasions.

The first National Poet of Wales was Gwyneth Lewis, who publishes equally in Welsh and English and whose tenure is marked by the bilingual inscription of her poetry on the Wales Millennium Centre in Cardiff. The second appointment was Gwyn Thomas, who writes predominantly in Welsh and whose tenure lasted for two years, from 2006–8. He was succeeded in 2008 by Gillian Clarke. On 31 March 2008 the BBC reported her appointment, quoting Clarke: 'I interpret Academi's chosen model for the role of national poet as being one of cumulative development, one poet's work building on another's, with careful attention paid to the bilingual nature of Wales.' The BBC also cited Peter Finch's assertion that the role required an ability 'to write well and often, and to have a regular route into that magic that makes verse work'. He concluded that Clarke, '"as one of our best-selling exports" was simply the best person he could think of for the job'.[67] Always alert to the sensitivities of a bilingual nation, Clarke's acceptance poem was called 'Mother Tongue', depicting the poet as a 'helmeted embryo afloat/in the twilight of the egg,/learning the language'.[68] Her contract with the Academi was initially for a one-year appointment, which was extended annually until she resigned from the position in 2016. The stipulated expectation of the contract is minimal: to 'take part in at least 4 events and produce 4 poems during the year'.[69]

Despite the modest demands, Clarke is widely recognised as having transformed the role during her eight years in office, not least through her energetic schedule, which has been just as demanding as those of her fellow National Poets. Interviewed after several years in post by the *Western Mail* on 26 October 2012, Clarke stated, '[w]hen I was made National Poet of Wales they told me that I didn't have to write anything, but I regard my work as mending bridges between North Wales and South Wales, Welsh and English language, England and Wales, Wales and the world. I feel that I need to cross boundaries.'[70] Her long experience in this relatively new role has enabled her to reflect on its nature and purpose, which she has set out in her annual reports to the Academi. In 2013 she reported,

> First, this is a diplomatic post. Wherever I have travelled – Scotland, England, Ireland, France, Italy, the USA, and in the previous five years Bangladesh, Mexico, India – not just I but my country was being watched, heard about, noted, so I had better be careful. Whatever I did or said would contribute something to Wales/Cymru's reputation . . . Second, it is not true that 'poetry makes nothing happen' . . . In fact, poets, and other artists, are the thorn in the flesh of tampering executives, as was so eloquently illustrated by speakers at the PEN international conference in New York, which I attended in May . . . Wales is much more visible than it used to be. The British press and media take notice of poetry, and of Wales, more than they used to. Radio Cymru has always asked its 'beirdd' to speak, but this is now becoming a British norm too.[71]

Clarke's urge to use her position to 'cross boundaries' has more than a geographical resonance. The cultural profile of Wales has been vastly enhanced by the position and her execution of it, and the political agency of poetry has been made stronger not only in Wales but also in the United Kingdom and beyond.

Shared Platforms

> There are now four female British laureates: Britain, Scotland and Wales are joined by Sinead Morrissey as Northern Ireland's poet, and a fifth, Paula Meehan is Professor of Poetry for Ireland. This is the breaking of another too-long silence, and a cause for great rejoicing.[72]

So Gillian Clarke records the 2013 appointments of Sinéad Morrissey to the Belfast Laureateship and Paula Meehan to the Ireland Chair. The concurrent tenures of women in all of these public offices are one of the most visible achievements of Clarke's ambition for poetry to drive cultural change. At the same time, the arrival of Sinéad Morrissey in this picture, proclaimed by Clarke as 'Northern Ireland's poet', is an example of poets outpacing the rate of change afforded by arts establishments. Sinéad Morrissey's post was a city laureateship, but in the context in which the Ireland Professor of Poetry was a native of the Republic, Morrissey is taken by Clarke to stand for Northern Ireland. Poets themselves are drawing attention to the potential under-representation of Northern Ireland in this particular configuration.

As national poets, Clarke, Duffy and Lochhead were often programmed to attend literary festivals, readings or workshops together in shifting kaleidoscopic combinations. For example, between September 2013 and November 2014, Gillian Clarke made eight appearances with Carol Ann Duffy in addition to at least twelve joint 'Poetry Live!' performances to GCSE students in large arenas across England. Liz Lochhead made at least fifteen appearances with one or both Duffy and Clarke during the five years of her tenure, in locations from Wenlock to Aberdeen.

Only twice, however, did all four appear on the same stage. This was partly because the period when their National Poet tenures overlapped was relatively short, from 2013 to 2016, but also because the Ireland Chair of Poetry serves mainly on the island of Ireland and internationally, seldom including the British mainland, and the mainland poets rarely attend readings in Northern Ireland or the Republic.

On 7 March 2014, all four performed at the Women of the World (WOW) Festival in London's Southbank Centre, where they also shared the platform with Sinéad Morrissey.[73] Paula Meehan records the day in her Trustees Report, her double entry conveying something of the role's hectic schedule:

> 7th March morning: Saol Project, Dublin – A project for young mothers coming out of addiction. Address for launch of their history project & to celebrate International Women's Day.

> 7th March evening: London, Queen Elizabeth Hall, Southbank. Gala Reading to celebrate the historical moment when laureates of UK and Ireland Professor of Poetry are all women as part of the *Women of the World Festival*. Reading were Carol Ann Duffy, Poet Laureate of England; Gillian Clark, Welsh National Poet; Liz Lochhead, Scottish Makar; Sinead Morrissey, Belfast Laureate; and myself in my capacity as Ireland professor of Poetry.[74]

The event announced the arrival of women at the helm of cultural establishments. It was trailed by the *Guardian* under the headline, 'The female poets who have earned their laurels', stating:

> All five poet laureates of the United Kingdom, Northern Ireland and the Republic of Ireland this year are women. On the eve of International Women's Day this Saturday, they will perform together for the first time at the Women of the World festival at London's South Bank Centre.[75]

The article printed 'Mrs Schofield's GCSE' by Duffy, 'Polar' by Clarke, 'In the Mid-Midwinter' by Lochhead and 'Hannah, Grandmother' by Meehan. Together these poems take on major themes in public and personal life: education, climate change, organised religion, intergenerational relationships, the value of tradition, and hope. They are powerful testaments of the agency of poetry in public life as well as its aesthetic enrichment of culture.

All five poets met again the following year, on 13 June 2015 in Sligo, for the Yeats 2015 celebrations, joined additionally by Aisling Fahey, the London Laureate. Paula Meehan records the event in her annual report to the Trustees:

> Gala reading with music introduced by Theo Dorgan. Guests of honour President Michael D. Higgins and Sabina Higgins. To celebrate 150 years since the birth of the poet and to mark a particular moment in the history of poetry by women in these islands with Sinead Morrissey (Belfast Laureate), Gillian Clarke (National Poet of Wales), Liz Lochhead (Makar of Scotland), Aisling Fahey (London Laureate), Carol Ann Duffy (Poet Laureate of England).[76]

Meehan's notice deftly balances the celebration between Yeats and poetry by her fellow laureates. President Higgins, introducing their readings, drew attention to the unusual fact that six women as National Poets and Laureates were leading the celebrations of Yeats and his legacy for poetry and Ireland.[77]

The platforms shared by Clarke, Duffy, Lochhead and Meehan at WOW 2014 and Yeats 2015 were unlike other joint readings. The first celebrated the groundbreaking achievement of these poets as women; the second assembled the laureate poets of Ireland and the United Kingdom to blazon the relationship between poetry and national self-understanding. The matrix of women, poetry and nation is placed centre stage by these two events, and the authority of the woman's voice is no longer in question.

Notes

1. Royal Collection Trust, 'Poetry for the Palace'; reviewed by Brown, 'Poets, palaces and butts of sherry'. A critical overview of much of Duffy's work as Poet Laureate has been outlined by Dowson in *Carol Ann Duffy: A Poet for our Times*, pp. 173–86. For a helpful overview of the role, see the Poetry Society website, <https://poetrysociety.org.uk/topics/poet-laureate/> (accessed 16 April 2020).
2. Royal Collection Trust, 'Poetry for the Palace'.
3. Panecka, *Literature and the Monarchy*, follows the same convention.
4. Timbs, 'The First English Poet Laureate'.
5. See <https://poetrysociety.org.uk/question/who-was-the-first-poet-laureate/> (accessed 16 April 2020).
6. Broadus, *The Laureateship*.
7. Hoffenberg, 'Landscape, Memory and the Australian War Experience', p. 113.
8. Anonymous, 'The English Poet Laureate and his love of retirement'.
9. Anonymous, 'The New Laureate at Work'.
10. Anonymous, 'Speech and the Radio'.
11. Lazebnik, 'Arise! Arise! The British Are . . . Acting!'
12. Paul Muldoon cited in Lane, 'I think, therefore iamb'.
13. Taylor, 'Scots appoint first poet laureate'.
14. Marsack, 'On the National Poet's First Year', p. 9.
15. Flood, 'Carol Ann Duffy becomes first female poet laureate'.
16. *Daily Mirror*, 'Carol Ann Duffy: "Poetry is in your everyday life"'.
17. Duffy, 'Poems for a wedding'.
18. Duffy, 'Preface', in *Jubilee Lines*, p. x.
19. Ibid. p. xi.
20. Ibid. p. 134.
21. Duffy, 'Talent Contest', *The Other Country*, in *Collected Poems*, p. 141.
22. Kennedy, 'Carol Ann Duffy poem celebrates Dover's famous white cliffs'; Carol Ann Duffy, 'White Cliffs', in *Collected Poems*, p. 517.

23. Duffy, 'September 2014'.
24. Dowson, *Carol Ann Duffy*, p. 173.
25. See <http://irelandchairofpoetry.org/history/> (accessed 2 September 16).
26. Ibid.
27. See <http://irelandchairofpoetry.org/history/>.
28. Unsigned notice, *Times*, 18 February 1998.
29. Johnston, 'Montague takes Chair of Poetry'.
30. See 'Bloomsday 2011 at UCD – celebrating Ireland's poetry tradition . . .', *YouTube*, <https://www.youtube.com/watch?v=7Dd9hIo2yEE> (accessed 2 September 2016).
31. Boland, 'Paula Meehan is named Ireland professor of poetry': 'Michael Longley jokingly referred to Meehan as the new "iPop" – letting the audience in on the academic nickname for the Ireland professor of poetry.'
32. This is widely quoted in print media, e.g. McClements, '"My passport's green"'.
33. Boland, 'Paula Meehan is named Ireland professor of poetry'.
34. See <http://www.artscouncil.ie/Initiatives/The-Ireland-Chair-of-Poetry-Trust/> (accessed 2 September 16).
35. Ibid.
36. Meehan, 'Ireland Chair of Poetry: Report to the Trustees 2013–2014'.
37. Boland, 'Paula Meehan is named Ireland professor of poetry'.
38. Gorman, 'Spirit of Heaney fills room'.
39. Editorial, 'A Poet of Solidarity', *Irish Times*, 14 September 2013.
40. *Belfast Telegraph*, 'Meehan is new poetry professor'.
41. Bob Collins, 'Foreword', in Meehan, *Imaginary Bonnets*, p. viii.
42. Meehan, 'Ireland Chair of Poetry. Report to the Trustees 2013–2014'.
43. Ibid.
44. Ibid.
45. Ibid.
46. Marsack, 'On the national poet's first year', p. 9.
47. An overview of the role of Scots Makar is given here, on the Scottish Poetry Library Website: <https://www.scottishpoetrylibrary.org.uk/poetry/our-national-poet/>. Information about the current National Poet of Wales and some history of the role is given on the Literature Wales website: <https://www.literaturewales.org/our-projects/national-poet-wales/> (accessed 3 May 2021).
48. Robyn Marsack quoted in Kennedy and Carrell, 'Liz Lochhead appointed as makar'.

49. Lord McConnell in Scottish Government video on the appointment of Liz Lochhead, posted on <http://www.gov.scot/News/Releases/2011/01/19141814> (accessed 30 August 2018).
50. Ibid.
51. Carrell, 'Scotland stalls on new poet laureate'.
52. Crown, 'The Contenders'.
53. Kennedy and Carrell, 'Liz Lochhead appointed as makar'.
54. Ibid.
55. English and Malvern, 'Poetic justice for the free-thinking Scots'.
56. The process for appointing her successor is outlined on the Scottish Poetry Library website: <https://www.scottishpoetrylibrary.org.uk/2016/02/how-make-makar/> (accessed 27 April 2020).
57. See <http://www.gov.scot/Topics/ArtsCultureSport/arts/CulturalPolicy/Literature> (accessed 30 August 16).
58. Lochhead, 'Opening the doors again'. This poem is not reprinted in her Makar collection, *Fugitive Colours* (2016).
59. The Scottish Poetry Library hosts Kay's poem: '"Threshold" was read at the opening of Fifth Session of the Scottish Parliament in 2016. It is the first poem written by Scotland's Makar Jackie Kay': <https://www.scottishpoetrylibrary.org.uk/poem/threshold/> (accessed 27 April 2020).
60. Lochhead performed at the food bank benefit, 'Away Game', in Summerhall, Edinburgh, on 15 January 2015.
61. Launch of the Living Voices project took place on 2 December 2013 at the Scottish Poetry Library. For an account of 'Living Voices' see <https://www.scottishpoetrylibrary.org.uk/project/living-voices/> (accessed 20 February 2021).
62. Lochhead, *Fugitive Colours*, pp. 88–90. 13 June 2012, Glasshouse, Edinburgh.
63. English and Malvern, 'Poetic justice for the free-thinking Scots'.
64. Ibid.
65. Price, 'New Calls for Wales to Have Poet Laureate'.
66. *BBC News*, 'Wales to get its own "poet laureate"'.
67. *BBC News*, 'Clarke named Wales' national poet'.
68. Clarke, 'Mother Tongue'.
69. Academi, 'National Poet of Wales 2010–2011'.
70. Quoted in *The Western Mail*, 'Poets are really nice to each other'.
71. Clarke, 'National Poet of Wales/Bardd Cenedlaethol Cymru, April-October 2013-10-20'.
72. Ibid.

73. The full event is available on *YouTube*, 'WOW 2014, Laureates Night': <https://www.youtube.com/watch?v=33-ujdN8aCE> (accessed 27 April 2020).
74. Meehan, 'Ireland Chair of Poetry: Report to the Trustees 2013–2014'.
75. *Guardian*, 'The female poets who have earned their laurels'. Further to the initial article, the following day the paper sought to clarify its representation of the public office held by Sinéad Morrissey: 'This article was amended on 4 March 2014 to correct a mistake in the sub-heading and to attach the following footnote: WOW Laureates Night features the four poets here, plus Sinéad Morrisey of Northern Ireland.'
76. Meehan, 'Ireland Chair of Poetry: Report to the Trustees 2014–2015'.
77. 'Yeats Day 2015', *Youtube*, <https://www.youtube.com/watch?v=Sb6yfOvw2Qg>, from 2.35 minutes (accessed 29 April 2020).

3
Gillian Clarke: From Woman Poet to National Poet

Breaking a Path

Before poetry by women could gain public acceptance it first had to gain currency within the poetry community. Much of this work was done in the pages of specialist poetry journals, and it was here that Gillian Clarke exercised a pioneering role. Her first poems were published in *Poetry Wales* in 1970, quickly followed by the publication of her first pamphlet, *Snow on the Mountain*, in 1971.[1] Her poems continued to appear in Welsh magazines, journals, and anthologies throughout the decade, leading to the publication by Gomer Press of her first full-length collection, *The Sundial*, in 1978.[2] In tandem with her work as a poet, she became Reviews Editor for *The Anglo-Welsh Review* in 1973, before taking on one of the most important gatekeeping roles in Welsh poetry when she succeeded Roland Mathias as Editor in 1976. Clarke was not only the first woman to edit a national poetry journal in Britain, she was also, throughout the period of her service, the only woman to do so. She left this position in 1984, two years after the publication of her second major collection, *Letter from a Far Country*. This came out with the Manchester-based press Carcanet, ensuring a readership beyond the borders of Wales. Throughout this period she exercised significant influence on English-language poetry in Wales by her own poetic practice, her editorial selection of material for publication, her nurturing of new talent ('[t]his is interesting. From a Welsh poet, too. This one could get better. Wait a minute, we've got something here'),[3] her editorials and her participation in wider debates about poetry. The following discussion explores the extraordinary leadership of Clarke's early career for the development of women's poetry, as it is reflected in the culture of Welsh poetry journals and beyond.

The four poems which mark the beginning of Clarke's career are 'Beech Buds', 'Nightride', 'Sailing' and 'The Fox', and they were published in *Poetry Wales*, 6.1 (1970). She was one of four women whose work appeared in that issue, alongside poetry by eighteen men.[4] Issue 6.2 featured twenty-three poets, of whom three were women; in 6.3 there were twenty poets, amongst whom Gillian Clarke was the only woman. The numerical imbalance between men and women at this time tells a microcosmic story of the obstacles women would have to overcome before their work as poets could be treated with the same regard which accrued to poetry written by men. Women faced not only the difficulty of having their work accepted for publication by the editors of journals, who were all men, but also of finding a readership. The overwhelmingly male environment, in which content was provided and curated by men, hardly encouraged any kind of participation from women. Whether as writers or readers, the world of small poetry magazines was hostile to women. Deprived of an environment in which to experiment and grow as writers, or to enter into dialogue with fellow poets, it is no surprise that it took decades for women to arrive on the poetry scene as equal partners with their male contemporaries. Yet the 1970s was a pivotal decade in the Anglo-American feminist movement, bookended by the first British publication of Kate Millett's *Sexual Politics* in 1971 (a year after the first Equal Pay Act in England and Wales) and the publication of *The Madwoman in the Attic* in 1979 by Gilbert and Gubar. This international movement exerted pressure on the practices of publication at every level, including poetry.

'Beech Buds' is a love poem structured by an extended simile of the likeness between the slow emerging buds and the speaker's feelings. It begins, 'The beech buds are breaking. I feel so happy.'[5] Even in this first line some of the hallmarks of Clarke's style are evident: the cohesive effects of alliteration and assonance, the orchestrated moment of reflection in the mid-line caesura, and imagery drawn from lived experience. 'The Fox' describes a walk taken from her remote smallholding, Blaen Cwrt, into a landscape that is red in tooth and claw, but not as Tennyson's lyric had configured it. The land is both wild and farmed, the sheltering place where the ewes give birth holds relics of life and death; the final stanza shocks as the speaker is touched, literally, by a vixen shot and hanging from a tree, 'Her beautiful head thrown back, her life stiffened,/Her milk dry, her fertility frozen. The reds grew cold'.[6] The 'fox' is a vixen, a deliberate feminising of the traditional farmland predator whose life-giving role is no less evident than that of the ewes, and whose destruction will play out across the next generation of her cubs. 'Nightride' describes a journey in which the woman is the passenger, holding the sleeping child as the road unwinds 'like a roll of foil', a kitchen simile to assert both the domesticity and the mystery of the experience.⁷ The lyric 'I' develops a new simile to liken the apple tree and its fruit to the relationship between mother and child, gliding into the surprise of metaphor in the last line of the poem, 'As I with Dylan's head, nodding on its stalk'. The closing image evokes a unity through shared fertility between the human maternal and the natural world. 'Sailing' describes a severance between the land-locked mother and her boat-borne children; the space of water, 'a sheet' between herself and their sailing father, becomes an emotional distance which remains after the boat has returned to harbour.⁸ The cumulative emphasis of these poems is an open concentration on woman in her closely observed relationships with children, husband and nature; these relationships encompass difficulty and mortality as well shared purpose, love and security.

If it was conspicuous that the perspective offered was, as Sam Adams noted, 'infrequently explored in poetry' when these poems appeared in Clarke's single-authored collection, then this was even more striking when they were compared with the poems that surrounded them in the journal.⁹ Representation *of* women was hardly more encouraging than the vanishingly small number of poems published *by* them.¹⁰ Justification for standard feminist complaints, that women are objectified, belittled, humiliated or mocked when they are represented in poetry written by men, is amply on display. For example, in the same 1970 issue of *Poetry Wales* which launched Clarke's career, B. S. Johnson published a poem about the end of a relationship which attacks not simply the speaker's former partner, but her mother too, under the title 'Good News for Her Mother! *probably the Last Poem I shall Write about Her Daughter*'. Johnson's poem contains metaphors of sex which progress towards violence, the disingenuous confusion of 'one girl' with another; the notion of sex as something to be consumed by the speaker. Perhaps most disturbing of all is the relegation of 'being a woman' to a stage of gestation in the man's development towards a superior form 'at which I have/never, even in the prenatal stages/of bisexuality, been very good'.¹¹ There is nothing here to attract women readers, let alone women poets.

At the end of the decade, the battle lines between genders were, if anything, more clearly drawn than at its start, because now there was critical debate to scrutinise poetic practice. In Autumn 1979 *Poetry Wales* published a remarkable issue, 15.9, devoted to an investigation of the state of 'Criticism in Wales'. Questions about poetry by women formed an important subsection. The issue contained a questionnaire about literary criticism and its responses from eighteen poets and critics (four of them women) amongst whom it had previously been circulated.¹² With specific reference to appraisal of the status of poetry by women, it published an article by Swansea-born academic Barbara

Hardy, professor of English literature at Birkbeck College, London, entitled 'Women's Poetry'. As if to illustrate or offset some of Hardy's findings, the issue also printed some of the most sexist poetry one could ever hope to find.

Gillian Clarke's work serves as an important point of reference throughout this issue of *Poetry Wales*, invoked from the very beginning by the Editor, Meic Stephens, in setting out his content: '[i]t is . . . noticeable that none of our leading poets – R. S. Thomas, Dannie Abse, Leslie Norris, John Tripp, Gillian Clarke, let alone Dylan Thomas or Vernon Watkins – are or were university teachers nor prolific in criticism.'[13] The only woman to be listed as a 'leading poet', Gillian Clarke stands out also because she is, on average, a generation younger than all the men listed here. The Editor does not state what exactly qualified these poets as 'leading'. Clarke's credentials seem slim by comparison with others on the list, particularly given the disadvantage of her relative youth: she had one collection and one pamphlet to her name, and she was three years in to her service as Editor for the rival journal *The Anglo-Welsh Review*. Even so, it is evident that she was already a formidable force in contemporary Welsh poetry. However, the difficulty of accepting her into this male club becomes apparent in Question 2 of the Questionnaire:

> What should our criticism be? Humorous/intelligent/domestic/affirmatory of Wales and very accessible? Or should it make some accommodation to new literary theory in the formal sense – structuralism, Marxism, linguistics etc? or should it be more concerned with current topics –women poets, American influence, pop poetry, poetry of violence, etc?[14]

So, on the one hand Gillian Clarke is named in the editorial as a 'leading poet', yet, on the other, by these terms of reference she must also be classed as a 'current topic' alongside 'pop poetry'.

Of the respondents, only John Tripp and Steve Griffiths took issue with the elision between 'women' and 'topics'. Tripp declared, '[y]ou mention "women poets" as if they were strange objects suddenly landed among us: the late Sylvia Plath and Anne Sexton, for instance, have had a shattering effect, not always for the best, on many students I have met.'[15] Griffiths stated: 'the "current topics", put in a list like that, sound like fads . . . I can see very challenging views coming perhaps from a woman who saw an essentially woman's perspective coming down from Sappho to the poets influenced by the new wave of feminism . . .'[16] But neither offers clarity. Griffiths seems somewhat fearful of the 'challenging views' of feminism, while Tripp simply points out that 'women poets' are not a new phenomenon. More outspoken was the poet Ruth Bidgood, who rejected the category 'woman poet' altogether: 'I don't see why there shouldn't be articles on any topics of poetic interest – the American influence, visual poetry and so on – which relate in any way to poetry in Wales. (Even articles on "women poets" if you insist, though I am one who thinks a poet is a poet is a poet!)'.[17] No others responded to this topic at all. Most replies were concerned with the nature of a specifically Welsh or Anglo-Welsh perspective in criticism.

Tony Curtis responded within entirely different parameters which nevertheless illuminate Gillian Clarke's unique status. He revealed that he was currently pursuing his craft some 4,000 miles distant from Wales by taking a Master of Fine Arts at Vermont University, and he longed for a similar opportunity in Wales:

I would like someone – Yr Acadmei Gymreig – *Poetry Wales* – The Polytechnic – The University – to try and create such a context. I would like to see John Tripp, Robert Minhinnick, Gillian Clarke, Dannie Abse, Leslie Norris, Jeremy Hooker and you and you and you and me around a table in a workshop. I want to show my poems and stories at manuscript stage to people whose work and opinions I respect; I want the chance to see their work laid bare in its formative stages.[18]

Again, Gillian Clarke is the only woman on the list, and Curtis has stated his principles of selection: 'people whose work and opinions I respect'. He goes on to describe difficulties he encountered when attempting to organise an exhibition of work in progress by fellow poets. One refusal to submit manuscript evidence of process came from 'a leading Anglo-Welsh poet' who 'apologised saying, "The Muse is a lady and she does not appear in public in her dressing gown."' Curtis' riposte was, 'No, no. The Muse is a whore and you earn her on your raw knees. It's surely time for the writers to Come Out.'[19] Had this league of gentlemen failed to notice Clarke's gender? Did they consider her Muse to be a lady or a whore? Did they fail to notice a link between objectifying and indeed eroticising their Muses, and an objectification of women in their company?

These are questions which readers today take for granted, but they are enabled by the feminist literary criticism which was in formation during the 1970s and in the absence of which Clarke and her fellow women poets had to make their way. Barbara Hardy takes as her point of departure in 'Women's Poetry' exactly this moot question of the identity of the Muse as objectified female form in the dynamic between male poet and his projections: 'Women poets have no Muses because they are Muses. The role of the Muse varies a little from man to man, and from time to time, but it combines the support and inspiration of mother, mistress, wife and secretary.'[20] Whoever she is, the Muse has worked well, because Hardy states categorically that '[t]he history of English and American poetry is the history of male poets . . . No woman poet has made a strong or significant contribution until the middle of our own century, with two exceptions which prove the rule.'[21] The exceptions, according to Hardy, are Emily Dickinson and Emily Brontë, before she turns to Sylvia Plath. Hardy identifies Plath's poem 'The Disquieting Muses' as 'a significant farewell to those ideals of accomplishment which finished off so many bright young ladies'.[22] Yet in assessing Plath's work Hardy asserts that her 'achievement is distorted by our mid-century feminism',[23] and her view of poetry emerging in this context is not particularly encouraging: '[w]omen's poetry is historically coloured and at present . . . frequently . . . doctrinaire. Women's poetry uses confession, crudity, candour, and aggression. It adds menstrual blood and cunts to the traditional erotic catalogue . . . It rewrites the myths, images and assertions of men's poetry.'[24] But apart from Plath, who is dead, and Adrienne Rich, who is far away, Hardy wisely refrains from naming any contemporary women poets. She was not leading the cavalry to Clarke's assistance.

Hardy's negative view of contemporary poetry by women is offset by her observation of the social and political factors which impeded women's progress in the composition of poetry over centuries. She goes so far as to personalise those constraints:

> Even for men, to declare poetic ambition has never been easy, but I remember the astonished envy I felt, as an adolescent growing up in Swansea, when a male contemporary said he intended to be a poet. To be anything, other than wife and mother, would be hard enough, but to want to be a poet showed a strange strong sense of self, power, and profession.[25]

Expectations, legitimate aspirations, role models, did not exist for Hardy's generation of British women born in the 1920s, and they were slow to arrive for those following close behind. 'I think we all need models,' Clarke stated in 1994, 'and I was both Welsh and a woman. The world wasn't very interested in either.'[26] A major impediment on the path towards a more balanced sense of self and a wide horizon of ambition was the way in which women were represented in texts written by men. Hardy does not mention this, although the critics Gilbert and Gubar were amongst those who demonstrated at exactly the same time that disempowerment of women through their literary representation, effected through their infantilisation, objectification and sexualisation, had long been commonplace. The same issue of *Poetry Wales* which aired these discussions also carried a poem which exemplified every one of these tendencies, despite the satirical self-irony of the speaker, and which suggests there had been little progress since 1970: this was British West Indian poet E. A. Markham's 'Cool (ii)'.[27] It was also published in Markham's collection *Love Poems*, of which the reviewer in *Poetry Review* stated, 'there is little passion in the manner of their telling despite the aphrodisiac subject matter'; the reviewer's disappointment normalises the subject matter rather than challenges it.[28]

While the Autumn 1979 issue of *Poetry Wales* is remarkable for its rich and conflicting contribution to the discussion of the status of poetry by women, the exactly contemporaneous issue of *The Anglo-Welsh Review*, edited by Gillian Clarke, affords a powerful counterweight on the same subject. It opens with Clarke's combative editorial:

> This is, almost by coincidence, a special number for women writers. There has always seemed a high proportion of women poets in the Anglo-Welsh magazines in comparison with other British journals, and here three out of twelve poets and three out of six prose writers are women . . . Women writers often disappear into obscurity after the heyday of their creative period is done. They have, traditionally, striven less for fame, even sought privacy and so avoided fame . . . Then there are the likeliest subjects of female writing, the domestic and familiar and the way of looking at relationships, places, objects and society, that is inclined to be minutely perceptive and detailed. It is an under-valued perception, and 'domestic' and 'familiar' are too frequently taken to be derogatory words. The 'domus' is under-rated and what women could be saying about it is one of our society's unheard messages, powerhouse as that place is for every emerging adult, the mine upon which all artists draw for the rest of their creative lives. Elsewhere in this issue a reviewer writes of domesticity's 'strong attendant risks of banality and/or sentimentality'. Why? Anthony Conran, in his article, describes Lynette Roberts as a 'War Poet'; not that she wrote of the battlefield, but of the home emptied by that war. Why indeed should the paraphernalia of trenches, guns and napalm, seem more sacred stuff of art than kitchen, cot and nappy sterilising fluid? Why the brotherhood of active suffering more suitable for literature than the sisterhood of passive loss? . . . This leads no nearer to a definition of women's art, nor of the special nature of female perception, but it would be helpful to literary criticism if the choice of motif and sign were freed from such prejudices.[29]

Lucid in her conviction of the equal value for art of differently gendered perspectives and spheres of experience, Gillian Clarke is unapologetic in her celebration of writing by women, pleased to publish it, and unhesitating in explaining contributions to the common good which women's poetry and prose could bring. Unlike Barbara Hardy, she does not write about the past, but about the present; and she offers immediate evidence to contradict Hardy's generalising claims that women's poetry is 'doctrinaire', 'crude' or 'aggressive', since none of these qualities are found in the material published in this issue of the *Anglo-Welsh Review*. Furthermore, Clarke's determination to contest pejorative evaluations of literary representations of the domestic launches an important and lasting subject that has pulled both women and men into its orbit. Robert Crawford has called 'home . . . one of the great themes, perhaps the major theme of late twentieth-century poetry in the English-speaking world'.[30]

Clarke's insistence, in this editorial, that Lynette Roberts was correctly classified as a 'war poet' even though she wrote about civilian life and not about active combat goes against critical conventions which have prevailed even into the twenty-first century. Her challenge of the assumption, voiced by one of her reviewers, that attention to the domestic always risks 'banality' was borne out of practice much closer to Clarke's own real and literary home. The reviewer who asserted this was Robert Nisbet, and the context was none other than his review of Clarke's own *Letter from a Far Country*, a joint commission by BBC Wales and the Welsh Arts Council, first broadcast on 22 March 1979.[31] Nisbet describes it as 'a housewife's musings' and a 'prolonged speculation on the traditional role of Woman'. He asserts that 'Gillian Clarke deals very much in domesticity with the strong attendant risks of banality and/or sentimentality. She avoided these dangers almost entirely here, and this was, I think, largely due to the impressive delicacy of the poem's phrasing.'[32] There is a barely disguised tone of surprise in Nisbet's review, that a housewife could be sufficiently articulate to be the speaker of the poem, and that the poet could have rendered a domestic environment without banality or sentimentality. His surprise is the sound of decades' worth of patriarchal conviction being rattled, and Clarke as both poet and Editor will not let it go unnoticed.

The normative sexism of Nisbet's review links to the second part of Clarke's editorial in which, having argued for literary criticism to free itself of gender prejudice, she turned to a new subject: Jean Rhys, who had died in May of that year, 1979. Clarke admires the writing, yet observes an alarming, even tragic, proximity between Rhys herself and the protagonist of *Good Morning, Midnight*:

> There is, even in someone so intelligent and talented, an alarming tendency to look up, out of huge, dark eyes, to flirt, to depend on the dangerous, dark side of femininity. In a television interview this image of Jean Rhys presenting herself as victim was greatly strengthened.[33]

While Clarke asserts that such dependencies are no longer in play, and even looks in to our own present with the aside, 'forty years on women might wonder what all the fuss is about', nevertheless her comments highlight collusion by women in the unequal power structures of patriarchy. Participation by both men and women in modes of gender inequality are drawn into focus by the two sections of Clarke's editorial; the causal links between societal expectations and their literary mirroring become clear, as do the constructed, culturally determined aspects of gender behaviour by both men and women.

When *Letter from a Far Country* was first broadcast, it was one of a suite of six works commissioned from poets for radio. Three men and three women contributed: Jeremy Hooker, Graham Allen, John Idris Jones, Sally Roberts and Ruth Bidgood: Gillian Clarke's poem was the only one which deployed a single voice and which was certain of its form as poetry rather than poetic drama or radio play. These features embody her singleness of vision, and her determination to focus in cohesive, uninterrupted fashion on the value of this perspective. Moreover, amongst the women, Clarke's was the only voice which handled themes of the present, even the future; Sally Roberts' 'A Waste of Heroes' represented a 'voice of myth and legend', while Bidgood's 'Hymn to Sant Ffraed' also dwelt in history. Clarke's choice was audaciously designed to represent the experience of contemporary women and to unite the many in her use of the lyric speaking 'I'. By contrast, all three men deployed multiple voices, allowed the present and the past to flow together and selected typically masculine domains of football match, pub or road (despite the no less evident risks of banality incurred by such locations, all passed without the reviewer's comment). The broadcast poem was marked not only by Clarke's written voice, but also by her spoken voice. No actors were employed for the delivery of *Letter from a Far Country*: Gillian Clarke read it herself. The musical score for the closing song, 'If we launch the boat', was composed by her son, Owain Clarke,[34] as if to illustrate her editorial assertion that the 'domus' was the 'powerhouse . . . for every emerging adult'. Identity between writer and protagonist, a value which Clarke questions in the case of Jean Rhys, was assumed with confidence here.

While, in her editorial, Clarke had argued for a truce in the battle between genders in the field of literary criticism, her deployment of the 'domus' as the setting for this poem was not a neutral act in the context of this debate. It was a move in a necessary readjustment which, in 1995, she suggested was well under way: 'The haunted indoorscape is as important now as the haunted landscape and the poet of family relationships is disturbing the war-poet's supremacy.'[35] Clarke brings war, as metaphor and history, into the contemporary arena of poetry, not simply by selecting for publication and taking time in her editorial to notice Anthony Conran's essay on the Second World War poetry by Lynette Roberts,[36] but also in her own writing. In *Letter from a Far Country* the speaker inhabits an empty house where memories linger: 'The minstrel boy to war has gone./But the girl stays. To mind things./She must keep. And wait. And pass time.'[37] Clarke's positioning of her perspective, as a critic and as a poet, in the 'secret interior',[38] which is a consequence of war and a service to it, was of immense importance in her campaign to allow equivalence of worth for differently gendered experiences. Menna Elfin applauded Clarke's conviction on the occasion of her sixtieth birthday in 1997: '[a]s a poet, Gillian has never denied the power of gender. Her exploration of womanist themes . . . offered a new understanding of subject matter that might in the past have been regarded as not central to life, or not profound enough to be the stuff of poetry.'[39] An alternative outcome of Clarke's early commitment to this subject matter is observed by Gwyneth Lewis, Clarke's junior by twenty years, who saluted Clarke's 'massive claim' for the 'high seriousness' of domesticity for poetry, 'which has meant that we are free *not* to consider that realm. I've been freed up by Gillian's work to look at other things.'[40]

Consolidating the Role of 'Women's Poetry' in the 1980s

Women as both critics and poets (sometimes, as here, the two were identical) were rapidly claiming space in poetry journals. The following year, Anne Stevenson used her review column in *Poetry Review* to venture into similar territory: 'What shall we say of women poets? Is there such a category? Is it not absurd to divide the ranks of the world's writers by sex?'[41] She mocks traditions of masculine literary history and judgement, she laments the absence of role models suffered by Edna St Vincent Millay, Elizabeth Barrett, Christina Rossetti. Stevenson asserts, 'I think it is possible that the poets of the future will look back on the second half of the Twentieth Century as an age when, for the first time in civilized Western history, women found multiple and original tongues of their own.' She posits: 'If we have to give *a* voice to the age, let it be that of Sylvia Plath,' admiring her 'experiential language for women which no poet would have dreamt of exploring before'. Crucial for arguments about the relationship between feminism and women's writing, Stevenson makes the towering assertion that '[t]he legacy of Plath was a perfectible art, not a political stance.'[42] Excited by the aesthetic avenues opened by Plath for poets who succeeded her, for Stevenson aesthetics take precedence over politics.

Gillian Clarke concurs:

Women's poetry isn't feminist poetry. Once in a while it is, but the two must not be confused. Political frustration marred the work of many an Anglo-Welsh poet until national self-confidence grew strong enough to allow us to write poetry instead of tracts. A poet's first duty is to poetry, and the increasing number of fine women poets does the feminist movement a deal of good too.[43]

Clarke returned to the promotion of poetry written by women, particularly by Welsh women, in her *Anglo-Welsh Review* editorial for Number 70 (1982), a move prompted by hearing two Welsh poets assert in broadcast media that 'there were almost no women writers in Wales'. Clarke observes, as she had in her 1979 editorial, that women writers rarely court fame; the consequence for poets such as Ruth Bidgood, Jean Earle, Sally Roberts Jones and Sheenagh Pugh was that 'their places on the stage are taken by men with smaller talents than theirs'. By 1982 the question was no longer one of existence but of visibility. For Number 70 Clarke used the full force of her power as Editor to throw light on poetry by women, both through selection – publishing poetry by nine women – and editorial comment. She noted how the normative use of the pronoun 'he' inscribes a masculine perspective, tending to elide women from the experience of reading and writing: she introduced the use of 'she' rather than 'he' to denote herself-as-editor:

> One problem that confronts an editor in the writing of an editorial is the avoidance of the word 'I'. In this editorial the third person singular is causing trouble. The solution is usually to use the word 'he', but in this case, women writers being the majority in the present issue of the *Anglo-Welsh Review*, I shall choose 'she'.[44]

Lack of female representation continued as a theme into Clarke's editorial for Number 72, in which she announced the formation of the 'Writers Union of Wales', but also that no women were invited to the first meeting, and few poets. She quoted from Janet Dube's postscript to the invitation to the second meeting:

> By no-one's deliberate intention, everyone at the meeting on May 22/23 was a man. Left to themselves men will inevitably tend to create organisations in which they feel comfortable and in which women who arrive later may feel less comfortable and effective . . . I am raising the issue to try to ensure that the meeting in September to establish the Union and confirm a constitution, is not a man's meeting.[45]

Clarke reported that the timing of the September meeting continued to exclude many who would have benefited from attendance, concluding: '[w]e wish the Union well, but hope it is still young enough to correct these early faults.' Her assuredness in the political arena matches that expressed, with an equal sense of natural justice, in her own poetry.

Clarke's departure from *The Anglo-Welsh Review* was marked by a valedictory issue, Number 78, the first of 1985. Its cover bore a black and white photograph of the buzzard's skull that inspired her poem 'Buzzard', the first two stanzas of which were printed on the inside cover. She sees, 'No sutures in the steep brow/of this cranium, as in mine/or yours. Delicate ellipse/as smooth as her own egg'.[46] As in 'The Fox', Clarke has chosen to make this predator, so readily connoting masculinity, a female; life-giver and death-bringer, the female predator embodies a microcosm of nature, focused in this stanza by the alignment of skull with egg. Clarke explores the buzzard's fertility, and, in the last stanzas of the poem, meditates on her blood's compulsion to risk. The subject of her poem, just as the editorial career saluted in Number 78, subverts gender stereotype and challenges status quo. The editorial of this number was an appraisal of her work for the journal, written by Roland Mathias, her predecessor in the role: 'She saw to it that poetry took the first place in her new numbers. Gone was the old admixture of prose with poetry: gone was the over-generous space for book reviews.'[47] One change that the incoming Editor, Greg Hill, was able to introduce immediately, was the publication of Clarke's poetry: 'it is fitting . . . that we should bid farewell to Gillian with an example of her own work, the more so because her strict editorial principles never allowed her to publish any of it while she was Editor'.[48]

Clarke's immediate task on stepping down from the editorship was again to foster work by new writers, this time through the foundation of the Lampeter Writers Group. Hilary Llewellyn-Williams joined in its founding year: '[t]hose first few months at Gillian's group were what turned me into a writer, rather than merely someone who sometimes wrote poems,'[49] she states, describing not only the professionalisation she learned from Clarke but also the way in which the arrival of a writers' group in rural west Wales, where young mothers suffered a particular isolation, offered a simple and exciting kind of hope. The group enabled Llewellyn-Williams to prepare her first full-length collection, *The Tree Calendar* (Poetry Wales Press, 1987), and to embark on a career which Clarke asserted a decade later was amongst those which 'helped change perceptions about subjects fit for poetry'.[50] The then unpublished Kathy Miles, poet, playwright and short story writer, was also a founder member, together with poet Sue Moules, who soon went on to publish her third collection, *Metaphors* (Spectrum, 1986). This was of course a mixed-sex group of writers, yet it seems that women in particular benefited from participation. The group, in combination with the gender politics of the era, brought women an opportunity to experience their professional potential.

With the increasing visibility of poetry being published by women it is hardly surprising that the poetry journals continued to take note. In the summer of 1987, *Poetry Wales* devoted itself to a 'Symposium: Is There A Women's Poetry?' The Editor, Mike Jenkins, expressed his anxiety about potential marginalisation or special pleading which might attend such a question, yet, he stated,

> I've chosen to focus on this upsurge in writing by women, not as a sop or to suggest it is some unified body of work, but as a belated recognition, and, hopefully, a step towards a situation where women's achievements are accepted and applauded, but no longer seen as a *phenomenon*.[51]

Articles by Sheenagh Pugh, Gloria Evans Davies, Christine Evans, Sally Roberts Jones and Val Warner were printed alongside substantial examples of their poetry, and a Review section which focused heavily on women's collections (e.g. Anne Stevenson's *Selected Poems*) or anthologies (e.g. *The Faber Book of Twentieth Century Women's Poetry*, ed. Fleur Adcock). Of the five women consulted, only Gloria Evans Davies found the segregation helpful for her own development. By contrast, Pugh stated, 'I object violently to . . . being judged as anything but an individual'; Evans, 'I don't accept that imagination is subject to limitations of gender'; Jones, 'I have never felt that I was writing as a woman rather than as a human being'; Warner, 'there is no such thing as women's poetry'.[52] Such statements of denial have recently been analysed by Toril Moi in her article 'I am not a woman writer' as defensive acts made under provocation within a sexist society, rather than as the expressions of freedom they may superficially appear to be.[53]

Although Gillian Clarke has never denied that her poetry is gendered and indeed has embraced the opportunities of sexual difference, two of the respondents to *Poetry Wales* cited her work to support their completely contrasting arguments. Jones, for example, asserted: 'It would be difficult to find any common link between Gillian Clarke, Ruth Bidgood, Sheenagh Pugh and Alison Bielski which had a special relevance in their being women – as distinct from their being parents, for instance, or interested in history or mythology or Wales'.[54] Christine Evans, on the other hand, placed Clarke's work at the heart of her discussion: 'I see poetry by women not as a separate development . . . but perhaps as part of the latest renewal of poetic sensibility . . . there is an extension of subject matter to include *work* and the small domestic rituals that bond us (what Jenny Joseph calls "dailiness" and Gillian Clarke "ceremonials": "As priests/we fold cloth, break bread, share wine,/hope there's enough to go round".)'[55] Evans states that in drafting her contribution she had begun to list aspects of women's work, 'until I realised how sub "Letter From a Far Country" it was beginning to sound. For men as well as women, honesty of perception and exact observation remain defences against sentimentality.' She quotes examples from recent poetry by women, noting that the 'images ring true, not clever', then develops her consideration of women's use of language by turning to an article by Gillian Clarke published in the 1987 Bloodaxe *Catalogue*:

> there are significant differences in the way women use language: girls, she argues, talk and read first and can therefore 'draw more deeply on the earliest animal sensations.' . . . The other suggestion, that most women convey a 'sense of moving from one image to another as if searching, as if not fully committed to a role, the metaphor not seen but felt' excited me . . . because I feel it is a central development . . . I liked the sensible suggested explanation for such 'fluid' imagery: 'Women are called on every day to be in transition. One minute we talk to the gas man, the next to a child.'[56]

We may question the philosophical sustainability of these views, as well as their embedded gender stereotypes, but that is not the point here. Instead, what Evans' reach for Clarke's practice demonstrates is that it was an important agent which facilitated and enabled the practice of other women in a workplace hitherto closed to them.

Within months of the symposium held by *Poetry Wales*, a sibling 'Symposium on Gender in Poetry' was conducted by the journal *Planet: The Welsh Internationalist* in which Gillian Clarke was one of the respondents. There Clarke argued, like Christine Evans, that poetry by women was bringing about a transition in poetic sensibility. She cited Eavan Boland's view that the woman poet confronted a dilemma 'inherent in a shadowy but real convergence between new experience and an established aesthetic'. In light of Boland's assertion, Clarke moves the discussion beyond consideration of gendered subject matter, theme or location, to focus instead on the new aesthetics introduced by women to poetry, observed, she argues, in syntax rather than subject. She proposes an 'impatience with the iambics and latinates of theory', positing in their place the introduction of a new tone, 'conversational, eloquent, suitable for talking to bright children'. Plath provides her touchstone, in whose voice she finds recognisable 'truth' and 'naturalness', a poetry based in experience of life. These qualities, she argues, are 'tendencies' in which male poets, Larkin and Heaney for example, also participate, so that collectively women and men are generating a radical 'shift that is reshaping taste'.[57]

Clarke may overstate her case here, and in her effort to promote what she sees as an innovative directness of expression, risks a new infantilisation of both poet and reader. But she is beginning to move the argument away from gender polarisation towards a vision of a more collaboratively devised practice in which neither subject matter nor style was ghettoised. Immediately prior to writing for the *Planet* 'Symposium of Gender in Poetry' she had served as editor for the 1987 Poetry Book Society anthology, in which she had attempted to offer readers, as well as writers, equitable exposure. Reflecting in 1994 on the editorial adjustments she made for that volume, she stated:

When I edited the Poetry Book Society anthology in 1987, there were fifty poets in it, and twenty-five of them were women. In 1986, the editor had six women in the anthology. In 1988, there were about ten women. In 1991 Anne Stevenson restores this balance again. I didn't do it on purpose when I was editor; I just chose the best of the poets. It's not to do with subject but with a way of seeing. My taste led me to those poets. If the editors are men, their sensibilities naturally turn towards what they favor, what they enjoy and respond to.[58]

While there is a tussle between the interests, no doubt political as well as aesthetic, of male and female editors during this period, perhaps a measure of the success of Clarke's strategy can be gauged from the fact that in 1993 the first all-female judging panel for the Arvon Poetry Competition, chosen 'to avoid the possibility of any prejudice',[59] selected Don Paterson's 'A Private Bottling' as the winning poem. There is no guarantee, of course, that women are prejudice-neutral – indeed there is ample evidence to the contrary – but what does seem remarkable, in terms of Clarke's avowed quest for a new aesthetic sensibility, is that together this panel of Eavan Boland, Gillian Clarke, Liz Lochhead and Penelope Shuttle awarded the prize to a male poet.

This chapter set out to explore how Gillian Clarke contributed to the acceptance of women into the arena of poetry, as the first necessary move towards women's acquisition of an authoritative and representative voice. The evidence considered here, which has looked well beyond her poetry itself into the realm of what might be termed the wider business of poetry, with its editorial personae, their decisions, their stimulation of debate, and the shaping contributions these have made to fast-paced cultural change taking place within and beyond the poetry world, demonstrates the extent to which she was an artificer of her own success as well as that of others. Without Clarke's dynamic professional interventions at every level, the journey from 1979, when men referred to 'women poets as if they were strange objects suddenly landed among us',⁶⁰ to 1987, when Mike Jenkins asserted that he wanted to help to create a situation 'where women's achievements are accepted and applauded',⁶¹ is likely to have been much more uncertain. Hitherto, critics have focused on Clarke's published poetry, particularly *Letter from a Far Country*, as the agent of change. Entwistle asserts, for example, that 'Clarke's letter crucially authorised the value of the woman-centred history and experiences it imagined and which, alongside peers . . . she would import into the literary and poetic traditions of her time.'⁶² This investigation demonstrates that while Clarke's published poetry was certainly an important instrument of change for poets and critics alike, it was not the only tool at her command, and that her agency as editor and activist has also been powerfully decisive. The outcome, however, is agreed: Entwistle concludes, '[t]he very role in which Gwyneth Lewis's gigantic millennial poem was commissioned from her, as first national poet for Wales, confirms the success of the shift which Clarke helped engineer.'⁶³

The Voice of the Tribe

The arrival of women as active participants in the creation of a vibrant poetry culture in Wales forced a slow readjustment amongst the puzzled male establishment of poets, editors, reviewers and readers. Gillian Clarke's leadership in this movement was unquestionably transformational, building the road towards acceptance which eventually enabled first Gwyneth Lewis and then herself to assume the cultural authority of National Poet of Wales. But this was not the era's only battle in which Clarke took a leading role. Argument about the legitimacy of English as a medium of expression for poetry claiming to be Welsh has been longstanding in Wales. Consequently, Clarke, as an English-language poet, has always been, or perceived herself to be, under implicit attack. Even her first publications in *Poetry Wales* threw her English-language practice into relief since this was a bilingual journal, printing poems in Welsh and English alongside one another. The following discussion, therefore, explores the ways in which she has negotiated the challenge this posed to her potential authority to speak as a national poet, to represent all citizens of a nation who have long been deeply divided about what their proper language should be.

She began by using her editorial position at *The Anglo-Welsh Review*, an exclusively English-language journal as its name suggests, to move the argument forward. While her Autumn 1979 editorial had promoted the 'domus' as a meaningful subject matter for poetry, in the previous issue she had addressed the cultural division of language duality in order to advance an understanding of home on the scale of nation. The date of her campaign was not random. Welsh national identity, what it was, how it was to be positioned in relation to the other nations of the United Kingdom, came under severe self-scrutiny before and after the referendum on devolution held in Wales on St David's Day, 1 March 1979. The question of whether the people of Wales wished to have a Welsh Assembly, phrased as 'Do you want the provision of the Wales Act 1978 to be put into effect?', was answered with 'Yes' by 11.9 per cent of the Welsh electorate; 46.9 per cent voted 'No', while 41.2 per cent did not vote.[64] This outcome was determined just three weeks before the broadcast of *Letter from a Far Country*, supplying for that poem a context in which the Welsh territory of the poem's 'far country' stands proud of the nuances of gender identity which have tended in critical interpretation to predominate as the location of that place. In her editorial for *The Anglo-Welsh Review* following the referendum result, written even before the snows of that spring had melted, Clarke numbers herself amongst the defeated. She offers a brief explanation for the result, and issues a warning:

> We hesitated because of our own divisions, our self-doubt ... the most frightening comment of all came not from a politician but from a businessman. He declared that Wales is not united as a nation; that North Wales has always looked, economically, to Merseyside; that Mid-Wales is connected, commercially, with the English Midlands; that South Wales businessmen look to London for their links. If this casually expressed belief is considered in all its implications the spectre of a Wales, carved up by businessmen, its culture and language totally disregarded, its doubts and divisions deliberately exploited, should terrify us into unity and teach those on either side of the language barrier to love and value each other. What if some future devolutionists decided to divide Britain into economically convenient strips, instead of nations? It is not romantic to consider Wales a whole if quarrelsome country or to wish the Referendum had been fought on cultural and not economic lines.[65]

Clarke was determined to overcome the 'language barrier', which, she argues, presented a dangerous obstacle on the path to national and cultural cohesion. In an act of extraordinarily percipient cultural diplomacy, she had prepared for the post-referendum situation, whatever it should be, by joining forces with the editor of the Welsh Language journal *Y Genhinen*. Together they had written to seventy-five of 'our best writers in Welsh and English, chosen for their achievement as writers' to solicit a declaration of 'support for the principle of Devolution'. Clarke reports that 90 per cent of writers had responded positively. She prints the bilingual declaration, unusual for this normally monolingual publication, and the names of all the signatories in her editorial, hailing 'a fellowship of some of the most creative and articulate people of Wales'.[66] It was a display of cultural unity, to demonstrate partnership across languages and to combat what she considered to be the most wounding of her country's internal divisions.

In that same post-referendum editorial she told a family story, in terms which render it both a fairy tale and a parable. As a narrative of blood lines, it enlarges upon the theme of cultural unity:

> [H]ere is a history of small importance, chosen because it is known, told because it is typical. In 1650 in Llanbedrog in Caernarfonshire there lived a farmer called William Jones. He had several children, among them two sons. One was clever and was sent to an uncle for care and education . . . He became a lawyer, a linguist, and went to London. Another son took his father's Christian name for surname, and was known as Williams Williams, farmer. The line continued, generations of Williams farming in Lleyn, moving no further from home than a few miles. But in the nineteenth century, Thomas Williams, born in Lleyn . . . took his line to the South, to Llangynog in Carmarthenshire . . . By 1934 the son of Wil Williams, a railwayman, was moving East to Cardiff where the British Broadcasting Company was opening its first studio in Wales and new jobs glittered. His mother tongue, Welsh, was that of all his forefathers. The geography of the landscape in which they lived made sure of it. Their work also had protected the language and held them to the land . . . Even the last Williams of the male line used Welsh as the language of his life and of his working day. But for his children, born in Cardiff in the Second World War, the mother tongue was English. Their mother was from a Welsh-speaking Denbighshire family, all farmers, all, by now, turning to English as the forces of the North-East of Wales give way to the weakness of its border position. What happened to those of the Williams of Lleyn who are here unchartered? Many, presumably, moved to Liverpool, Birkenhead, Birmingham. One thing is certain, that a multiplying tribe could not have found work . . . in twentieth-century Wales . . . (The exiled Welsh had no vote in the Referendum.) A map traced with the movements of just one family across three centuries covers the whole of Wales with lines like marks on the snow-bound hills, yet just as strangely, the tracks of this branch-line stay within the country, as if Offa's dyke were a sea and there were no traversing it . . . The Williams tribe, as do all our tribes, belong, in reality, to the whole nation of Wales.[67]

By showing the metamorphoses of traditional ways of life under pressure from economy and industry, personal ambition and migration, Clarke demonstrates that the cohesion of the Welsh 'tribe' is maintained across such forces of change, and that it is a kinship which accommodates pluralities of language, economy or location. At the beginning of this story she places home 'no further than a few miles from Lleyn'; by the end, home includes 'the whole nation of Wales'. Her careful phrasing of the relationship of ownership, the 'belonging' between the 'Williams tribe' and 'the whole nation of Wales', erases hierarchy and asserts in its place an equivalence between family tribe and whole nation, Welsh speaker and English speaker.

The Williams story is of course easily recognisable as the story of Clarke's own family: her father, John Penri Williams, was the Welsh speaker whose wife renounced her own language and switched their daughters, Gillian and her sister, to a 'mother tongue' of English. It is also the narrative that would give rise to Clarke's long poem 'Cofiant', for the research of which she was awarded an Arts Council of Wales Bursary in 1981, and which she published in *Letting in the Rumour*, ten years after this post-referendum editorial. 'Clarke relocates the cofiant's emphasis from the public realm of history to the home, not to replace one with the other but to show their inextricability,' argues Michael Thurston in his compelling essay on this poem.[68]

Clarke's familial proximity to questions of language difference inform her rebuttal of hierarchical inequality between English- and Welsh-language poetry. Primed for action by her personal circumstances, her strategic response to the referendum stands in striking contrast to any adopted by fellow poetry journal editors, including J. P. Ward at *Poetry Review*, who, as Matthew Jarvis has recently observed, barely noticed it at all.[69] However, its aftermath in Wales entailed an almost inevitable polarisation of positions such that two years later, in 1981, even the name of the journal Clarke edited was under fire. Again, she speaks with the authority of the editor of a national poetry journal, patiently setting the scene before staking out her territory. 'Since Saunders Lewis concluded in 1939 that there could be no such thing as an Anglo-Welsh literature the question of the validity of the term has been almost continually debated,' she explains, continuing, '[t]he magazine *Arcade* . . . shuns the term altogether . . . "We are not Anglo-anything" they argue, "we are Welsh."' Clarke is assured in response to the question she is forced to ask, 'Where . . . does that leave *The Anglo-Welsh Review*?'

> Wales is our home ground and our main aim is to cover a range of material which has some relevance to the cultural life of the nation . . . Whether that life is lived primarily in Welsh or in English is a matter on

which it would not be prudent to pronounce without further space for qualification. But so far as it is lived in English our job is to be an expression of that life.[70]

Clarke's deft sidestepping of judgements concerning relative artistic merit or political resonance of each language is inclusive, pragmatic and respectful of aesthetic choice. She shows herself to be as unwilling to allow nationalism an overriding place in poetry as she had feminism.[71] Even so, the topic remains amongst the most painfully divisive for citizens of Wales. In 1987 Richard Poole contended in the pages of *Poetry Wales*, '[d]oes not writing in English actively retard the nationalistic interest, since it is the prevalence of English which is unacceptable?'[72] There was not, and there would not be, a benign cohabitation of languages of the kind Clarke seeks to represent amongst the bitter accusations and counter-accusations flying in the wake of the referendum. As recently as 2013, Gwyneth Lewis, who embraces the creative tension of working in and between two native languages, testifies to the perceived treachery of bilingualism itself: '[i]t's still regarded in some quarters as a betrayal of the Welsh language, because immediately you enter into a relationship with the English, it's taking the place of the Welsh.'[73]

Gillian Clarke's response to the competition between English and Welsh is to generate a poetic practice that resists the binary choice of 'either/or'. This is not to suggest that Clarke's occasional Welsh-language poetry qualifies her as a bilingual poet. Nor is it to inflate the significance of Clarke's occasional use of Welsh words in her English-language poetry, though it does require attention to this element of her practice. And neither is it to rely on the way in which her poetry in English is structured by traditions and practices that derive from the oral corpus of the Welsh bards rather than the textual corpus of the English lyric. It is, however, to accord due weight to the way in which Clarke has embraced the bi-cultural opportunities of her situation and negotiated its conflict: 'I live in a land with two languages. Twice as lucky . . . It's an edge. There's no moment of life in Wales that hasn't got that edge, unless you decide you're not Welsh.' Alternatively, '[b]eing Welsh but brought up in English adds that edge that loss gives to writing. It may be another example of the power of absence,' she stated in an interview in 2001.[74] For Clarke, luck and loss figure as equal opposites. They are mutually conditioning: '[t]o speak two languages is to be in two minds, to see both sides. Welsh means them, the strangers; its translation, "Cymry" means us, we who belong.'[75] Clarke's dual language situation positions her as a perpetual outsider, magnetised between the poles of 'us' and 'them', in a constant state of 'otherness'. Bakhtin, as Robert Crawford has pointed out, represents this as a necessary condition for 'creative understanding': '[i]t is immensely important . . . to be located outside the object of his or her creative understanding – in time, in space, in culture . . . our real exterior can be seen and understood only by another people, because they are located outside us in space and because they are *others*.'[76] This creatively enabling perspective is the given of the culture which Clarke brings to the fore.

As powerfully as her mother sought identity with the ruling class, so Clarke celebrates difference, measured both internally and externally: 'There are people who live here . . . who might as well be living in the London suburbs . . . That doesn't include all those who don't speak Welsh, but it includes all those who don't accept the fact that Wales is different.'[77] The subject is addressed directly in 'Border', a politically resonant poem about speaking Welsh in Wales. Written in English and therefore freighted with estranging irony, the speaker announces, 'I'm foreign in my own country'.[78] In the last stanza, '[a]t the garage', the speaker is met with '"Sorry love, no Welsh"', and '[a]t the shop I am slapped/by her hard "What!"'. John Kerrigan points out of the poem that, 'this "Border" is nowhere specified as the cartographic and administrative line that separates England from Wales . . . it runs internally and locally through fields and pockets of Welsh-speaking groups'. The poem, Kerrigan contends, captures 'the divisions that . . . exist within Welshness as well as along the edges that run through it'.[79] Clarke's rejection of the binary choice between the civic and aesthetic legitimacy of English or Welsh entails the straightforward decision to place the tension between languages at the heart of her practice. She seizes the opportunity for naming the loss of division which is, after all, common to speakers on both sides of the 'language barrier', and she revels in the linguistic and conceptual gains. Across her corpus this is expressed as an audacious confrontation of cultural duality, seeking always to display rather than hybridise difference and entailing her service to traditional Welsh social and cultural functions of poetry.

By embracing doubleness, Clarke's work fashions the culture of Wales as a 'debatable land', or what Robert Crawford has named 'a shifting, dynamic border territory'. Crawford elaborates, citing Bakhtin: 'the realm of culture has no internal territory: it is entirely distributed along the boundaries.'[80] Her work recognises the 'edge', or the 'power of absence', as a constitutive element of Welsh culture which conditions not only herself but also the nation at large: 'this was an area of tension, a minefield of pride and loss that language had become in our tribe'.[81] It leads her practice into what Homi Bhabha has called 'those spaces that are continually, contingently "opening out", exposing [how] difference is neither one or the other but *something else besides*, in-between'.[82] Her refusal of the binary choice between languages enables her to exploit the fact that, as Robert Crawford puts it, '[i]n the postmodern world, home has no one pure language; its language is heteroglot, richly impure.'[83]

The 'edge' location of a land with two languages is inscribed in Clarke's family biography, 'Cofiant', through repeated juxtaposition between the Welsh proper names of people and places and the English narrative in which the poem embeds them. Michael Thurston offers a fine-grained interpretation of 'Cofiant' which concludes that Clarke, ultimately, presents an 'evacuative' picture of national identity, in which it is presiding absence that supervenes over any lasting claim to geopolitical place. Thurston's reading attends to both the form and the content of the poem, in which, he argues, a 'self-interrupting lyric sequence' repeatedly traces ancestral lines back to vanishing points. Yet the sequence has a double ending: first, a lyric which announces that 'the sea wastes words . . .//It drafts and redrafts the coast/and is never done/writing at the edge//its doodle of scum'; and second, a memorial genealogy which begins with 'Daughter of Penri Williams, wireless engineer of Carmarthenshire and Ceinwen Evans of Denbighshire', which reaches back through thirty generations of sons to 'son of Gwaethfoedd of Cibwr in Gwent and Morfudd, d. of Ynyr Ddu'. Focusing on the English lyric which ends the sequence in a shifting space of littoral record-keeping, Thurston concludes that, 'Clarke remains in the liminal space between the desire for a distinctive Welsh culture and Welsh nation and the desire for commitments that supersede the national.'[84] Thurston pushes his observation towards a reading of this poem which claims an effacement of conviction in national identity in favour of 'writing at the edge',[85] positioning self, family and nation on the restless shoreline of time and tide. An alternative interpretation of the poem's ending can be elicited by looking at the juxtaposition between the shoreline lyric and the family biography. These two lyrics face one another on the open page of *Letting in the Rumour*, verso against recto, the book's spine separating, or joining, them, to make the 'edge' a destination, a place of positive arrival.[86] The materiality of the book, and the positioning of these two lyrics on facing pages of a single opening, affords an aesthetic replication of what Clarke sees as the physical landscape of Wales, which she also configures in terms of a book:

> From where I write I see a landscape open like a book, a landscape of valleys and hills . . . Valleys, and a land that is tilted to face its neighbour, make for familiarity and open lives . . . It encourages an already talkative people . . . to question the stranger.[87]

The spine of the book, the space between pages and between lyrics, provides the structure which enables the mutual interrogation of self and stranger, of self as stranger. The pendulum swing between these two forms of otherness, generated by the spatial relationship between the two last poems of the sequence, defies poetic closure and assures openness. 'The space between languages', Clarke contends, 'is as dynamic as the huge currents of the Severn estuary between the two shores.'[88]

The idea of 'the space between' looks, in turn, towards the lyric sequence which Clarke composed after the completion of 'Cofiant', namely 'The King of Britain's Daughter' (1993). Like 'Cofiant', this sequence blends Welsh legend with family memory, and it too ends on a shoreline: 'Walking the beach/ we felt the black grains give/and the sun stood/one moment on the sea/before it fell.'[89] Entwistle suggestively considers the factors which are held in balance here: '[t]he poem's final stanzas implicitly weigh the quasi-tidal provisionalities of its own textualities (the sea writes on sand/. . ./It discards, draft after draft,/ each high tide a deadline') against the suddenly vulnerable-seeming materialities (of footprint and rocking stone) . . . on which her father's storytelling depended.'[90] The energy, and indeed the substance, of this lyric sequence is fuelled by movement between polar opposites: Branwen's 'eloquent starling' brings word, the single untranslatable word of a name, across the Irish sea to call for rescue.[91] Eloquence crosses the gulf of separation.

Also like 'Cofiant', the composition of this lyric sequence was triggered in response to a specific cultural event. The origin story of 'The King of Britain's Daughter' was first told by Clarke in an essay written for the book *How Poets Work*, edited by Tony Curtis (1996); it has been frequently reprinted, usually under the title 'Cordelia's Nothing', and retold by others.[92] In 1990 she took part in 'the first of the Hay-on-Wye Literary Festival weekend "Squantums"': six poets were each commissioned to write an oratorio on the subject of:

> 'Border: Fatherland, Motherland'. What I saw at once was that border country in the self where mother and father meet, an edge where there is tension and conflict. At the same time it was the border where the two languages of Wales define themselves and each other.[93]

But the origin story that Clarke does not tell here, which accounts more vitally for her vision of the given metaphor as a border specifically between languages, is the story of her personal relationship with the languages of Wales, already outlined in her 1979 editorial. Her parents were both Welsh speakers; while her father cherished his native tongue as much in ancient legends as in the language of daily life, and spoke Welsh everywhere except in the home from which his wife had banished it, her mother refused to speak Welsh from the moment their first daughter, Gillian, was born. 'A child of a tenant farmer, she noted that her father's landlords were rich, privileged, and English, and she made up her mind in bitterness to escape her own heritage.'[94] Her mother's internalisation of the imbalance of power between nations expresses not merely a colonised oppression but the wholesale denial of a culture. 'A lost language represents the obliteration of a culture,' Clarke asserts in her important essay on the role of poetry in a country with two languages, 'Voice of the Tribe'.[95]

The banishment of Welsh from her home stood for the young Gillian Clarke as a proxy for national identity. Being Welsh was, therefore, to understand oneself as the coloniser dictated: displaced and precarious, neither here nor there. Determined to access the language of 'speech, thought, and dream' of her ancestors, Clarke, in deliberate defiance of her mother, taught herself Welsh during her teenage years.[96] The Welsh-language poet Menna Elfin summarises the momentum of this late-coming: 'Gillian Clarke's sense of loss at being denied the language at an early age has been distilled into a deep understanding of Welsh identity in all its variety, and into a desire for its survival and growth.'[97] Clarke herself confronts it directly in the first collection she published as National Poet of Wales, *A Recipe for Water* (2009). The first five poems of that collection, 'First Words', 'A Pocket Dictionary', 'Glas y Dorlan', 'Not' and 'Otter', meditate on the acquisition of Welsh as a conduit to insight and fullness of being. But it is the experience of learning to see the world through both languages, not Welsh at the expense of English, and the recognition of difference, that are inscribed and embodied by these poems, and that come to rest figuratively in the last line of 'Not', in the liminal space of 'the *ll-ll-ll* of waves on the shore'.[98] These opening poems establish a leitmotiv that sounds throughout the volume as a whole. The poem 'Fflam', for example, addressed to her immediate predecessor as National Poet, the Welsh-language poet Gwyn Thomas, celebrates their shared responsibility 'to speak in tongues/ to pass on simple truths'.[99] The choice of Welsh to name a poem written in English embodies the Welsh duality of 'tongues', while the mystical connotations of the image also invoke what Carol Rumens identified as the Academi's 'un-nerving job description' for National Poet: 'an ability to communicate, to write well and often, and to have a regular route into the magic that makes verse work'.[100] Alternatively, the poem 'Welsh' meditates on what a younger generation in Wales can take for granted, 'as if it's ordinary/to shake the dust off a rumour,/to shimmy and shout in Welsh in a Cardiff square'.[101] The 'two minds' of the heteroglot are simultaneously present, observing and observed, belonging and alien.

The opening poems of *Recipe for Water* and indeed the title poem itself, 'Recipe for Water', are a reprise of 'The Water Diviner', an early poem published in *Letter from a Far Country* which Clarke explained was about 'finding language, finding poetry'.[102] In that earlier poem, Clarke described the act of divining water during the drought of 1976, discovering how 'a thorough bass too deep/for the naked ear, shouts through the hose//a word we could not say, or spell, or remember,/something like "Dŵr . . . dŵr"'.[103] Beyond conscious apprehension, this buried, hidden source of life shouts its name in Welsh, erupting into the surface of the English poem. It is an image of something concealed, which is found, and as such it communicates simultaneously loss and recovery. The unassimilated, untranslated word asserts its difference from the English lyric it intersects. There is a risk of political essentialising here, of claiming that Welsh water in a Welsh garden can only speak in Welsh, that the land and its elements have a specific cultural identity, buried under a superficial crust of Englishness. But as a metaphor for 'finding poetry', this risk is superseded by insistence on the value of linguistic difference, together with the life-giving energy of the acknowledgement of difference. In one of the later poems, 'A Pocket Dictionary', which describes the speaker's use of her father's Welsh–English dictionary fifty years after his death, the energy of colliding languages has been entirely absorbed by metaphor, in which 'definitions, ambiguities' of words resurface as 'a seepage in the earth, a gleam of meaning,/a sudden uprise of remembering'.[104] The absence of Welsh, and of the father, emerge in the figurative presence of poetry itself, bringing new life out of bereavement. The third lyric of the title sequence, 'A Recipe for Water', savours '[t]he second word for water./*Dŵfr. Dŵr. Dyfroedd*. Dover.'[105] The list of words moves from Welsh to English, ending with the English place name which contains in its etymology the Welsh word for 'water', 'reminding us', Clarke states elsewhere, 'that the British language was Welsh'.[106] While buried in the English place name is the Welsh word for water, much as 'dŵr' was buried in Clarke's garden, the place name also crucially asserts difference and change. '*Dŵfr*' is not the same as 'Dover', though the charm is in observing the trace of ancient migrations and shifting geopolitical territories contained in the relationship between the two words. The next lyric of 'Recipe for Water' lists words for water, '*wysg, uisc, dŵr, hudra, acqua, agua, eau, wasser*',[107] revelling in the sonic specificity of each word, the quiddity of its embodied form in the speaker's mouth, and recognising the untranslatability of the meaning-containing sound.

Philip Owens observes of Clarke's work, 'she knows that words have a *real* power; that they don't merely describe but effect. Her poetry is as much an exploration of this as it is of the subject of any one poem.'[108] The agency of words is nowhere more evident than in what emerges as the impossible act of translation. Clarke's poem, 'Translation/after translating from Welsh, particularly a novel by Kate Roberts', in the collection *Five Fields* (1998), reflects on the irreducible particularity of one language in relation to another.[109] The poem is a two-stanza lyric, as if to suggest the twinned connection of translation between origin and copy. The first stanza is heady with eroticism, opening, 'Your hand on her hand – you've never been/this close to a woman since your mother's beauty'. The embodied thrill of the intimate manipulation of words is palpable, the linguistic intercourse of the act of translation emphasised through the insistence of duality in the poem, 'two up, two down, too small'. Yet what emerges is the untranslatability of one language into another. The '*real* power' of words is specific to a given language:

> . . . But you're lost for words,
> can't think of the English for *eirin* – it's on the tip of your –
> But the cat ate your tongue, licking peach juice
> from your palm with its rough *langue de chat*,
> *tafod cath*, the rasp of loss.[110]

Clarke's 'translation' catches the ache across difference. She turns to a third language, French, as a way of gesturing away from binary choice. The perpetual tension of living between two languages is caught too in the mid-line caesura of the last line, the comma, the breath, that separates Welsh and English. The poem may seem to announce failure, but its act of so doing creates a particular belonging which owns the pain of internal division as a constitutive element.

A further refinement in Clarke's confrontation of the untranslatability of two intimately known languages emerges when she explores, as she does repeatedly across her corpus, the Welsh word *glâs*. This word denotes a colour which is both green and blue. There is no English equivalent and therefore no Anglophone perception of this particular colour nor of its connotations. The word *glâs* opens a realm of sensory perception to a Welsh speaker which is simply not available to an English speaker. In the early poem 'Neighbours' Clarke uses the word to augur a new covenant of the world cleansed after the poisoning of Chernobyl, deliberately recalling the dove's olive branch after Noah's flood: 'one bird returning with green in its voice//glasnost/golau glas/a first break of blue'.[111] She places 'glas' to mirror the sound of the Russian word 'glasnost', which she also does not translate, though it is traditionally interpreted to mean 'openness'. Three different languages articulate together a hope for a recovering world, the completeness of which depends on juxtaposition.

She returns to the word *glâs* in 'Pigeon House Wood', a poem written for the Aberglasne estate, in *Nine Green Gardens* (2000):[112]

> Pools turn
> to eels of light oiling between fern
> and water's soft mutations. *Aber*, a confluence
> and *glas*, a blue-green sound, after reflection's silence.[113]

The poem eludes the enterprise of defining its terms, instead relegating explanation to her own editorial notes. It prefers the densely layered pun of 'reflection's silence', for which *glâs*, the colour and the sound, as well as the echo of the English homonym 'glass', provides the mirror surface for meditation and doubling, resulting in paradoxically voiced 'silence' rather than speech. For a later poem, from the collection *Ice* (2012), entitled 'Gleision/ for the four miners killed at Gleision drift mine, 15 September 2011', Clarke explains that 'Gleision' is not simply a place name but also the plural of *glâs*. This establishes an organic relationship between language and place, much as her comment on 'Dover' had done. Language becomes a means of orientation, a map of belonging which, figured by oxymoron, places the duality of absence and presence at its core:

> *Glâs* of rivers and rain and waterways
> where streams and heroes are lost
> in the hill's dark hollowed heart.[114]

In this collection, Clarke devotes an entire poem to 'Glâs' in which again the Welsh word sits unassimilated within the English poem given over to its exploration. The final couplet of this sonnet announces a concealed presence: 'like those rivers, reservoirs, aquifers underground/invisible silvers silent as ultrasound'.[115] The subterranean network of waterways, familiar from 'The Water Diviner' and serving a similar metaphorical function of 'discovering poetry' here, can only be '*glâs*' when it reaches the light above ground. The poem is another assertion of the 'power of absence', the articulation of which is so central to Clarke's method and aim.

These are, however, largely literal instances of duality: juxtapositions, collisions, a reaching for and across two languages. They are concerned with content, with vocabulary and its connotations, and this lexicon opens at a fresh page with every new subject matter. These examples are partnered by her development of poetic craft which she deliberately learned from Welsh-language poetry. This has a structural value for her practice; it provides an instrument for the treatment of any subject matter, and as such underwrites her entire corpus. Early in her career she described certain technical qualities of Welsh-language poetry which she set out to assimilate with her own professional craft:

> I'm very fond of the seven syllable line, and I've got that from Dafydd ap Gwilym, and from others like him, though not necessarily consciously. And I don't use rhymes at the endings of lines, but at other places in the line, and that, too, is a very Welsh characteristic. I love using *cynghanedd*. I don't do this regularly as the Welsh language poets do, but I let it happen and find a private pleasure in it. It is something that puts an extra tremor or richness into the line. Also, occasionally, the word that comes in to a poem is a Welsh one, as in one poem where I use the word 'dŵr' instead of water, because it was the right one to use on that occasion.[116]

Dafydd ap Gwilym was a fourteenth-century poet admired for his sophisticated craft, which proved an inspiration for successive generations. As a measure of his continuing significance, in 1973 Meic Stephens chose to mark the close of his career as Editor of *Poetry Wales* with a special issue dedicated to the study of Dafydd ap Gwilym. The last section of that issue, entitled 'A Garland for Dafydd ap Gwilym', published poems commissioned in response to his work. Gillian Clarke was the only woman amongst the contributing poets, and her poem, 'Dyddgu Replies to Dafydd', voices a lover's perspective, the only poem in this 'garland' which lets a woman speak. Dyddgu imagines a path of poetry open to her sex, which Clarke makes real in the self-referential act of writing the poem:

> The feet of young men beat, somewhere far off
> on the mountain. I would women
> had roads to tread in winter
> and other lovers waiting.[117]

The last two lines of this quotation have the seven-syllable line, Clarke's fondness for which she attributes to Dafydd ap Gwilym. Her mid-line positioning of the rhyme words 'feet' and 'beat', which pun as technical descriptors of poetic metre, follow a bardic rather than a lyric tradition which she deliberately acquires.

Clarke's use of *cynghanedd* takes many forms, and has a far-reaching presence throughout her work. It is this which primarily conditions and announces the national belonging of her poetry, at the same time refusing an 'either/or' response to Welsh or English as the language of poetry.[118] In an article to introduce British readers to contemporary Welsh poetry, 'A Musical Nation', written for *Poetry Review* in 1982, Clarke describes *cynghanedd* as 'a system of consonantal repetition and internal rhyme' best known in English through the poetic techniques of Gerard Manley Hopkins.[119] In her own work it can be seen in the sensuous abundance and the sonorous patterns of her diction; it is evident in her coinages, metaphors and epithets, descriptions that work in the tradition of *dyfalu* or riddling. *Cynghanedd* gives her poetry a musicality which communicates exuberance or 'joyful vitality' much as that credited to Dafydd ap Gwilym.[120]

This quality places Clarke's work in another, cognate and core Welsh tradition: praise poetry derived from the legendary sixth-century poet Taliesin. Anne Stevenson notices these twinned qualities of *cynghanedd* and praise poetry in her review of Clarke's *Selected Poems*: 'I don't think there exists a book of poems today so abundant in its imagery or so generous in its acceptance of the world as it is.'[121] A playfully self-referential example of the praise poem tradition can be seen in a more recent poem from the collection *Ice*, 'Taliesin. *Frank Lloyd Wright 1867–1959*', in which Clarke praises the achievements of the architect whose mother emigrated from Clarke's home county of Ceredigion. He named his summer home in Wisconsin 'Taliesin' and this has been adopted as the name for the school of architecture he founded in Arizona:

> Raised in the old language, the old stories,
> he learned his lines from the growth-rings of trees,
> . . .
>   his favourite red
> the rusting zinc of old Welsh barns, of *twlc* and *beudy*.
> . . .
> He sang a new architecture
> from the old, in perfect metre.[122]

Clarke's attention to the fabric of her poetry, the 'new architecture' of her own practice which embodies its liminal location and declares its cultural belonging in the very act of its making, writing or singing, guarantee that the landscape, place names, legends in her work are never merely scenic backdrop or local atmosphere for English poetry, but cohere organically with the artifice through which she reconfigures the geography of her country and the spirit of her nation.

Linden Peach has posited of Welsh poets who write in English that 'their aesthetic is so Welsh, despite the fact that they write in English, that it is more profitable and illuminating to focus upon what is un-English in their work rather than upon what is not Welsh. Ultimately, the former leads us back to Wales.'[123] As Michael Thurston argues, Peach's attempts to ascribe a polyglot aesthetic to the work of Welsh poets writing in English repeatedly measure

English-language poetry against an 'almost primordial Welshness'.[124] Peach's argument thereby falls into exactly the binary trap which his plea for 'more polyphonous models of identity' purports to eschew.[125] Clarke's practice refuses to choose. Her recourse to the structures of Welsh-language poetry within her English-language corpus mounts a deliberate display of the mutually informing presence and absence of two languages. Her voice acquires authority by appropriating forms and techniques from both English and Welsh and makes a virtue of destabilising their conventional associations. If it was the case, as Alice Entwistle argues by citing Emry Humphreys, that the Welsh story-teller's ancient function was to 'celebrate and sustain the social order',[126] then Clarke flies in the face of tradition. Her insistence on the positive value of duality disrupts the social and aesthetic status quo by forcing tension into the foreground.

Alice Ostriker's statement that '[t]o be a creative woman in a gender-polarised culture is to be a divided self' can be rephrased in the case of Gillian Clarke, as 'to be a creative woman in a language-polarised culture is to be a divided self'.[127] Clarke herself has long been alert to the way these twinned divisions of gender and nationality have fashioned her work: 'I am certain . . . since writing *Letter from a Far Country* that the right way forward is to be more not less oneself. If I'm Welsh, and if I'm a woman, then what I must not try to be is a perfect English man poet and to model myself on what's going on amongst the men.'[128] Others have reinforced her self-perception: 'Adrian Henri once said to me, "you're in two political situations, being both Welsh and a woman poet." A useful warning. I determined to skate too swiftly over both sheets of thin ice to fall through either.'[129] The extent to which she embraces the dynamic 'otherness' in which her appreciation of difference positions her can be seen from the concluding lyric of 'Cofiant'. At the head of the genealogical table is 'Daughter', the only one, to front thirty generations of 'sons'. This is not an elision or hybridisation of difference; it is a deliberate display which rides on a double source of energy, 'rediscovering Welshness and pride in it, which is somehow parallel to the new confidence of women and the women's movement'.[130]

While her refusal to compromise on either side of the division has been significant for the development of her personal practice as a poet, it also entails what she views as the responsibility of the poet towards the public:

> Out of all this pleasure and the need to feel again and again the electric connection between the deepest waters and the hovering hand with its hazel twig or pen, come a poet's responsibilities to mediate the world between those who'll be reading the poems and those whose world is being voiced. A poet is the voice of the tribe.[131]

The experience of living in a country where two languages are spoken is therefore a theme and a mode which Clarke is compelled to articulate. She determines to speak for 'the tribe' as it traverses the painful terrain of language difference, to name and locate that difference rather than to try to suppress it, or to privilege one over the other.

This flows together with her early decision to promote the 'domus' as a subject for poetry. As is evident from her biography, her own home was a place where language divisions were a source of constant tension. At the same time, her configuration of home on the larger scale of nation and cultural belonging, radiating across her career from the three early major lyric sequences, 'Letter from a Far Country', 'Cofiant' and 'The King of Britain's Daughter', brings this tension out of the private and into the public sphere. 'The two literatures of Wales have been the people's journal,'[132] she asserts, arguing that in Wales the poet is traditionally at the service of citizens as well as religion and the court. Clarke draws a distinction, admittedly generalised, between the service of the poet to the 'ordinary' in Wales and the 'grander purpose' which poetry has played in English Literature. Her insistence that the proper subject matter of poetry is the ordinary and local, be it the home, or a Welsh–English dictionary, or a mining tragedy, includes as well the frank admission of the cultural divisions encountered there, and this is a further alignment of her practice with a specifically Welsh tradition, whatever language she chooses to use. In so doing she turns what could have been a double disadvantage, being a woman and being Welsh, into a double advantage on her journey towards the acquisition of a voice which had the authority to speak for all the citizens of her divided nation. That road towards acceptance was longest, not with the Welsh public, but with the Gorsedd of the Bards. Menna Elfin notes that in 1997 when Clarke was sixty, despite her indisputable achievements as poet, editor, teacher, and her ambassadorial role for Wales beyond its borders, she was still ineligible to the Gorsedd of the Bards, which would elect only Welsh-language poets.[133] Clarke was eventually appointed to this body in 2011, a year after she received the Queen's Gold Medal for Poetry and three years after she began her tenure as National Poet of Wales.

Notes

1. Clarke, *Snow on the Mountain*.
2. 'Selective Bibliography: Gillian Clarke', in Elfin (ed.), *Trying the Line*, pp. 96–9.
3. 'Interview with Gillian Clarke', in Lloyd (ed.), *The Urgency of Identity*, p. 30.

4. The other women were Ruth Bidgood, Molly Owen and the Welsh-language poet Gwenieth Davies.
5. *Poetry Wales*, 6.1 (1970), p. 18, and Clarke, *The Sundial*, p. 33.
6. *Poetry Wales*, 6.1 (1970), p. 19 and Clarke, *The Sundial*, p. 18.
7. *Poetry Wales*, 6.1 (1970), p. 19 and Clarke, *The Sundial*, p. 40.
8. *Poetry Wales*, 6.1 (1970), p. 20 and Clarke, *The Sundial*, p. 28.
9. Sam Adams, 'Introduction', in Clarke, *Snow on the Mountain*, p. 6.
10. As a measure of the minority interest in poetry by women, it can be noted that the only women discussed in Michael Schmidt and Grevel Lindon (eds), *British Poetry since 1960* (Manchester: Carcanet, 1973), were Sylvia Plath and Elizabeth Jennings.
11. *Poetry Wales*, 6.1 (1970), pp. 26–7.
12. There were eighteen respondents, four of them women: in order of appearance, Brian Morris, Glyn Jones, Peter Elfed Lewis, John Idris Jones, Desiree Hirst, Steve Griffiths, Tony Curtis, Bryan Martin Davies, Roland Mathias, Belinda Humphrey, Ruth Bidgood, Robert Minhinnick, Ian Gregson, Diane Davies, John Pikoulis, John Tripp, Greg Hill, G. M. Watkins.
13. *Poetry Wales*, 15.9 (1979), p. 6.
14. Ibid. p. 7.
15. Ibid. p. 36.
16. Ibid. p. 20.
17. Ibid. p. 29.
18. Ibid. p. 23.
19. Ibid. p. 23.
20. Hardy, 'Women Poets', p. 83.
21. Ibid. p. 84.
22. Ibid. p. 84.
23. Ibid. p. 86.
24. Ibid. pp. 86–7.
25. Ibid. p. 83.
26. Lloyd, *The Urgency of Identity*, p. 29.
27. Ibid. p. 47.
28. Markham, *Love Poems*; reviewed in *Poetry Review*, 69.2 (1979), p. 50.
29. *The Anglo-Welsh Review*, Gillian Clarke and Tony Bianchi (eds.), 65 (1979), p. 1. The women poets were Alison Bielski, Liz Cashdan and Margaret Toms.
30. Crawford, *Identifying Poets*, p. 14.
31. 'Letter from a Far Country' was later published in the summer 1980 issue of *Poetry Wales* before it gave the title to her collection of 1982; see *Poetry Wales*, 16.1 (1980), pp. 7–19.

32. Nisbet, 'Poems for Radio'.
33. *Anglo-Welsh Review*, 65 (1979), p. 2.
34. *Radio Times*, Welsh edition, 22 March 1979. The singer of 'If we launch the boat' was Olwen Rees.
35. Clarke, 'The Traders and The Troubadours'.
36. Conran, 'Lynette Roberts: War Poet'.
37. Clarke, *Letter from a Far Country*, p. 8.
38. Philip Owens, '*Letter from a Far Country* by Gillian Clarke', *Anglo-Welsh Review*, 75 (1984), p. 103 and the last words of 'Bluetit and Wren', in Clarke, *Letter from a Far Country*, p. 26.
39. Elfin, *Trying the Line*, p. 8.
40. Alice Entwistle, 'Entwistle/Lewis Interview, 2006', in *Poetry, Geography, Gender*, pp. 7–8.
41. Stevenson, 'Houses of Choice', p. 57.
42. Ibid. p. 59.
43. Clarke, 'Beyond the Boundaries', p. 60.
44. Editorial, *Anglo-Welsh Review*, 70 (1982), p. 3. The poets were: Anne Stevenson, Alison Bielski, Jean Earle, Pamela Gillilan, Lesley Grant-Adamson, Joyce Herbert, Bridget Joseph, Sheenagh Pugh and Rosamond Stanhope.
45. *Anglo-Welsh Review*, 72 (1982), p. 3.
46. Clarke, 'Buzzard', in *Letter from a Far Country*, p. 47.
47. *Anglo-Welsh Review*, 78 (1984), pp. 1–2.
48. Ibid. p. 1.
49. 'Through the Telescope', in Elfin, *Trying the Line*, p. 25.
50. Clarke, 'Traders and Troubadours', p. 12.
51. 'Editorial', *Poetry Wales*, 23.1 (1987), p. 2.
52. Ibid. p. 31; p. 45; p. 52; p. 56.
53. *Feminist Theory*, 9.3 (2008), pp. 264–7.
54. *Poetry Wales*, 23.1 (1987), p. 52.
55. Ibid. p. 44.
56. Ibid. p. 45.
57. Clarke, 'Beyond the Boundaries'.
58. Lloyd, *The Urgency of Identity*, p. 28.
59. *Times Literary Supplement*, 28 May 1993.
60. *Poetry Wales*, 15.9 (1979), p. 36.
61. 'Editorial', *Poetry Wales*, 23.1 (1987), p. 2.
62. Entwistle, *Poetry, Geography, Gender*, p. 7.
63. Ibid.
64. See <http://www.bbc.co.uk/news/special/politics97/devolution/scotland/briefing/79referendums.shtml> (accessed 7 April 2016).
65. *Anglo-Welsh Review*, 64 (1979), p. 3.

66. Ibid. p. 4. The full list of signatories is: Ruth Bidgood, Euros Bowen, Gillian Clarke, Anthony Conran, Pennar Davies, Brian Martin Davies, Anerin Talfard Davies, Marion Eames, Donald Evans, Islwyn Ffowc Elis, Jane Edwards, Gwyn Erfyl, Raymond Garlick, Jeremy Hooker, Emyr Humphreys, John L. Hughes, A. G. Prys Jones, Elwyn Jones, Sally Roberts Jones, W. S. Jones, Bobi Jones, T. Llew Jones, John Gwilym Jones, Dic Jones, Harri Pritchard Jones, Gwilym R. Jones, Rhiannon Davies Jones, R. Tudor Jones, Clifford Jones, D. Tecwyn Lloyd, Derec Llwyd Morgan, T. J. Morgan, Elaine Morgan, Roland Mathias, Jan Morris, Leslie Norris, W. Rhys Nicholas, Gwenlyn Parry, Thomas Parry, Bernard Picton, Keidrych Rhys, Kate Roberts, Eigra Lewis Roberts, Dafydd Rowlands, Meic Stephens, John Tripp, Gwyn Thomas (Bangor), Ned Thomas, R. S. Thomas, Harri Webb, Emlyn Williams, Raymond Williams, Alun Llywelyn-Williams, Rhydwen Williams, John Griffith Williams, R. Bryn Williams, Gwyn A. Williams, Gwyn Williams.
67. *Anglo-Welsh Review* 64 (1979), pp. 1–2, p. 3.
68. Thurston, '"Writing at the Edge"', p. 288.
69. Jarvis, 'Repositioning Wales', p. 22.
70. *Anglo-Welsh Review*, 69 (1981), pp. 3–4.
71. Clarke, 'Beyond the Boundaries', p. 60.
72. Richard Poole, 'Poetry and Nationalism in Wales – A disinterested view', *Poetry Wales* 23.2 (1987), p. 64. This was a special issue on Poetry and Nationalism.
73. Gwyneth Lewis, cited in Entwistle, *Poetry, Geography, Gender*, p. 95.
74. Rees-Jones, Deryn, 'The power of absence', p. 56.
75. Ibid. p. 55.
76. Bakhtin, 'Response to a Question'; Crawford, *Identifying Poets*, p. 12.
77. Lloyd, *The Urgency of Identity*, p. 27.
78. Clarke, 'Border', in *Letting in the Rumour*, p. 21.
79. Kerrigan, 'Divided Kingdoms', p. 16.
80. Crawford, *Identifying Poets*, p. 11.
81. Clarke, 'Voice of the Tribe', in *At the Source*, p. 56. This essay was first published in Lothar Fietz, Paul Hoffman and Hans-Werner Ludwig (eds), *Regionalität, Nationalität und Internationalität in der zeitgenössischen Lyrik: Erträge des Siebten Blaubeurer Symposions* (Tübingen: Attempto Verlag, 1992), pp. 168–78.
82. Bhabha, *The Location of Culture*, p. 219; cited in Entwistle, *Poetry, Geography, Gender*, p. 11.
83. Crawford, *Identifying Poets*, p. 15.
84. Thurston, '"Writing at the Edge"', p. 298.

85. Clarke, 'Cofiant', in *Letting in the Rumour*, p. 78.
86. Ibid. pp. 78–9.
87. Clarke, 'Voice of the Tribe', p. 62.
88. Ibid. p. 58.
89. Clarke, 'The King of Britain's Daughter', in *The King of Britain's Daughter*, p. 20.
90. Entwistle, *Poetry, Geography, Gender*, p. 124.
91. Clarke, 'The King of Britain's Daughter', p. 15.
92. Clarke, 'The King of Britain's Daughter', in Curtis (ed.), *How Poets Work*; see also Gillian Clarke, 'Cordelia's Nothing', in *At the Source*, pp. 30–46.
93. Clarke, 'Cordelia's Nothing', p. 31.
94. Clarke, 'Beginning with Bendigeidfran', p. 289.
95. Clarke, 'Voice of the Tribe', p. 55.
96. Ibid. p. 56.
97. Elfin, *Trying the Line*, p. 10.
98. Clarke, 'Not', in *A Recipe for Water*, p. 12.
99. Clarke, 'Fflam', in *A Recipe for Water*, p. 18.
100. Rumens, 'A Huff of Rain'.
101. Clarke, *A Recipe for Water*, p. 47.
102. Clarke, 'Voice of the Tribe', p. 59.
103. Clarke, 'The Water Diviner', in *Letter from a Far Country*, p. 33.
104. Clarke, 'A Pocket Dictionary', in *A Recipe for Water*, p. 10.
105. Clarke, 'A Recipe for Water', in *A Recipe for Water*, p. 21.
106. Clarke, 'Voice of the Tribe', p. 59.
107. Clarke, 'A Recipe for Water', p. 21.
108. Owens, '*Letter from a Far Country* by Gillian Clarke', p. 104.
109. Clarke, 'Translation', in *Five Fields*, p. 84.
110. Ibid.
111. Clarke, 'Neighbours', in *Letting in the Rumour*, p. 8.
112. This poem is not included in the selection from *Nine Green Gardens* printed in Clarke, *Making Beds for the Dead*, pp. 36–40.
113. Clarke, *Nine Green Gardens*, p. 31. Clarke's notes in the same volume for this poem explain that 'in the language of Welsh landscape, *glas* means both blue and green, like the colour of hills and waters. The estate lies close to the confluence, *aber*, blue-greeness, or *glasne*, of several streams: Aber-glasne.'
114. Clarke, *Ice*, p. 62.
115. Ibid. p. 43.
116. Butler, *Common Ground*, p. 196.

117. *Poetry Wales*, 8.4 (1973), pp. 81–2 and Clarke, *The Sundial*, p. 21.
118. Matthew Jarvis argues that it is Clarke's subject matter, her inflected representations of the landscape of Wales, rather than her use of language, that place her in the tradition of Anglo-Welsh writers. See Jarvis, 'Repositioning Wales'.
119. *Poetry Review*, 72.2 (1982), p. 48.
120. Thomas, 'Dafydd ap Gwilym the Nature Poet', p. 31.
121. Stevenson, 'Review: Gillian Clarke, *Selected Poems*', p. 64.
122. Clarke, *Ice*, p. 60.
123. Peach, 'Wales and the Cultural Politics of Identity', p. 375; cited in Thurston, '"Writing at the Edge"', p. 280.
124. Thurston, '"Writing at the Edge"', p. 280.
125. Peach, 'Wales and the Cultural Politics of Identity', pp. 374–5, cited in Thurston, '"Writing at the Edge"', p. 279.
126. Entwistle, *Poetry, Geography, Gender*, p. 116; citation of Emry Humphreys, *The Taliesin Tradition: A Quest for the Welsh Identity* (Bridgend: Seren, 2000), p. 6.
127. Ostriker, *Stealing the Language*, p. 60.
128. Butler, *Common Ground*, p. 197.
129. Clarke, 'Beyond the Boundaries', p. 60.
130. Butler, *Common Ground*, p. 195.
131. Clarke, 'Voice of the Tribe', p. 61.
132. Ibid.
133. Elfin, *Trying the Line*, p. 11.

4

Paula Meehan: Poetry across Boundaries

Born in 1955, Paula Meehan is almost a generation younger than Gillian Clarke. Yet she too found herself writing into a poetry world populated by very few female role models. Midway through her tenure as Ireland Chair of Poetry she reflected on the conditions which prevailed at the start of her writing life, 'I wouldn't have even bothered sending work out. In the journals I was opening at home, you might occasionally see a woman's name. I certainly didn't feel there was a place in Ireland for my work, that there was a place where I could aspire to being published. So I never sent work out.'[1] And even when she did start submitting work, she met with gender-based 'resistance'.[2] The turning point came when Meehan made contact with Eavan Boland, who, in 1983, was the external examiner for her Masters in Fine Art (MFA) at Eastern Washington University, becoming a mentor and later a friend and collaborator. It was Boland whose activism on behalf of women and whose personal encouragement gave Meehan the confidence to submit work with the expectation that it would be published. In 2002 Meehan spoke in more detail about Boland's agency:

> Eavan went into committees and fought: she argued, she proselytized, she fought for the right, the human right, if you like, as citizens, for women to have more space to speak, for the kinds of and number of grants that went to young women writers, to the amount of space they got in the literary magazines, to representations in anthologies – right across the board. She fought the frightening disparities between the quality of the work being done by women and the number of women who were writing, and the attention they were getting in the business . . . She was an amazing member of the Arts Council . . . She was a great champion for poetry for both men

and women. She was very articulate and persuasive and eloquent at a time when it was really important that someone did it.[3]

The transformation of arts institutions was a precondition for enabling women poets to take a generative part in culture. For women as writers, it heralded the professionalisation of their practice, and entry to this work place. This in turn permits Meehan's presentation of herself and other artists as 'cultural workers', and it facilitates her important view that poetry is 'a tool of culture'.[4] Without the active interventions of Clarke in Wales and Boland in Ireland, poetry by women would have been more delayed in finding acceptance within the poetry community, with funding bodies and ultimately with readers.

The success of this strategic feminism enabled Meehan's rapid move from silence, enforced however unintentionally by the inertia of patriarchal practices, to a place from which, in 1992, she could describe her poetry as 'public speech',[5] be credited by others with writing political poetry and praised for practising a communal art. Since her earliest publications, as Pilar Villar-Argáiz observes from an interpretation of the poem 'Dialogue' in *Return and No Blame*, she strove to establish continuity between the poet's contemporary role and its ancient communal function.[6] Meehan states in interview with Jody Allen Randolph that she understood this to mean 'the idea of the poet as holder of public memory, community memory, tribal memory, which has been our job for most of the possibly 40,000 years we've had poetry as a tool of culture'.[7] She goes so far as to assert that 'I'm the professional memory of the tribe.'[8] The important word here, for a consideration of the arrival of women poets as figures of cultural authority, is 'professional'. It announces assurance that her voice is not only heard but that it also has cultural status, a far cry from her beginnings in a world indifferent or deaf to poetry by women.

Just as Clarke's early poetry liberated the next generation of women, as Gwyneth Lewis asserts, from taking the necessary feminist step of addressing the domestic in their work, so too Boland's poetic attention to the place of women within a national tradition of poetry enabled younger women to focus elsewhere. Meehan regards herself as 'part of a bridging generation in that as a child I was raised and educated by people who still had a colonial mentality and all the fractures in identity that brings'.[9] The trajectory of her work is to reject 'any narrow nationalist project',[10] to 'by-pass the nation stage'[11] and to focus on the 'post-national'[12] by attending to 'our connectedness to the web of life'.[13] Her work crosses borders by noticing them as points of exchange and interpenetration rather than of separation, and holds up poetry as a model of 'spiritual culture'[14] to offset the exploitative materiality of global corporations and the divisions of nationalism. In this sense there is an unusual alignment between the drive of her subject matter and her tenure in the public office of Ireland Professor of Poetry: 'My job crosses the jurisdictions, and that is part of the ethos of the job, to hold open a space that crosses the border because poetry specifically, but also other kinds of cultural engagement, right through the war in the North, kept open a cross-border space for communication . . . Cultural workers can provide a template for other kinds of cooperation in the bodies politic.'[15] The Ireland Professor of Poetry is unlike the other offices of National Poet within the UK in that it is not, and has never been, an instrument of state. It is notable, for example, that when the Royal Irish Academy and Ireland's permanent mission to the United Nations sought a poem to mark the centenary of Irish women's suffrage in 2018, they did not commission it from the serving Professor of Poetry, but looked outside this framework and selected, in this instance, Eavan Boland.[16] The separation of the Irish Chair from state ceremonials has enabled, in Meehan's case, a particular synergy to develop between her preferred subject matters and the public office itself. Kirkpatrick even suggests that the collection *Geomantic*, published at the end of Meehan's tenure, 'became a counter-commemorative act in a year of official celebrations of the Easter 1916 Rising'.[17]

Paula Meehan's relationship with the island of Ireland has always contained a perspective of detachment. Geographical separation was her initial step in overcoming the conditions of self-division imposed by her post-colonial and gendered subjectivity. Ideological distance followed, as she began to draw inspiration from the poetry and Buddhist practice of her abiding poetic mentor, Gary Snyder. She has taken up the battles of her class and her gender against impoverishments enacted by government, Church or custom. Though always distrusting 'on-behalfism',[18] Meehan has used her poetry to advocate for a country she could feel at home in, one which nurtured her and made her strong as both a working-class woman and as a poet. Most recently she has configured home in a cosmic dimension, exploring temporal relationships between the human and the non-human, in her articulation of a home place for the many: 'there'll come a day I'll be dust in wind,/Irish dust in Irish wind, a hundred/and a hundred million years from now'.[19] This chapter explores Meehan's negotiation of boundaries and borders in their many manifestations, whether considered as sites of relationship between places, between human and non-human, between past and present, life and death, power and powerlessness, inside and outside.

Creating Distance

The native land from which Meehan began her childhood emigration was 'the north inner city' of Dublin.[20] Her family lived in a Corporation tenement flat on the corner of Séan MacDermott Street and Gardiner Street, and during the 1950s she was often left in the care of her grandparents while her parents worked as migrants in London. When it was time for her to start school, she was sent to join them in Kingston upon Thames: 'learning to sing "God Save Our Gracious Queen", and longing, longing, to be back'.[21] In Dublin during the 1960s she attended the Central Model Girls School on Gardiner Street, where in preparation for the fiftieth commemoration of the Easter Rising in 1966 '[o]ur little girl hearts were bursting with ideas of the heroic; we were ready to die for Ireland.'[22] In her early teens the family moved to Finglas, a new council estate in Dublin; she attended the local convent school, led a rebellion and was expelled. At seventeen she left home and became a student at Trinity College, Dublin, where she read English, History and Classical Civilisation from 1972–7. Four years later she went to America to develop her craft as a poet under the direction of Jim McAuley, who led poets on the MFA at Eastern Washington University.

Already this is a narrative of real and symbolic fractures. The corner position of Meehan's childhood tenement placed her home directly between the forces of Republic and Empire. Séan MacDermott (Seán Mac Diarmada, 1883–1916) was one of the seven signatories of the Proclamation of Independence read from the steps of the Dublin General Post Office on Easter Monday 1916. He was sentenced to death by firing squad for his part in leading the uprising against British rule. Luke Gardiner (1745–98) was the first Viscount Mountjoy, from the Irish landowning and political class, who died leading his regiment to quell Irish insurgence at the Battle of New Ross in Wexford. Both men whose names are given to the streets where Meehan was raised were killed in the conflict between Republic and Empire. Their legacies were built into the streets of Meehan's first neighbourhood.

Her separation from her parents as they sought work in England, coupled with her longing for home when she was united with them in Kingston, indicates how quickly in this post-colonial environment it became impossible to settle in one unitary place called home. Being expelled from the convent school of her teenage years was an achievement on the way to creating an ideological distance between herself and her birthplace. Her decision to attend Trinity College, Dublin, was another, since Trinity is a Protestant, Anglo-Irish foundation and if Paula Meehan was to defy the expectations of her class and gender to attend university at all, then surely she would have enrolled at the Catholic foundation of University College, Dublin.

Meehan's first collection, *Return and No Blame* (1984), was published a year after her MFA graduation. Its title and thematic core reflect the emotional complexity of these internalised distances. She describes the origin of the title in one of the lectures she delivered as Ireland Professor of Poetry. While she was living on the Shetland island of Papa Stour in 1978, with winter approaching, she consulted the *I Ching* on the question 'would I go home to Dublin?': 'I got the hexagram Fu – Return. One of the lines in the hexagram was a moving line with the interpretation – Noblehearted return. No remorse.'[23] *Return and No Blame* explores the dynamics of the rejection of home twinned with longing for its embrace. This is achieved not in a narrative sense, but as a resonating harmonic relationship between poems which express sharp awareness of the tension between the need to leave, the impossibility of leaving, and the risks of homecoming: 'Oh sister, I am afraid of my face in the mirror/Lest it stay when I have gone'.[24] The multifaceted theme is central to the title poem, 'Return and No Blame'. Here the speaker, '[b]lown about the planet', abandons her wanderings in order to go home.[25] On arrival she is temporarily robbed of language. She cannot tell her stories to her father, who figures both as the speaker's real familial father and as a patriarchy which cannot hear her or to which she has nothing to say. Slipping back into wordless domestic routine, she watches him fry the breakfast bacon. She must,

> . . . sit here quiet . . .
> And watch awhile the flames flicker
> The story of our distance on the wall.[26]

The last poem of *Return and No Blame*, 'Chameleon', reflects on the poet's many identities and seeks to capture the transformation into an authentic self. Looking through photographs, the speaker points out her previous guises: 'That was me . . .', 'That was me . . .', 'I was definitely not . . .'. The concluding words of this poem are the closing words of the collection as a whole, and hold out a promise for a future home place: 'Boy, you should see me when I feel safe:/I turn golden, I shine'.[27]

The topic of necessary and impossible departure spills into Meehan's second collection, *Reading the Sky*, which followed just two years later (1986):

> I walk through an American university
> In a day so Irish (wet windy grey)
> I wonder why I travelled all the way
> Across the grave Atlantic to know it.[28]

The collection strives for an integration of self and other: the poles between home and away explored in *Return and No Blame* resurface in *Reading the Sky* as metaphors of a divided self, the separate parts of which demand acknowledgement but not a false convergence. The poem which gives *Reading the Sky* its title concludes,

> I will forever wait
> At the brink of the winter
> Holding off the dark
>
> That you may escape.[29]

The speaker is both the 'I' and the 'you', both guardian and escapee. The collection assembles the signs by which it augurs integration of selves from all manner of materials found in nature, in politics and in the psyche. 'Hunger Strike', for example, addresses the events of 1981 when Bobby Sands and other republicans in the Belfast Maze prison went on hunger strike as a means of negotiating new terms for their captivity; Sands died on 5 May 1981, the first of ten republican prisoners to die in the Maze before the hunger strikes were called off on 3 October 1981. The poem makes no direct reference to these events. Instead it describes the anxiety of waiting for news, the signs by which it would be communicated, 'that din of stick on dustbin lid',[30] there are indictments of a bankrupt religion, or political oppression glimpsed in embedded emblems of the Easter Rising. The final stanza of the poem overlays the Irish Famine with the hunger strike through the metaphor of the speaker's wasting garden, observed by 'an old neighbour woman':

> She remarked I was losing weight
> And looking through the window asked
>
> Did I feel no shame at the rotting harvest.[31]

Like the legend of the Fisher King, the ailments of a leader, the land and the population reflect one another and wait for healing revelation. As with *Return and No Blame*, a thematic resonance is established across the poems of the collection which cumulatively offer a cohesive vision to integrate nature, self and history.

Meehan's third collection, *The Man Who Was Marked by Winter* (1991), marks a new and combative phase for her articulation of her relationship with home. No longer seeking an escape, the predominant tone is of anger and its method is attack. While nine of the thirty-four poems contained in this collection had appeared, subject to greater or lesser revision, in her two previous collections, the volume is far more than a reprise of earlier work.

'The Pattern', for example, a version of which dates from an early American journal publication in the 1986 special edition of Irish Women's Writing of the *Midland Review*, published in Stillwater, Oklahoma, and which appeared again in revised form in *Reading the Sky*, is extended here into eight short poems of address to the memory of the speaker's dead mother,

> . . . We might have made a new start
>
> as women without tags like *mother, wife,*
> *sister, daughter,* taken our chances from there.³²

Like the father figure in 'Return and No Blame', the mother here has mythical proportions; larger than life, she represents a nurturing Ireland which was not available to Meehan or others of her class and generation, and opportunities for structuring a new relationship have been foreclosed. The last lines of this suite of poems are, 'she'd say, "One of these days/I must teach you to follow a pattern"'.³³ Both liberation and loss are contained in the implied daughterly resistance against 'pattern', which irrigate the tone of the entire volume. The collection as a whole expresses refusal to conform with convention or expectation, stripping away prejudice, superstition, stereotype, the complacencies of convention, in order to make visible what these things hide from the light of scrutiny.

Gary Snyder and Meehan's Poetry of Breath

Eavan Boland observes that *The Man Who Was Marked by Winter* came out of a decade of intense turbulence for Ireland, the 1980s, when old certainties, both political and aesthetic, were overturned. Within this period, Boland argues, the Irish poem itself became a migrant, 'its aesthetic constantly being revised by other cultures, other countries'. Paula Meehan, she asserts, was 'already a pilgrim soul in this new terrain, finding sustenance in other cultures, other poetries.' This enabled her to write, Boland states, 'a poem shaken by the local, but shaped by a wider aesthetic. The public poem. The political poem.'³⁴ Nowhere are these qualities more clearly on display than in one particular poem in *The Man Who Was Marked by Winter*, around which the entire collection arranges itself: the towering dramatic monologue, 'The Statue of the Virgin at Granard Speaks'. In order to understand the dynamic interplay of 'local' and the 'wider aesthetic' which gives this poem its stature, it is necessary first to explore the major encounter of Meehan's years in America, which brought new focus to her previous geographical and literary journeying. This was her meeting with Gary Snyder, who came to deliver a masterclass to the MFA students at Eastern Washington University in 1983, galvanising her craft, her vision and her ambition.

Snyder's work was not new to Meehan. She had already encountered it in Dublin, where as a teenager she had been captivated by the countercultural poetry of the Beats, responding in particular to the 'Buddhism and environmentalism' of Snyder's poetry.[35] While it would be a mistake to single out any one poem as a primary source of inspiration, it is nevertheless the case that Snyder's 'What You Should Know to Be a Poet' from his collection *Regarding Wave* (1970) made a particularly deep and lasting impression on her. Meehan returns to it repeatedly throughout her work, in poetry and interviews, and dwells on its impact in each of her three Ireland Chair of Poetry lectures. In her important 2009 interview with Jody Allen Randolph, she states of Snyder's poem, 'I would have taken the injunctions literally. "At least one kind of traditional magic, tarot, astrology, the book of changes." It was an opening out into a perception of a world where there could be integration.'[36]

Any account of Meehan's work must acknowledge her deep commitment to the practice of writing as a means of divination, undertaken to achieve the 'integration' she so ardently desired. A simple scan of the titles of each of her collections confirms this: *Return and No Blame* (1984) is derived from her experience of consulting the *I Ching*, or 'book of changes', about her future; *Reading the Sky* (1986) invokes astrology; *The Man Who Was Marked by Winter* (1991) reads seasonal force from its markings on the human body; *Pillow Talk* (1994) tricks the expectation of the reader with sleight of hand; *Dharmakaya* (2000) is named from *The Tibetan Book of the Dead* to herald the co-extension of individual with cosmic life force; *Painting Rain* (2009) speaks of the artist's magic in conjuring the visible from the invisible; *Geomantic* (2016) summons the art of divination from signs in the earth. Throughout, as she states in 'Odds On' in *Reading the Sky*, she wants her poems to be 'bursting with magic'.[37]

Snyder has been associated with the poets of the Beat Generation since he read 'The Berry Feast' alongside Alan Ginsberg's performance of 'Howl' at the San Francisco Six Gallery in October 1955, but it was his trajectory as a poet of the environment that has compelled Meehan's most profound response. Snyder's poetry attends to nature and the cosmos, the trace of the human, the quest for transcendent vision through Buddhist meditation, and a view of the poet as shaman. These are the aspects of his work which would become abiding resources for Meehan, along with his demand in 'What You Should Know to Be a Poet' for a 'watchful and elegant mind'. The expression of her engagement with his vision began early in her career. Her poem 'Southside Party', published in *Return and No Blame*, already reveals his influence. 'Southside

Party', a satire of class division located in Dublin, opens with three questions: 'Whose landscape?/Whose trees?/Whose sky?'[38]

They recall Snyder's provocation, 'Who owns the land?' from his poem 'What Happened Here Before', published in *Turtle Island* (1974). Meehan's elaborations are the fundamental questions of any colonised people, although in 'Southside Party' they direct her quest for belonging towards dispossessions meted out primarily by class and gender. While there is always a colonial or post-colonial connotation to the question of land ownership, there is also, from the seer's perspective to which Meehan is always alert, an irony to that question which is given by the transient and contingent relationship between the human and the non-human, which she notes in interview in 2009: 'I would have tried to find a way to write about nature that actually took into account the fact that I was part of it. I suppose similarly to what Eavan Boland says about women as the object in the poem, equally "nature" is an object, it's a kind of imperialism to use it. So I was always trying to find a way to integrate nature that didn't privilege me.'[39]

What changed for Meehan during the workshop which Snyder delivered in person was her understanding of the importance of breath. 'Physically to make a poem is to shape breath in space. The text is the record of that,' she explains.[40] It is Snyder's Buddhist practice which gives breath a spiritual significance, and following the workshop, Meehan began to read more widely in Zen, Taoist and Tibetan Buddhist thinking. Although she has never fully identified with Buddhism, part of its strength for her, she asserts, was that 'it did give me a powerful support system at a time when I couldn't have had any kind of a spiritual life within Catholicism'.[41] She took on the view that 'we're all dust in the wind eventually, that transience is at the heart of the life.'[42] She embraced the holistic vision of Buddhism, its celebration of 'the interpenetration of all species and all creatures on the planet'.[43] For Meehan it was also important that Buddhism did not require belief 'in a god' but instead encouraged the discipline of 'a practice'.[44] This complex of ideas underwrites Meehan's own practice as a poet. Poetry, through its control and production of embodied sound, is a means of orchestrating breath; the text, she explains, separating the spoken from the written form, is a notation of breath. The act of breathing, for Meehan, is an act of exchange between the individual and the planet, so that the body itself becomes a kind of border place, a liminal zone between self and world. Poetry is a means by which the spiritual dimension of this necessary physical act can be brought to the fore, a paradoxical record of transience and a statement of the porous interdependence of life. Providing a powerful counterweight to Catholicism at a time when Meehan was detaching herself from the beliefs of her home, and unifying the discipline of her spirituality with her craft, the Buddhist thinking which Meehan learned from Snyder vastly fortified the ideological and aesthetic innovations with which her 'pilgrim soul' returned to Ireland.

Meehan's understanding of the physical, symbolic and spiritual dimensions of poetry as scripted breathing within a non-Christian belief system equips her with a powerful instrument to challenge the *mores* of home which she invokes throughout her career as both a reader and a writer. She turns not to Catholicism but to reading aloud Ginsberg's elegy 'Kaddish', for example, 'to make peace with my own dead mother': 'I always feel purged and that my demons are driven out afterwards. My body feels transformed by the breath-work of the lines.'[45] In her own writing, the opening poem of *Dharmakaya* is an elegy dedicated to Thom McGinty, a well-loved Dublin street artist and campaigner for gay rights, which explores the moment of death as transition of breath from one state of being to another: 'Breathe/slow-//ly out before the foot finds solid earth again'.[46] The pacing of exhalation and inhalation is marked by the coincidence of word break with stanza break before the assimilation of individual with planetary breath. Alternatively, the opening poem of *Painting Rain*, 'Death of a Field', which has become one of Meehan's most celebrated poems, contains an incantatory list: 'The end of dandelion is the start of Flash/The end of dock is the start of Pledge . . .'[47] This is the means by which the reader's breath is orchestrated into a kind of liturgical chant designed to generate a consciousness which transcends the destruction and asserts a unity with nature even while articulating primal loss. Meehan has stated in interview that 'Death of a Field' draws on Christopher Smart's 'Jubilato Agno',

> a fantastic synthesis of listings of herbs, minerals, the great families of Britain, a huge synthetic vision that pulls it all together. And because of the chant elements, what it does to your breath, it's a litany, pure litany, prayer of the highest order. If you actually read it aloud you will be transcendentally elevated.[48]

Jordan Smith, reviewing *Painting Rain*, focuses on the liminal zone into which Meehan leads her readers, noticing her attention to 'the intense marginality of even the living'. Smith states, '[s]he locates herself at the unravelling edges of things: . . . in "Death of a Field", the places where the old border between city and country frays into the new and indifferent suburbs'.[49] Meehan herself has said of this poem that she was 'playing with the idea of Mother Ireland and the Four Green Fields and the serious environmental damage we're doing to the island', indicating that the border at stake operates on a much larger scale than simply the boundary between city and country.[50] Her orchestration of the reader's breath here leads the poem into what Jody Allen Randolph has identified as Meehan's method of 'setting local history against a scale of archaeological or deep time'.[51]

Meehan's trust in the relationship between poetry and breath also enters her own practice as a workshop leader, which she described in an article for the *Irish Times* in 2009:

> The physical experience of the poem is the reading of it aloud. Its breath patterns and rhythms move through the body and mind, effecting a pure change.
>
> I go in (to prison, psychiatric facility, hospital, rehabilitation project) as a poet, not as a therapist, not as a healer.
>
> There may be a therapeutic dimension, there may even be occasions of healing, there is very often transformation. But it is the craft of poetry I teach. It is poetry I bring to the group.[52]

She reflects on the therapeutic dimension of her workshops in the sombre poem 'Literacy Class, South Inner City'.[53] All the class participants have been injured by the beliefs and strictures of the community which should have nurtured them; the tone of the poem blends anger with grief. Through the act of creating poetry all are charting an 'unmapped world', to find, the poem concludes, 'the sad flag of the home place newly furled'. Remaking home requires new perspectives, and for Meehan herself these are mediated by her engagement with Snyder's multifaceted vision as she brings the 'local' into new focus via her practice of a 'wider aesthetic'.

Three Female Images of Ireland

One of the most powerful means by which Meehan adjusts understanding of the 'home place' is by reconfiguring the icon of woman. Eiléan Ni Chuilleanáin attests to the 'identification of the female with the sovereignty of the land' in the Irish Gaelic-speaking tradition,[54] while Eavan Boland has extensively developed the view that '[w]omanhood and Irishness are metaphors for one another' and 'if you consistently simplify women by making them national icons in poetry or drama you silence a great deal of the actual women'.[55] By changing the significance of one, Meehan changes understanding of the other. Her dramatic monologue 'The Statue of the Virgin at Granard Speaks' in *The Man Who Was Marked by Winter* is the first of three iconic female figures which represent Ireland that Meehan published during the 1990s. Each of these figures achieves more than a simple subversion of female stereotype. Instead, Meehan's reach to her Buddhist-informed vision enables her to completely reconfigure the significance of the iconic Irish woman. Each is powered by chthonic forces and dispassionate towards the destruction of her own people. As emblems, each seems at first to project a typical man-made woman of the kind so bitterly decried by Eavan Boland. Yet as each character unfolds, she reveals herself as a personification of the non-human, akin to the figure of Winter in 'The Man Who Was Marked by Winter'. Alongside the Virgin, there is the speaker of the poem 'Pillow Talk' (1994) and the character of Alice Kane in Meehan's play *Cell* (1999). All demonstrate how Meehan's Buddhist thinking destabilises the oppressive agency of conventional images of women, in order to revitalise the spiritual life of her nation.

'The Statue of the Virgin at Granard Speaks' responds to the death in childbirth of a fifteen-year-old convent-school girl, Ann Lovett, and her baby, alone in a grotto dedicated to the Virgin Mary in the girl's home town of Granard, Co. Longford, on 31 January 1984. They died four months after the 1983 referendum on abortion in Ireland. Ann Lovett's case was remembered again during the 2018 referendum on the same topic, during which Meehan campaigned directly and in which the outcome was a reversal of the 1983 result. Meehan describes the background to her writing the poem when it was shortlisted in the competition launched by RTE in March 2015 to find 'A Poem for Ireland':

> 'There was a devotion to iconography' during the era that her poem addresses, 'but nobody seemed to see the suffering or exercise compassion,' she said. 'It is a very strange experience to find it in the competition – it was written out of respect – her family suffered, and I sat for a very long time before publishing it, because I knew that behind the public outrage there was very private grief . . .'[56]

The jury, selecting from over 440 poems nominated by the public and briefed 'to choose those poems that told a story of Ireland over the past century', gave first place to Seamus Heaney's sonnet 'When all the others were away at Mass'.[57] Meehan's 'The Statue of the Virgin at Granard Speaks' was voted in joint second place,[58] confirming by popular poll Boland's earlier claim that the poems of *The Man Who Was Marked by Winter* implied 'community'.[59]

For Boland, Meehan's ability to write both for and from a community entailed an awareness of its 'flawed nature'. In this poem the community flaw is expressed by the vocal silence of the statue towards the girl, 'though she cried out to me in extremis'.[60] Neither organised religion nor its icons have any help to offer the suffering, just as Lovett's pregnancy had been overlooked and denied by all around her. The community and its gods are equally indicted by this dramatic monologue. Meehan inscribes the ethical shock of that silence as an aesthetic disruption to the rhythm of the monologue, so that the statue's silence is perceived as an unexpected vacancy, a gap in the foreshortened line in the recollections of this otherwise garrulous speaker:

> I did not move,
> I didn't lift a finger to help her,
> I didn't intercede with heaven,
> Nor whisper the charmed word in God's ear.[61]

Instead of intercession, the role of the statue is to bear witness. More attuned to the processes of nature and the weather, the statue likens the burial of the dead to the fall of ripe fruit. 'Death is just another harvest/scripted to the season's play'.[62] Even the colour symbolism of its painted dress, 'pure blue, pure white', is presented in terms of the natural world, 'as if they had robbed/a child's sky for their colour'.[63] The speaker longs for the sensuousness of being human, and female, for carnal knowledge, its word made flesh, 'incarnate' and 'tousled in a honeyed bed'.[64] The interpenetration of human and divine celebrated by Yeats in 'Leda and the Swan' are not for this Virgin Statue, which views the religious ceremonies that take place in the grotto as pageants. With a detached, alien eye the statue observes its own role in them: 'They fit me to the myth of a man crucified;/... They name me Mother of all this grief... They kneel before me and their prayers/fly up like sparks from a bonfire/that blaze a moment, then wink out'.[65] The statue has no agency in these rituals but over everything exercises what might be considered a 'watchful and elegant mind'.

Glossing this line of Snyder's '*ars poetica*' in the last of her Ireland Chair of Poetry lectures, Meehan explains that she considers 'watchful mind' to be like 'a hunter who must recognise tracks and trails and scat patterns, a voyager who reads current and wind patterns, who recognises and interprets with all the senses engaged'. The 'elegant mind' she views as 'mind shaped by human practice but aware of animal self'.[66] For Snyder, and for Meehan, the poet is a traveller in the unknown, a figure always external to circumstance and situation yet seeking to interpret them. The voice of the Statue of the Virgin at Granard is likewise that of an observer, alert to divination, 'shamanic and individuated at the same time'.[67] It can be taken as a cipher of the poet herself, making good Meehan's claim that 'the witness of individual suffering is of value'.[68] Elaborating, she asserts that '[p]oetry ... in the traditions I've worked in, is ... a kind of holding up against the mass totalitarian type states we live in now, of the witness of a single human life,'[69] and the role of the poet is 'someone who is keeping the watch'.[70] She seeks to demonstrate 'how dangerous private memory is to the state', and to be the 'holder of the individual private conscience'.[71] Through the voice of the Statue, Meehan channels the provocation of watchfulness.

The full detachment of the speaker from what is witnessed comes to the fore only in the last stanza of the monologue. Here, and with the full weight of irony conferred by its own words, the statue intercedes in prayer. It invokes not the Christian God, but the sun, as the poem itself seeks enlightenment for a benighted era:

> O sun,
> centre of our foolish dance,
> burning heart of stone,
> molten mother of us all,
> hear me and have pity.[72]

The rhythm of these lines separates them from the rest of the poem. With their echo of the liturgy and their chanting, they tilt the reader towards meditative integration with the non-human life of the planet in which acceptance must take the place of redemption.

In *The Man Who Was Marked by Winter* this monologue resonates with 'Home by Starlight', not simply for its night-time setting ('The Statue of the Virgin at Granard Speaks' is set on All Souls' Night), but more importantly for its view of the cosmos. Spoken by an astrologer or Magus, 'Home by Starlight' reflects on the significance of '[t]he light they later called the Christos/and the terror, the blood cost of that Logos',[73] assigning Christianity a relative position, rather than an absolute, on the road towards revealed truth. The astrologer, like the poet, journeys through the dark and finds meaning by observation. 'Home by Starlight' compounds the profoundly uncanny nature of 'The Statue of the Virgin at Granard Speaks' by casting another perspective on the source from which the speaking voice comes. The statue may look virginal, may seem by appearance and association to offer comfort, but as a conduit of the primordial it is indifferent to the destiny of individuals. It observes the bringing forth of death where there should have been life, the deaths of girl and newborn at the altar, with blank impassivity, and as though they were nothing more than part of the seasonal darkness, noting simply: 'I number the days to the solstice/and the turn back to the light'.[74]

Three years later, in the title poem of the collection *Pillow Talk* (1994), this spirit made itself known again. The poem 'Pillow Talk' is not, Meehan explains, 'something to do with the Doris Day movie', as her aunt first thought, but a reprise of a bedtime conversation between Queen Medbh of Connacht and her husband Ailill, King of Ulster. It is taken from *The Táin*, a narrative contained in the twelfth-century manuscripts of the Ulster Cycle, a collection of epic material composed as early as the seventh or eighth centuries.[75] 'I like the fact that they are talking about cattle; they aren't murmuring sweet nothings,' she states.[76] 'In choosing *Pillow Talk* as a title for my book, I wanted to show that battles are fought in bedrooms as well as in public places.'[77]

The Táin, also known as 'The Cattle Raid of Cooley', tells of battle between the warrior queen of Connacht, the ancient western province of Ireland, and her lover, king of the northern province Ulster. The competition between Medbh and Ailill is for possession of cattle which signify status: Aillil claims the magical white-horned bull for his people, but Medbh arranges a border raid to capture from his territory the even more talismanic brown bull of Cooley to secure her superiority despite her soothsayer's warning that the raid is doomed. Medbh's warriors are held off by the heroic prowess of the Ulster warrior Cúchulainn, who battles for three days single-handed against his beloved foster brother Ferdia, previously exiled and now fighting for Connacht. Although the army of Ulster is victorious, the brown bull of Cooley was captured by Medbh's warriors and it defeats Aillil's white-horned bull before a truce is called by both sides.[78] Medbh and Ailill, Cúchulainn and Ferdia, Ulster and Connacht, white bull and brown bull: *The Tain* tells of bitter competition and intimate connection, its legendary significance chiming with political battles on the island of Ireland during the 1980s and 1990s.

Meehan attests that Snyder's exploration of Native American traditions as a route to holistic spirituality opened a door for her own poetic practice: 'Snyder ... helped me look at our own past in a different way. Because if you look at the *Táin*, the great cowboy epic of the Bronze Age ... Snyder was showing me ... vestiges of the hunter-gatherer traditions right up until a hundred years previously, pre-colonization.'[79] Snyder's discovery of pre-colonial cultures in America, much more recent than the pre-colonial culture in Ireland, brought Meehan the possibility of imagining an unfractured native culture for her own land in which human and non-human interact in harmony. The speaker of 'Pillow Talk' incarnates ancestral connection with the land. A medium, she foresees the bitter territorial battles of Ireland and is helpless to protect her beloved from them. In constructing the speaker of 'Pillow Talk' as a divided self, conflating Medbh with her soothsayer poet Fidelma, and a primal spiritual force, the dramatic monologue draws on established tropes of Meehan's writing. 'The Other Woman' and 'Autobiography' in this collection alone explore the tensions of a divided self, developing themes of a subject split between home and away presented in her earlier work.[80] The title poem 'Pillow Talk' resounds with the heightened sensuality of erotic passion, itself a route to divination in Meehan's work; it thrives on risk and draws the natural world into its service. The poem is a spell. Yet it is not only the addressed beloved, and the reader, who fall victim to the enchantment: the speaker herself is possessed by an occluded power,

> I fear
> not all my healing arts can salve
> the wound she has in store for you.[81]

That demonic, irresistible force is the ancient spirit of the land, present through Meehan's invocation of the *Táin*, and seen inside the poem: 'My stomach turns at the hot/relentless stench of her history'.[82] 'Her' people are in thrall to the voice which 'speaks through me/beyond human pity or mercy'.[83] A chthonic spirit of place, or primal energy that forms briefly into sexual encounter, seizes the speaker and her lover, or the subject and the land of her birth, and cannot be resisted. The poem invites the reader into a charmed circle of vision in which a transcendent apprehension is possible, and in which experience is stripped to an uncanny but transfiguring core. Meehan's treatment of the epic offers a post-feminist counterweight to the heroic narratives of Cúchulainn's masculine prowess with which Yeats and Lady Gregory sought to invigorate a young Ireland during the formation of the Abbey Theatre and the Celtic Revival.

This spirit takes on a new shape in Meehan's play *Cell*, written for Calypso Productions, staged in 1999 at the City Arts Centre, Dublin before touring Ireland.[84] It was published in 2000 and revived in New York in 2009 by Aedin Moloney's Fallen Angel Theatre Company. *Cell* draws directly on Meehan's experience in working with the Writers in Prison Foundation, holding writing workshops in the women's prison Mountjoy and other state prisons of Dublin for a decade from 1985:

> This play would be my way of acquitting my huge debt to the women I've worked with over the years; and might act as a channel of the anger and frustration I've felt in the course of working with women prisoners ... Most were victims of social forces, of the same class background as myself. For many, the outside world was as much a prison as Mountjoy.[85]

While this is a drama rather than a poem, in dialogue, setting and action the play shares its rich economy of expression with Meehan's verse. The title word 'cell' puns prison with the smallest unit of biological life: in the compressed environment of the prison cell, the life of its four female inmates becomes a power struggle to the death. The dialogue is realist with the flare and wit of Dublin demotic, yet it simultaneously encompasses a mythical cosmos in which even the characters' names are resonant with metaphorical significance. Dolores Roche, the controlling drug dealer of the cell and the prison, has a Satanic emblem of the Fall, a snake, tattooed on her arm. This is her pet 'Snakey' which is conjured into life to bend the others to her will. Lila, a nineteen-year-old Dublin woman sentenced to three years for possession of heroin, strains her gaze out of the window. 'I wish I could see more of the garden. The bit of the tree is the only growing thing. No. There's stuff on the wall. Weeds in the cracks. They had a little blue flower . . .'[86] The poem 'Buddleja' of 'The Lost Children of the Inner City', written at the same time as *Cell*, is recalled: 'When they break into blossom – so free, so beautiful./I name them now as flags of the people'.[87] The inmates of the prison cell can only glimpse such signs of free flourishing in their exile from the garden.

Dolores' regime is disturbed by the arrival of a new inmate in the cell who replaces the dead and haunting Annie, who had been driven to her death by Dolores' brutal bullying. The outsider is Alice Kane; she is forty-nine years old and sentenced to life for murder. She sings Irish folk songs and tells inconsistent stories about her murderous past. It is Alice Kane, her name a homophone with Cain, the first murderer in the Bible narrative when he killed his brother Abel, who embodies in a different form the chthonic force which also speaks in 'Pillow Talk'. Alice announces, 'I feel like I'm about two thousand years old.'[88] Having murdered Dolores in the cell, she explains to fellow inmate Martha that she will take sole responsibility for the death: '[t]his whole episode is so familiar to me: like I saw it once in a dream or I lived through it in another life . . . Even the palms of my own hands with her life's blood on them.'[89] Alice, like Lila, is banished and in exile from the Garden of Paradise: 'I think I've loved my garden more than any human.'[90] Yet, Alice has a final vision of possible redemption. Looking out of the window she sees, 'There's a frost over everything! . . . And Lila's tree has turned to pure silver in the moonlight. Glittery and shiny. It's a Christmas tree for sure . . . It's so beautiful it would take your breath away.'[91] This last line of the play is equivocal, since the implication of death is enfolded in the response to beauty.

The Christmas tree which 'would take your breath away' signals not only the possibility of new life, but is also a darker invocation of the suffocating inflexibility of Christian morality which assigns sinfulness to the imprisoned women. Alice's closing line of the play completes its underlying biblical narrative, which moves from expulsion from Eden, through murderous experience, to her martyrdom. At the same time it presents the natural world as a force of beauty and life for its own sake, knowledge of which is mediated by Alice, here no less than midway through the play when she extolled her pleasure in her garden immediately on telling her first version of the murder story. 'And I went about taking great handfuls of herbs and breathing them deep into me.'[92] The action recalls Meehan's Buddhist appreciation of the act of breathing as an exchange between the human and the non-human, as well as her practice as a poet to orchestrate such exchanges.

Meehan has reflected on the meaning of 'breathtaking' in relation to poetry in her Ireland Chair lecture, 'Imaginary Bonnets with Real Bees in Them':

> If poetry makes *nothing* happen, maybe it stops *something* happening, stops time, takes our breath away. Though, strange that taking our breath away, being breathtaking, is associated with achievement, accomplishment. Maybe it's like the negative space in a painting by which what is there is revealed, to be apprehended by human consciousness.[93]

The 'negative space' in *Cell* is the space around the staged set, the world beyond the claustrophobic cell where the action takes place, mediated only through dialogue, tantalisingly glimpsed through the cell window or referred to in conversation. This vanishing world of natural beauty beyond the prison, whether held in the memory or seen as a blue flower growing from a crack in the wall, puts pressure on the life within and displays itself vividly through its absence. It also, as Meehan suggests, lifts the action of the play out of the immediate present and gives it an emblematic significance, connecting the women with the world beyond by their very separation from it. Life, in *Cell*, as the title indicates, is apprehended in its most reduced form and in its limitless potential.

Alice is a shape-changer, a vessel for non-human energy that encompasses a planetary animus sweeping through history and connecting all life. As an ancient spirit of place she is present throughout Ireland's murderous past, and seems therefore to be an agent of it, as though the place itself were actively sacrificing human lives. In allowing this implication, Meehan couples the animism of her Buddhist thinking with her socialist politics, to draw attention to the toxicity of the 'social forces' which have criminalised and incarcerated the cell's inmates. Alternatively, when this spirit manifests through the voice of the Statue of the Virgin at Granard, Meehan points at what she considers to be the dangerous forces of organised religion which control or condemn women. And when it appears in the guise of the speaker of 'Pillow Talk', the critique is of tribal conflicts which have riven lives and communities on the island of Ireland in the more recent colonised and post-colonial past. Kathryn Kirkpatrick has observed how Meehan's engagement with the work of Gary Snyder, and Buddhist philosophy, facilitates her 'willingness to weave pre-colonial and premodern ways of knowing with a modern secular rationalism and a socialist politics'. This enables her to address, Kirkpatrick contends, 'our historical moment of social . . . crisis, when a change of consciousness and a shift in paradigm require intelligent retrievals and artful appropriations of alternative cosmologies'.[94] Shape-changing is an act of resistance, a refusal to be trapped in a fixed identity or mode of being, as well as an assertion of interconnection. The animus Meehan presents in these three uncanny representations of a female Ireland embody renewal and transformed understanding. They are, furthermore, confident subversions of what Boland has identified as 'the tendency' in Irish poetry 'to fuse the national and the feminine, to make the image of the woman the pretext for a romantic nationalism'.[95] As if taking up Boland's call, Meehan's configurations of an implacable yet female spirit of Ireland are powerful examples of how '[a] poetic landscape which had once been politicized through women was now politicized by them.'[96]

Inside History: A Jobbing Poet of the 1990s

The 1991 publication of *The Man Who Was Marked by Winter* launched a decade of focused public engagement for Paula Meehan which brought her to the centre of the cultural arena, and which diversified both her practice and her audience. During this decade she published two further collections of poetry; she wrote two plays for children and two plays for adults; her poetry was interpreted by dance, visual art, song and documentary film; she gave readings at world charity events; her poetry was placed on the Irish national curriculum and examined in the Leaving Certificate.[97] These developments signal the professionalisation of Meehan's practice, her generative participation in an evolving culture, and therefore mark a radical shift from her starting position.

In July 1992 Dublin's Rubicon Gallery opened its summer exhibition, 'Balance and Imbalance': invited artists had been commissioned to collaborate with selected poets, and Eithne Jordan made 'two small paintings' to accompany Meehan's poem 'Pillow Talk'.[98] Next, in October 1992, came Rubato Ballet's dance performance of Meehan's poem sequence 'The Wounded Child' at the RHA Gallagher Gallery. Choreographed by the founder of Rubato, Fiona Quilligan, with music for piano and violin commissioned from Fergus Johnston, this piece was performed by four dancers (representing the wounded child, the mother-image, father and woodman) and a chorus of trees. The production drew praise from the *Irish Times*.[99] Meehan read 'The Wounded Child' as part of the twice-daily performance, which ran 7–10 October 1992 as part of the Dublin Theatre Festival.[100] The sequence of five poems was later published in *Pillow Talk* (1994), where it is dated 25 February 1992.[101] The poems explore an inward journey of the adult woman, looking 'strange' to herself and arrayed in 'battledress', to find the wounded child within, 'Curled/ to a foetal grip in a tight place,/sobbing her heart out'.[102] The internal mental landscape is figured as a fairy-tale forest where the child is threatened by an ambiguous woodman, quietened by discovery and the telling of a tale about a Russian doll which transforms the surrounding birch wood into a whittled emblem of self. 'The Wounded Child' works with themes already evident in Meehan's work: the divided self, the harnessing of forces of nature for good, necessities of difficult journeys and healing power of artful expression. The first two poems of the sequence deliberate on suitable dress for this journey: 'First – gird yourself. Put on/a talisman', both protection and an outer display of inner conviction which estranges the self: 'Whatever you wear you'll be strange./ This is battledress. Paint your face,/put feathers in your hair, arrange/your skirts, your skins, your lace'.[103] The sequence as a whole points directly to the underlying enterprise of *Pillow Talk*: Meehan chose a depiction of the goddess Athene in armour for the front cover of this collection. Katie Donovan in the *Irish Times* commented,

> Meehan has referred to her poetry as autobiography that must be arrayed with the 'battle dress' of poetic form 'to survive': 'The formal qualities of a poem, such as rhyme and rhythm, are its protection, the battle dress it wears in order to become public speech,' she explains.[104]

The collaboration with Rubato facilitated a bodying forth of the private in the public, in which the formal movement of the dancer and the rhythm of music brought Meehan's battle dress and its vulnerable core into new and complementary media.

Just one month later, in November 1992, her arena shifted dramatically in magnitude when she took part in 'a monster rock gig in aid of Concern for Somalia at the Olympic Theatre' in Dublin.[105] Bands taking part included the 'Frames, Dignam and Goff, Blink and Hada to Hada', and Meehan shared the stage with fellow poets Theo Dorgan and Gabriel Rosenstock, using her poetic arsenal in an instrumental fashion to raise funds for charity. The next large public platform on which Meehan appeared was on the stage at the Abbey Theatre, Dublin, in March 1993, to celebrate International Women's Day and to raise funds for Women's Aid. The President of Ireland,

Mary Robinson, introduced the twelve women poets, nine of them from Ireland, with one each from England, France and Poland. This three-hour reading 'was intended, in President Robinson's words, to "fulfil a practical purpose as well as to feed our souls"' and was one of the earliest platforms Meehan shared with Carol Ann Duffy, who was the representative poet from England.[106] The following month Meehan's poem 'She-Who-Walks-Among-The-People', commissioned by Combat Poverty Agency to honour Mary Robinson, was presented to the President on 19 April 1993,[107] and was published in *Pillow Talk*.[108]

In June 1993 the multiple strands of Meehan's experience in performance came together when the company Rough Magic, in an effort to boost new writing for the stage by women, secured funds from Gulbenkian to finance five women in their script development.[109] For Meehan this led to the play *Mrs Sweeney*, which opened on 7 May 1997 at Project@the Mint in Dublin.[110] The first signs of her treatment of the theme appear in *Pillow Talk* with the poem 'Mrs Sweeney', an invocation spoken by Mrs Sweeney to her lover, who has metamorphosed into a bird. She seeks reunion with him and prays to achieve this by transforming herself into an element of nature: 'Flash of beak as you stoop to pierce'.[111] The short lyric has a setting which is at once elemental and metaphysical. Outwardly it could not be more distant from the play *Mrs Sweeney*, which is set in 22A Marie Goretti Mansions, a version of the Corporation tenements where Meehan once lived. Recalling her early life, Meehan states, 'I grew up in the tenements and when I was a young one reading an O'Casey play was like the news of the day. It was exactly what was going on . . . the same wonderful things and the same heart-breaking deprivation.'[112] The heartland of *Juno and the Paycock* is palpably recalled in *Mrs Sweeney*, which portrays the way in which Lil Sweeney deals with her pigeon-fancier husband's sudden departure into insanity when his beloved pigeons are destroyed overnight in an act of savage vandalism. As he turns into one of the birds taken from him, Mrs Sweeney confronts anew the loss of their daughter, who died from AIDS in the heroin epidemic sweeping Dublin's urban poor. The play is buoyant with the Dublin humour of an inner-city community in the throws of decimation, yet it turns on Meehan's sense of accelerated cycles of life and death seen already in *The Man Who Was Marked by Winter* and given here a material setting and political explanation. These are captured in the resonant stage picture recalled by Mrs Sweeney of her daughter, lit by spring sunshine as she stands on the doorstep and announces, 'Ma . . . I'm dying.'[113]

Meehan's poetry continued to find its way into other media. In 1994 her poem 'Well' – first published in *The Man Who Was Marked by Winter*,[114] again in the *Irish Times* on 5 September 1992, and once more in Meehan's Bloodaxe anthology *Mysteries of the Home* (1996)[115] – was interpreted as dance to a musical score by J. J. Vernon, with bodhran for percussion. 'Well' is a sixteen-line lyric in tight rhyming couplets about the speaker's capture by the spirit of the well, returning to show,

> in my bucket – a golden waning moon,
> seven silver stars, our own porch light,
> your face at the window staring into the dark.

The dance was choreographed by Adrienne Brown and performed by a solo dancer, Ella Clarke, as part of the New Music, New Dance Festival in June 1994 at the Project Arts Centre in Dublin. The poem was read aloud during the performance by Mary O'Driscoll.[116] The piece was repeated in December the following year in the larger space of the Samuel Beckett Centre.[117]

In 1996, the hugely beloved Irish folksinger Christy Moore took one of Meehan's prose poems 'Folktale' (reminiscent of Wilde's poems in prose) from *Pillow Talk* as the lyrics for the song 'Folk Tale' in his album *Graffiti Tongue*.[118] This won both the poem, a fable about a young man who fell in love with Truth, and Meehan herself, the stamp of popular approval. It was a credential frequently invoked by the Irish press when it announced Meehan's appointment as Ireland Professor of Poetry in 2013; *The Irish Daily Mail*, for example, stated, '[c]ritics say her poetry – which has been set to music by Christy Moore – is marked by its wit and beauty.'[119]

It is evident that when *Pillow Talk* was published by the Gallery Press in 1994 many of its poems had circulated not simply, as is often the case when a collection is published, in specialist poetry journals, but also in more popular or outward-facing modes of communication, while others, as exemplified by Christy Moore's song, would soon find their way into alternative embodiments. Paula Meehan was thirty-nine when this, her fourth collection, appeared; the volume was firmly embedded in a matrix of creative production at the centre of Irish culture. With it, she took her place amongst Ireland's 'standing army of 10,000 poets', as Patrick Kavanagh had satirically dubbed the propensities of his nation and which Meehan cited in 'The Standing Army', a poem she wrote for May Day 1990.[120]

The review of *Pillow Talk* in the *Irish Times* was, despite the note of caution already cited with regard to the poem about Mary Robinson, astute in its praise. It singled out 'the sequence "Berlin Diary, 1991"' for particular note, observing that it shows how 'the kind of concentration needed "for reading the street" sharpens the focus and releases her sense "of danger at the edges" of things'.¹²¹ This is a resonant observation. The quotations are taken from the second poem of the sequence, 'On Being Taken for a Turkish Woman'.¹²² On the surface, the poem mediates a social commentary on suspicion of strangers and looks for camaraderie amongst the ostracised. But it also slots into Meehan's wider interest in the porousness of one culture to another, one era to another, in pursuit of holistic understanding. Her vigilance at 'the edges' fosters her literal and metaphorical efforts to find 'the margins moving to the centre',¹²³ just as her aesthetic practice has sent her own career as a poet on the same trajectory.

However, even in 1994 Meehan's own marginal status as an Irish woman remained a professional threat to the cultural authority of her poetry. Evidence of this can be read in the London-centric *Times Literary Supplement* review of *Pillow Talk*. Both her gender and her nationality are invoked as a means of placing, and belittling, the achievement of her poetry:

> As befits an Irishwoman, Meehan does sacred and profane to perfection – 'dancing wantonly in silk' and fellating her sleeping lover, but with equal vigour addressing prayers to the great beyond of Supernature.¹²⁴

There is no appraisal of the lyric conceit, while the failure to distinguish the speaker of the poems from the identity of the poet leads to the stereotyping sexism and racism of whatever this reviewer deems to 'befit an Irishwoman'. From this review, it appears that Meehan's warrior mode of belligerent defiance throughout *Pillow Talk* is both necessary and just as a means of protecting what she articulates. It is worth remembering that Eavan Boland's volume of essays, *Object Lessons: The Life of the Woman and the Poet in our Time*, reflecting on the sources and consequences of the prejudices captured by the phrase 'as befits an Irishwoman', was still a year away from publication.

Meehan's last decade of the twentieth century drew to a close with the publication of *Dharmakaya* (2000), which, prior to *Geomantic*, was her most explicitly Buddhist work. The collection contains a sequence of seven poems, 'The Lost Children of the Inner City', which was written for a documentary film about Dublin's north inner city communities, *Alive, Alive O: A Requiem for Dublin*. Made by Sé Merry Doyle, it was broadcast on RTE 1 on 4 September 2001. The film footage records the demolition of the site of Meehan's first home, Séan MacDermott Street and Gardiner Street.¹²⁵ 'If you blink you'd miss it,/your own life passing/into memory, frame by frame', she writes in 'Window on the City', the penultimate poem of the sequence.¹²⁶ Transience and dust, those two truths which Meehan embraced at the heart of her Buddhist exploration, are recorded here, as the physical evidence of her own childhood passes into the trace memory of an urban tribe. Doyle explains that the film was 'not a strident social realist type of documentary but rather an attempt at something more lyrical'.[127] Of the first of Meehan's accompanying poems, 'Molly Malone', he states: '[t]he poem was written as if the spirit of Molly Malone was looking down on her own community, on kids smacked out on heroin and on traders being run off the streets.' The impassivity of this statue is not far removed from that of the statue of the Virgin at Granard with which this decade opened. While, therefore, the sequence is an act of spiritual commemoration, like 'The Statue of the Virgin at Granard Speaks', it is also an act of also political resistance: 'Pray for us who have lost our wings'.[128]

While this account of Meehan's decade-long participation in the creative culture of her home city Dublin and of her nation is neither comprehensive nor complete, it is sufficient to indicate how intricately her own practice as a poet was becoming woven through manifold expressions of Ireland's self-understanding. By the time the twenty-first century dawned, Meehan was no longer an outsider but had become a keenly respected cultural leader. The difference between Meehan's position and that of her predecessor Eavan Boland is identified by Boland herself in the contrasting titles of the two essays which recount her own development and that of her younger colleague. Boland calls her autobiographical account 'Becoming an Irish Poet', as opposed to 'Paula Meehan: Being an Irish Poet'.[129] The distance between 'becoming' and 'being' may have been made traversable by the transitional role which Boland herself adopts, yet Meehan's belonging has also grown from the margins. Kate Conboy contends that 'Boland's portrait of female marginalisation is unwilled, but potentially powerfully communal'; Meehan has built on exactly this potential of her literary and social inheritance, creating community even as she articulates its absence or its needs.[130] She has espoused the social, political and spiritual causes rooted in her home place, real and symbolically evident in that corner flat between Séan MacDermott Street and Gardiner Street, and indeed by its subsequent physical erasure. Meehan's articulation of the rife afflictions and thriving passions inhabiting that place means that her poetry has grown from the social ground up. In doing this she has, as the Northern Irish critic Edna Longley urged in her plea for a non-unitary sense of Irish identity, created a 'web . . . "female, feminist, 'connective'"', which not only permits but valorises 'mixed, fluid, and relational kinds of identity' that are not rooted in political territory but which imply an enlarged signification of human place.[131]

Notes

1. Knittel and Meehan, '"Nature Doesn't Stop"', p. 77.
2. O'Halloran et al., 'An Interview with Paula Meehan', p. 7.

3. Ibid. pp. 23–4.
4. Randolph, 'The Body Politic', p. 260.
5. Dorgan, 'An Interview with Paula Meehan', p. 269.
6. Villar-Argáiz, '"Act Locally, Think Globally"', p. 181.
7. Randolph, '*Painting Rain*', p. 49. This interview is an extract from the longer interview, Randolph, 'The Body Politic'.
8. Ibid. p. 50.
9. O'Halloran et al., 'An Interview with Paula Meehan', p. 5.
10. Ibid. p. 5.
11. Ibid. p. 12.
12. Randolph, '*Painting Rain*', p. 49.
13. Janna Knittel, *New Hibernia Review*, p. 70.
14. O'Halloran et al., 'An Interview with Paula Meehan', p. 5.
15. Knittel and Meehan, '"Nature Doesn't Stop"', p. 84.
16. See <http://webtv.un.org/watch/launch-of-the-eavan-boland-poem-our-future-will-become-the-past-of-other-women/5975983194001/?term> (accessed 5 March 2020). Boland reads from 20 to 27 mins. The poem itself, 'Our Future Will Become the Past of Other Women', appears in Boland, *The Historians*, pp. 63–7.
17. Kirkpatrick, '*Geomantic* by Paula Meehan (review)', p. 149.
18. Randolph, 'The Body Politic', p. 247.
19. Meehan, 'The Graves at Arbour Hill', in *Geomantic*, p. 59.
20. Boland, 'Two Poets and a City: A Conversation', in *A Poet's Dublin*, p. 99.
21. Meehan, 'The Solace of Artemis', in *Imaginary Bonnets*, p. 35.
22. Ibid. p. 37.
23. Meehan, 'Planet Water', in *Imaginary Bonnets*, p. 67.
24. Meehan, 'Journeys to My Sister's Kitchen', in *Return and No Blame*, p. 19.
25. Meehan, *Return and No Blame*, p. 40.
26. Ibid. p. 40.
27. Ibid. p. 63.
28. Meehan, 'The Garden of a Sleeping Poet', in *Reading the Sky*, p. 19.
29. Meehan, 'Reading the Sky', in *Reading the Sky*, p. 14.
30. Meehan, 'Hunger Strike', in *Reading the Sky*, p. 9.
31. Ibid. p. 10.
32. Meehan, 'The Pattern', in *The Man Who Was Marked by Winter*, p. 17.
33. Ibid. p. 20.
34. Boland, 'Unfinished Business', p. 19.
35. Knittel and Meehan, '"Nature Doesn't Stop"', p. 81.
36. Randolph, 'The Body Politic', p. 247.
37. Meehan, 'Odds On', in *Reading the Sky*, p. 46.

38. Meehan, 'Southside Party', in *Return and No Blame*, p. 16.
39. Randolph, '*Painting Rain*', p. 49.
40. Randolph, 'The Body Politic', p. 250.
41. Ibid. p. 248.
42. Ibid. p. 249.
43. Ibid. p. 249.
44. Ibid. p. 249.
45. O'Halloran et al., 'An Interview with Paula Meehan', p. 20.
46. Meehan, 'Dharmakaya', in *Dharmakaya*, p. 11.
47. Meehan, 'Death of a Field', in *Painting Rain*, p. 13.
48. Randolph, 'The Body Politic', p. 267.
49. Smith, 'Review: Poetry Books'.
50. Randolph, '*Painting Rain*', p. 49.
51. Ibid. p. 49.
52. Meehan, 'Poetry and the power of healing'.
53. Meehan, *Dharmakaya*, p. 51.
54. Hurtley et al. (eds), *Ireland in Writing*, p. 83.
55. Wilson and Somerville-Arjat (eds), *Sleeping with Monsters*, p. 84; p. 87.
56. Dalby, 'A Contest Honors Ireland's Poets and Past'.
57. Ibid.
58. 'Readings were a "celebration of poetry"', *Wexford People*, 10 March 2015.
59. Boland, 'Unfinished Business', p. 18.
60. Meehan, 'The Statue of the Virgin at Granard Speaks', in *The Man Who Was Marked by Winter*, p. 42.
61. Ibid.
62. Ibid. p. 41.
63. Ibid. p. 41.
64. Ibid. p. 41.
65. Ibid. pp. 40–1.
66. Meehan, 'The Solace of Artemis', p. 64.
67. O'Halloran et al., 'An Interview with Paula Meehan', p. 10.
68. Randolph, '*Painting Rain*', p. 48.
69. Ibid. p. 48.
70. Ibid. p. 49.
71. Ibid. p. 50.
72. Meehan, 'The Statue of the Virgin at Granard Speaks'.
73. Meehan, 'Home by Starlight', in *The Man Who Was Marked by Winter*, p. 46.
74. Meehan, 'The Statue of the Virgin at Granard Speaks', p. 42.
75. Donovan, 'Passion's Battles'.

76. For a translation of this bedroom conversation see <http://www.askaboutireland.ie/reading-room/life-society/irish-language-legends/the-tain/maeb-and-ailill/> (accessed 6 February 2020).
77. Donovan, 'Passion's Battles'.
78. See <http://www.askaboutireland.ie/reading-room/life-society/irish-language-legends/the-tain/short-summary/> (accessed 6 February 2020). The epic was translated by Thomas Kinsella in 1969.
79. Randolph, 'Body Politic', p. 248.
80. Meehan, *Pillow Talk*, p. 18; p. 40.
81. Paula Meehan, 'Pillow Talk', in *Pillow Talk*, p. 33.
82. Ibid. p. 32.
83. Ibid. p. 32.
84. Reviewed by Mic Moroney, *Guardian*, 25 September 1999.
85. See <http://homepage.eircom.net/~calypso/production/last.html> (accessed 21 October 2015).
86. Meehan, *Cell*, pp. 20–1.
87. Meehan, *Dharmakaya*, p. 31.
88. Meehan, *Cell*, p. 27.
89. Ibid. p. 90.
90. Ibid. p. 45.
91. Ibid. pp. 90–1.
92. Ibid. p. 45.
93. Meehan, 'Imaginary Bonnets with Real Bees in Them', in *Imaginary Bonnets*, p. 19.
94. Kirkpatrick, '"A Murmuration of Starlings in a Rowan Tree"', p. 195.
95. Boland, 'Outside History', p. 151.
96. Boland, 'Subject Matters', in *Object Lessons*, p. 196.
97. MacMonagle, 'Conference Preview'.
98. MacAvock, 'Poets and Painters at the Rubicon Gallery'.
99. Swift, 'Dance Strokes 11'.
100. See also <http://iol.ie/~rubato/dancewks.html> (accessed 9 November 2015).
101. Meehan, 'The Wounded Child', in *Pillow Talk*, pp. 55–9.
102. Ibid. p. 56; p. 57.
103. Ibid. p. 55; p. 56.
104. Donovan, 'Passion's Battles'.
105. Boyd, 'Hot Licks'.
106. Donovan, 'Poetry with a Purpose'.
107. Combat Poverty Agency was an NGO founded in 1986 and integrated with the Department for Social Inclusion in 2009 and subsequently,

in 2010, with the Department of Community, Equality and Gaeltacht Affairs.
108. This poem (*Pillow Talk*, pp. 60–2), unusually public and heraldic in Meehan's corpus, has received a certain amount of negative criticism including in [Peter Sirr], 'Power, anger and the ordinary', *Irish Times*, 8 October 1994. Both the title and the line divisions of the poem are misquoted in the review article.
109. White, 'Trojan work for change'.
110. From <http://www.roughmagic.ie/News-and-Updates-from-Rough-Magic/January-2013/Rough-Magic-Archive-15>.
111. Meehan, 'Mrs Sweeney', in *Pillow Talk*, p. 63.
112. González-Arias, '"Playing with the ghosts of words"', p. 194.
113. Meehan, *Mrs Sweeney*, p. 415.
114. Meehan, 'Well', in *The Man Who Was Marked by Winter*, p. 60.
115. See Helen Dunmore, 'The Week in Reviews', *Observer*, 5 January 1997. *Mysteries of Home*, an anthology of her work, was Meehan's first publication of poetry on the British mainland and was designed to widen her readership outside Ireland.
116. Swift, 'New Music, New Dance'.
117. Swift, 'Fire in the Soul'.
118. See 'Folk tale Christy Moore', *YouTube*, <https://www.youtube.com/watch?v=ZokGbD2Xmtk> (accessed 10 November 2015).
119. *Irish Daily Mail*, 'Poet Meehan honoured with top accolade'.
120. Meehan, 'The Standing Army', in *Pillow Talk*, p. 17. Patrick Kavanagh's saying is frequently quoted and misquoted in the press – see for example Joe Lowry, 'Coming out of the garret', *Irish Times*, 9 February 1993, or Andrew Martin, 'The man who planted Dublin in our heads', *Daily Telegraph*, 12 June 2004.
121. [Peter Sirr], 'Power, anger and the ordinary', *Irish Times*, 8 October 1994.
122. Meehan, 'On Being Taken for a Turkish Woman', in *Pillow Talk*, pp. 46–7.
123. Meehan, *Imaginary Bonnets*, p. 19.
124. KJ, 'Pillow Talk', *Times Literary Supplement*, 3 March 1995.
125. See 'Excerpt: Alive Alive O – A Requiem for Dublin', *YouTube*, <https://www.youtube.com/watch?v=7zm5SuWfOgU.>. In this extract, Meehan's poem 'Grandmother, Gesture' is at 5.08 mins (accessed 26 November 2015). Meehan reads the sequence at <https://www.youtube.com/watch?v=JZhgzjL0tpM> ('Paula – The Lost Children', YouTube, accessed 26 November 2015).
126. Meehan, 'Window on the City', in *Dharmakaya*, p. 30.

127. Maire Kearney, 'Broadcast News', *Irish Times*, 1 September 2001. See also IMDB, <http://www.imdb.com/title/tt2815472/> (accessed 3 May 2021).
128. Meehan, 'Pray for Us', in *Dharmakaya*, p. 26.
129. Boland, 'Becoming an Irish Poet', in *A Journey with Two Maps*, pp. 45–60, and 'Being an Irish Poet: The Communal Art of Paula Meehan', ibid. pp. 219–31.
130. Conboy, 'Revisionist Cartography', p. 199.
131. Longley, *From Cathleen to Anorexia*, p. 23; cited in Conboy, 'Revisionist Cartography', pp. 198–9.

5

Liz Lochhead: Performing Scotland

Mapping Scotland

Scotland, its present, past and future, has been at the heart of Liz Lochhead's work since her earliest publications, *Memo for Spring* (1972) and *Islands* (1978). Both collections begin the lifelong enterprise of mapping her home country. As a young poet, aged twenty-four when *Memo for Spring* came out, she was finding her own place within Scotland at the same time as finding her place within the business of poetry. Lochhead, like Gillian Clarke, entered a culture where she was routinely the only woman present. 'There were no Scottish women poets writing in English when I got started really. Well, there must have been but they weren't getting into print, weren't quoted.'[1] The point is reinforced by Carol Ann Duffy in her introduction to Lochhead's Selected Poems of 2011, *A Choosing*, where she observes that *Memo for Spring* 'blossomed out into the very male landscape of Scottish poetry and somehow managed to make that landscape female'.[2] Looking back, Lochhead identifies a public appetite for the unheard woman's voice, as well as an emerging sense of political correctness in the industry: 'I got gigs because the organisers would think: I suppose we should have a woman on the bill, and then, there was only me.'[3]

This is one of the factors which distinguishes Lochhead's Scotland from the outset. The country contains women. Not only that, but the female speakers of her dramatic monologues, lyric poetry and recitations for performance, are women who talk, and who articulate what had silenced them. Their reasons for voicelessness range from self-evasion through internalised reticence to out-and-out frustration at the cloth-eared deafness of their menfolk. Lochhead acknowledges that the vocal presence she gives to her vast cast of female speakers is 'a political act', particularly because 'it's not done often, especially in Scotland'.[4]

The opening poem of *Memo for Spring* is 'Revelation'. It takes a childhood memory[5] of encountering a chained bull in a farmyard and magnifies it to monstrous proportions, from which a metaphor is generated for the relations between masculinity and femininity, threat and safety, knowledge and ignorance, adult and child. 'Revelation' works entirely through symbols. Nothing is directly stated, everything is shown, as the reader becomes active in making the meaning of the poem. By the end of the lyric, only 'hens' remain 'oblivious' of the threat posed by the sheer 'Black Mass' of the bull.[6] The child, who would be herself a 'hen' in the colloquial term of endearment for girls and women in the West of Scotland, flees in terror, noting the gratuitously murderous play of the 'big boys' in the lane, as she seeks to preserve the integrity of her eggs and the 'placidity' of her milk. There could not be a more resonant opening statement for Lochhead's critique of the relations between men and women in the Scotland of the 1970s. Nor, as Dorothy McMillan contends, could there be a more powerful example of the energy Lochhead's work derives from encounter with threat; 'it is a darkness that attracts, even compels the child and a darkness that neither the poet nor the poem can do without'.[7] The generative power of nightmare is indeed evident across Lochhead's mature corpus, reaching implicitly into *Dreaming Frankenstein* and explicitly acknowledged, however humorously, in the later poem, 'Hell for Poets': 'Hell itself's pure inspiration'.[8] *Memo for Spring* as a whole does not focus explicitly on danger, nor on male/female relations; instead it does this work obliquely, by attending to the vulnerable and outsiders in society, those who are in some way endangered. The collection is populated, for instance, by a homeless beggar, a bedridden grandfather, an evicted wife, inpatients of a mental hospital, an immigrant Asian woman. Throughout it all runs the thread of a lovelorn young woman who sees her country from the American side of the Atlantic, strives to feel at one with her vocation and at home in her city, discovering that 'something compels/me to forge my ironies from a steel town'.[9]

By the end of the collection, the frightened child of 'Revelation' takes her place amongst many who are 'out on a limb',[10] each depicted with sufficient observational detail to convey individuality, yet who also serve as representative types. The gendered identity and often broken-hearted voice of the lyric 'I' across the collection is a vital element of the innovative strength of *Memo for Spring*. The beggar of 'Poem for Other Poor Fools' is not objectively observed, but described from the speaker's very specific point of view, as she begins the poem, 'Since you left I've only cried twice'.[11] The homeless man, like the waving grandmother who affords the first occasion for tears in the poem, is a substantial presence, but he is also a vector of the speaker's irony, an image of her self-denial, another version of her vulnerability. The reader is simultaneously aware of the persona of the lyric 'I', her subjects, and the dynamic between them. Alternatively, the Asian woman described in 'Something I'm Not' is not a neutrally observed figure in the urban landscape, but a relational being, the speaker's neighbour on the same tenement close who takes her turn, unlike the speaker, at washing the stairs.[12] The subjectivity of the perceiving eye, the lyric 'I', is as evident and as dynamic an emotional presence in the poems as the conventionally foregrounded figures. By placing her speakers as active in the dramas of these lyrics, Lochhead draws attention to women as perceiving subjects. She makes women as visible as the often overlooked figures which the poems observe. And, through the knowing communication of the vantage point of the gaze, Lochhead makes the perspective from which she writes part of the subject matter she writes about. Place, then, has been an embedded subject of her work since the beginning.

Islands continues the exploration of diversity within Scotland. Dominated by two lyric sequences, 'Outer' and 'Inner', this collection arranges itself around an exploration of the ancient cultures and contemporary *mores* of the outer and inner Hebrides, Lewis and Skye. The 'Outer' island is home to weaving, all-consuming weather, and rumours of witchcraft. Here too an immigrant population is observed, in the 'Pakistani draper's shop',[13] sharing the island with those born there from whom the speaker-visitor learns Gaelic. The sequence of six lyrics ends with the repetition of 'Is e seò tigh ban' and 'Is e seò tigh dubh', the Gaelic for 'white house' and 'black house'.[14] The speaker's teacher is an eleven-year-old girl, who announces that 'she'd rather be here than Glasgow anyday'.[15] The language lesson, with its black and white words for dwellings, conveys the inhabitants' centre of self which makes the speaker, and the Anglophone reader, alert to their own otherness.

Lewis and the Gaelic are contemplated afresh from the perspective of Skye, the 'Inner' island, which too embodies an otherness that defies Anglophone naming, 'Skye flowers are too wild to call/Seapink . . .'[16] The speaker notes that the experience of visiting Lewis, and learning Gaelic words for colour in the place itself, compelled a realignment of perception with language. Like Gillian Clarke, Lochhead dwells on the Gaelic word 'glàs', concluding that the colour words convey 'more a chroma of the weather/colour of the mind'.[17] The view that language makes sense of place and place makes sense of language, and that therefore a sense of place alters the speaker's perceptual range, stretches deep into Lochhead's poetic practice. It shapes the way she conveys not only geographical location but also social place, the positions of gender, and national belonging. It is a performative view of language: words are only fully communicative in the localised utterance where the mutually informing relationship between language and place can be experienced.

Two things stand out about these lyric collections of the 1970s. The first is the poet's engagement with modes of representation, which entails both her self-reflective awareness of craft as process, and sensitivity to the ethics of how artifice is deployed. The second, which grows out of the first, is the attention to Scotland as a place of work. Artifice is the poet's work, which Lochhead aligns with the occupations (or their lack) of other 'city dwellers' in the predominantly urban focus of her canvas.[18] Even when she is in a rural location, such as the Isle of Lewis, what she brings to notice is people's labour, women scattering 'henmash', men 'shut in with the bare bulb/and the clattering in the blacktarred hut/where weaving gets done'.[19] Lochhead's Scotland is a place of production in which men, and now conspicuously women, play their parts.

She was writing at this time not only in light of the Anglo-American feminism of the 1970s, but also in light of the increased vigour of the Scottish National Party. In the general election of February 1974, the SNP, using 'It's Scotland's Oil' as a slogan, increased their number of MPs in Westminster from one to seven. In the second general election of that unusual year, the SNP went on to win 30 per cent of the Scottish popular vote, returning eleven MPs to Westminster in October 1974. The 1979 referendum on the creation of a Scottish Assembly returned a slim majority in favour (51.6 per cent of the votes) but, as less than 40 per cent of the electorate had voted, the Scotland Act 1978 was repealed. Even so, these were much higher numbers in favour of devolution than had emerged in Wales and Northern Ireland at this time. Both international sexual politics and the national politics of the era play into the way Lochhead positions her subjects. The Scotland she discovers in these early collections is heterogeneous: the Gaelic speaker and the English speaker, woman and man, city dweller and rural inhabitant, immigrant and native. All are strangers to each other, but collectively they are manifestly distinct from their English neighbours.

Lochhead's *Islands* metaphor, that words convey 'colour of the mind', recurs emphatically throughout her work. In an interview given in 1987 while she was writing *Mary Queen of Scots Got Her Head Chopped Off*, Lochhead states, '[m]y language is female-coloured as well as Scottish-coloured.'[20] Elaborating, she explains that '[b]eing a feminist writer was stopping writing as if I might be a man, so being a Scottish writer is stopping writing as if I might be English.'[21] The binaries are striking. For Lochhead it was enough simply to stop 'writing as if I might be a man' to be a feminist writer, irrespective of the political subject matter of her poetry. Merely the act of being a writing woman was, as Kathryn Kirkpatrick has argued, a defiance of patriarchy. At the same time, Lochhead does admit to discovering an overt feminist strand to her work: 'I was surprised to find how feminist my writing was.'[22] Equally stark in

Lochhead's account of her writing identity is her assertion that being a Scottish writer is defined simply in opposition to being an English writer. She does not even bother with the pretence that Britain was more diverse than a hegemony of England, or that there could be more ways of expressing Scottishness, or that Scotland itself could be defined as anything other than not-English. By appropriating these binaries, she pushes against the homogenising drive of English/male dominance. As Gonzalez contends, '[t]he different gazes directed at Scotland, whether from colonial discourse or in the form of nationalistic justifications, have tended to offer a homogeneous view of its multiple realities.'[23] Articulation by a Scottish woman of the vocabulary used to control both her national belonging and her gender was itself a subversive act. And immediately she starts to inflect her identity: 'It's about what colour your English is.'[24]

Lochhead's colour metaphor for positioning her work chimes with that used by the Scottish critic Cairns Craig in his resonant statement, '[i]t is not by our colour . . . that we have stood to be recognised as incomplete within the British context, it is by the colour of our vowels.'[25] But while Craig uses the metaphor to diagnose perceived lack, Lochhead embraces the energy of difference: '[i]t's defining what you really are so that you can more honestly relate with the world.'[26] Her primary aim is to use her gender and her Scots language to generate a centre of self from which to trade. Crucially, Lochhead is looking out, while Craig is looking in; Lochhead is describing an internal 'colour of the mind', Craig is assessing how this colour is valued externally. Of course Lochhead is well aware of external perspective, of the 'double exclusion' which may afflict the Scottish woman writer, a condition arising, Marilyn Reizbaum argues, when 'the struggle to assert a nationalist identity obscures or doubly marginalises the assertion of gender ("the woman's voice")'.[27] Lochhead's alignment of Scotland with woman has long been recognised as one of her primary instruments of self-assertion for both nation and women, as Reizbaum herself has argued. But Lochhead brooks no traffic as a subaltern.

The metaphor of colouration is pursued into her 2003 collection, which is named, paradoxically, *The Colour of Black and White*. This volume, Laura Severin argues, 'traces an evolving Scotland from the anglicised black and white world of World War Two . . . to a more vibrant contemporary Scotland, transformed by art'.[28] Lochhead's Makar collection of 2016 refracts the metaphor further into the title *Fugitive Colours*, while on the cover is a coloured crayon sketch by Lochhead herself of a rainbow across water. Lochhead trained as a fine artist at Glasgow School of Art during the 1960s. The act of representation for the visual artist must include colour, even when it is absent, as the title *The Colour of Black and White* makes apparent. Lochhead transfers what is a literal means of representation in the visual realm, to a metaphorical mode of representation in the domain of language. What is made evident through the application of colour, in both media, is the process of artifice. Reflecting on the act of representation in 'Notes on the Inadequacy of a Sketch at Millport Cathedral, March 1970', Lochhead writes, 'it's plain/setting down in black and white/wasn't enough'.[29] As a writer she craves release from binary oppositions, just as she points up poetry's gift of imaginative flight from the material constraints of black typeface on the white page.

Lochhead's female-coloured language takes to the stage exactly contemporaneously with the publication of *Islands*. In 1978 she joined forces with Marcella Evaristi to produce the first of her choreographed poetry readings and revues, *Sugar and Spite*, at the Traverse Theatre, Edinburgh. This launched what has become her trademark genre, poetry written for performance. The articulate woman's voice, manifest in the lyric poetry of *Memo for Spring* and *Islands*, becomes a three-dimensional reality, loud, lewd and impossible to ignore. Jackie Clune has written about the feminist potential of Lochhead's revue work, its creation of a new genre which is politically transgressive in the way it crosses boundaries between the high culture of poetry readings and the popular culture of the variety show. As a genre it resists the closed, highly coded, complex plotting of bourgeois theatre, being more inclusive and accommodating of a socially diverse audience.[30] At the same time, Lochhead's revue is neither simple nor unsophisticated. Yet S. J. Boyd lamented what he saw as Lochhead's move 'down-market', assessing this work as 'not only unworthy of the author of *Memo for Spring* but also unworthy of the lavatory wall'.[31] He failed to find either 'subtlety' or 'substance' in it, asserting that Lochhead's interest in the 'monsters' of her lyric poetry is both more worthy than her revue work, and separate from it. However, one could instead recognise that the monstrous women of her revues, and their misshapen language, are judged so according to stereotypes of gender and culture, and that they are contiguous with the explorations of the lyric poetry. *Sugar and Spite* calls out the stereotype 'woman', calls out prescriptions for womanly behaviour, turns gender-polarisation on its head and asks audiences to recalibrate the measure by which culture encodes value in differences between 'high' and 'low'.

'The Suzanne Valadon Story (Rap)'[32] affords a microcosm of the enterprise as a whole. Lochhead's 'rap' form predates widespread circulation of British rap music, and as Laura Severin contends, it exemplifies 'an earlier meaning of rap within the African-American tradition – that of using verbal play to rewrite one's status'.[33] To rap, Lochhead states, means 'to talk back'.[34] Suzanne Valadon talks back in Franglais with as little regard for the rules of English grammar as for the rules of passivity supposed to govern the conduct of the artist's model. She begins, 'I could of been a laundress', and puns in the next line on the word 'scrubber'. Her salvation? 'I'd have ended in zee guttair as a clapped out lush/Eef I hadn't seized mon courage and a number seven brush'.[35] Valadon's transition from model to artist, narrated by herself with such uninhibited zest, mirrors the shift from object of poetry to its author which Eavan Boland articulates as the woman poet's climactically difficult journey. Valadon's switch from being the observed to the observer also anticipates the shifting balance of power scrutinised in Carol Ann Duffy's early dramatic monologue 'Standing Female Nude'.[36] Most importantly, Valadon is the author of her own story, controlling the very same 'clapped out lush' language of patriarchal systems which had previously been used to keep her in her place. She is not just an artist with language as colourful as her palette, but also the artificer of her own fate, emblem of the liberated woman. Lochhead's script for *Sugar and Spite* extends Valadon's stance into practice since the dramatic monologues empower women performers with new stage roles and exhort audiences to action.

The monologue 'Phyllis Marlowe: Only Diamonds Are Forever' exhibits another strategy of feminist disruption of gender norms. This prose piece is spoken by a young woman in the voice of Raymond Chandler's detective Philip Marlowe. Set in 'sixty-six' when 'the world was a more innocent place',[37] the speaker recounts her visit to a family planning clinic to get a prescription for the contraceptive pill. But none of this is directly stated. Instead she disguises her succession of social embarrassments and medical humiliations, including an internal speculum examination, in the faux-brash language of a streetwise woman, diverting attention from the purpose of the mission with intimate details about her preparation and confidently superior observational judgements about others in the waiting room: '[d]ame opposite was wearing laddered black Beatle nylons – Jesus, nobody had worn Beatle nylons since sixty-four Chrissakes. She was reading *The Uses of Literacy*.'[38] The voice captures the pacey swagger of the period, its love of fashion, its liberation from the old rules of propriety, all of which are undercut by the trivia of what is actually observed. But smuggled into the bluff voice is acknowledgement that the contraceptive pill enabled women to invest in education by remaining childless. The uses of contraception are directly linked with the uses of literacy. The liberation to pursue careers is glanced at by the fact that the 'Doktor' is a woman, conveyed lightly by the almost inaudible use of the pronoun 'she'.[39] Reactionary assumptions that the pill would only serve to make women promiscuous are deftly rebuffed.

The speaker locates her ordeal precisely in the West End of Glasgow, referring to the Mitchell Library and Kelvingrove Park as well as city shops of the period such as C&A and Galls. Her language is at complete odds with her location. She is a perfect mimic, describing women as 'broads', 'dames' or 'this old bird'. The cross-dressing of the voice juxtaposes forcefully with her gendered vulnerability to bring home, literally, the objectification of women and their status as lesser beings. The alienation between voice and location is a measure of the speaker's socially enforced alienation from sex and society.

Cultural references abound and assume high levels of knowledge of both literary and popular culture in the audience, as well as detailed local knowledge of place. Making no hierarchical judgements between, for example, acquaintance with *The Ancient Mariner* or Frank Sinatra, the intertextual acrobatics of this monologue are part of its strategy to transgress traditional cultural boundaries and to show women fully able to control these disruptions, even if the trajectory of the narrative itself suggests a more anticlimactic outcome. This technique is typical of Lochhead's revue works. They are steeped in contemporary feminist politics (Susie Orbach's *Fat is a Feminist Issue* (1978) underwrites 'Fat Girl's Confession'); national politics (the development of the oil fields in the North Sea underwrites the Verena monologues); high culture (art history underwrites 'Vymura: The Shade Card Poem'); they exhibit a particular fluency in popular and media culture ('Scotch Mist (The Scotsport Song)'; 'Look at Us'; 'Page Three Dollies'; 'Gentlemen Prefer Blondes'), and threaded throughout is a playful manipulation of the linguistic politics of cliché (flaunted particularly in the list poem, 'What-I'm-Not Song'). Lochhead produces a densely layered, sophisticated art form which challenges and enriches her audience in equal measure. Throughout the period 1978 to 1985, Lochhead's choric female voice continues the process of reclaiming the language and attitudes which had silenced women in the past. Her 'raps' are irrepressibly articulate about how women are restrained within patriarchal systems. They create and validate a social space for women to inhabit, and they are emphatically Scottish in language and location.

Over time and working with different groups of writers and performers, the songs, monologues and raps which were written for single performers diversify into short scripts for several performers. One such is 'Usherette Scene', written for *Red Hot Shoes*, the Glasgow Tron Theatre's Christmas show of 1983. The overlapping dialogue of the three young women who work as usherettes and ice cream sellers at the symbolically named Regal cinema is a piece of complex verbal choreography. The girls gossip, prepare for the intermission and lament the confines of their lot. Nettie is the most dissatisfied: 'Ah'd dae onything, tae get oot of this dump . . . Night school. Only therrs nae night school durin' the day. An' at night Ah'm workin.'[40] Their options are limited. Constantly interrupting each other with prompts for what is missing from their trays ('you mibbe need merr Mivvis . . .'),[41] they reflect on what is missing from their lives. Circumscribed by social class and gender, their boundaries are policed by the Regal manager, for whom they are not just employees but also sexual quarry. He embodies the patriarchal social structures which limit the possibility for these three young women to realise their ambitions. The vividly delineated conditions of their lives, conveyed by Lochhead's precise rendering of West of Scotland vernacular, resonate with both literal and metaphorical significance. Figuratively, the usherettes' desire for self-determination expresses the ambition of a nation, Scotland, for freedom from the marauding constraints imposed by the Westminster government. Their subaltern status is plain to the audience. Here, as in Lochhead's later plays *Perfect Days* (1998) and *Good Things* (2004), the audience, as Adrienne Scullion points out of those dramas, is 'rewarded for insider knowledge' of the represented locations.[42] Gender, social class, geographical place and national belonging are all exactly sited in the 'Usherette Scene', and the rewards of in-jokes and recognition serve to turn the audience into a community which shares political restiveness with the three girls.

Asked in 2011 'what first turned you on to poetry', Lochhead's response is unhesitating: 'Louis MacNeice.'[43] The answer might be surprising. She goes on to explain that it was hearing MacNeice recite 'Bagpipe Music' as the late-night sign-off poem for BBC2 in 1966 that instantly spurred her to begin writing poetry herself. From MacNeice, and from the Liverpool Beat poets, Lochhead understood that 'you must say this stuff out loud, that was what it was for'.[44] Performance, then, saying it out loud, has been core to Lochhead's poetic practice ever since she started writing. As the preceding analysis of the three pieces from *True Confessions and New Clichés* suggests, performance tilts easily into the performative. These poems and sketches do not remain as static objects on the stage for contemplation by the audience, but instead create a dynamic, inclusive relationship which gives the audience permission for action and exhorts to social change. Her more literal response to MacNeice's 'Bagpipe Music' is the 'recitation' 'Bagpipe Muzak, Glasgow 1990', published in her second collection of revue work, *Bagpipe Muzak*, in 1991. Written to critique the cynical marketing of an *ersatz* Glasgow during its year as 'City of Culture' in 1990, mirroring the way MacNeice's poem had observed the decimation of culture in the Western Isles by the economic decline of the 1930s, Lochhead's poem ends with a threat. She warns the political leaders Margaret Thatcher and Neil Kinnock to 'tak' tent' (watch out), 'Or we'll tak the United Kingdom and brekk it like a bannock'.[45] The political leaders of the United Kingdom would hear a similar message from Lochhead twenty-four years later at the time of the 2014 referendum on Scottish independence.

What separates the raps and songs of *Sugar and Spite* from the recitations and characters of *Bagpipe Muzak* is a decade of extraordinary artistic productivity during which Lochhead becomes increasingly vocal about Scottish identity. Her stage adaptations of *Frankenstein* (*Blood and Ice*, Traverse Theatre, Edinburgh, 1982) and *Dracula* (Royal Lyceum Theatre, Edinburgh, 1985) are assertively feminist in interpretation, a political focus which dovetails with her lyric collections of the same period, *The Grimm Sisters* (1981) and *Dreaming Frankenstein* (1984). Her interest during this period is in writing about 'unconscious people' and in exploring 'gaps' between what is said and what is heard.[46] The poem 'Storyteller', which opens *The Grimm Sisters*, describes how normative narratives lodge themselves in the subconscious, 'they/hung themselves upside down/in the sleeping heads of the children'.[47] Her artfulness as a poet is in delineating individual struggle with the fairy tales that shape her society. It is a drive which she pursues into her theatre-making of the period, first with her exuberant adaptation into Scots rhyming couplets of Molière's *Tartuffe* (Royal Lyceum Theatre, Edinburgh, 1986), bringing this iconic French script home to Scotland with all the verbal panache of *True Confessions and New Clichés*. The following year, with the drama *Mary Queen of Scots Got Her Head Chopped Off*, she explicitly articulates the two politicised conditions of gender and nationhood as twinned and cognate in her practice, and deconstructs the prevailing narratives that control their boundaries. As Marilyn Reizbaum has argued of that play, 'Lochhead involved the historical linkage of cultural marginalization, gender, and religion, but she disrupts the essentialist fiction by suggesting it is a loss of autonomy that joins them.'[48] It is also in 1987 that Lochhead begins to assert in interview that she feels a 'slightly-gathering-steam nationalism' and links this with her feminism.[49] To Colin Nicholson she says, 'until recently I've felt that my country was woman. I feel that my country is Scotland as well.'[50] By 1990 her internalisation of dual identity had swivelled round to accommodate the external view: 'Scotland is like a woman. The Scots know they are perceived from the outside.'[51]

Lochhead's likening of Scotland to woman risks the invocation of a tradition promulgated by Matthew Arnold's *On the Study of Celtic Literature* (1867) by which marginal Celtic nations are feminised and thereby weakened in relation to the dominant English centre. Yet Lochhead's move is a way of pushing back against the assertively masculinised national identity born out of the Scottish Literary Renaissance since the 1920s.[52] And her simile is deeply invested in contemporary feminist scrutiny of the male gaze, which she merges with the English gaze. Yet being looked at brings opportunities, particularly when the observed is confident and canny enough to lock eyes with the beholder. This is what happens in Lochhead's most dramatic of dramatic monologues, the opening speech of *Mary Queen of Scots Got Her Head Chopped Off*. La Corbie, the talking crow with the French name, embodies a Scotland costumed in all the clichés of *Macbeth*. She is the fourth of Macbeth's three witches, an English projection of Scotland. La Corbie wears the 'black glamour'[53] of the compelling darkness seen already in 'Revelation'. She represents Scotland's otherness to itself, encompassing a wildness glimpsed in *Islands*, and pointing up the dangers of Scotland's complicity with English constructions of itself whereby Scotland is liable to get lost in a 'smirr' of 'nostalgia'. Even at this early stage of the drama, she does, however, challenge the audience to imagine its own Scotland: 'Ah dinna ken whit like *your* Scotland is. Here's mines.' La Corbie controls both of the '*twa queens*', presenting them to the audience at the start of the drama.[54] They are her creatures, just, it emerges, as are the citizens of present-day Scotland for as long as they play along with the masculine structures of power that dictate the fates of both queens. Until the fakery of La Corbie is exposed, nothing will change. But her self-display gives readers and audiences every opportunity to see through her.

Fulfilling a similar function to La Corbie, in the compressed medium of revue recitation, is the speaker who opens *Bagpipe Muzak* with 'Almost Miss Scotland'.[55] A feminist conversion narrative, this dramatic monologue by a beauty queen recounts her disenchantment with her parade of Scottish tits ('like nuclear missiles') and teeth ('I'd larded oan lipgloss').[56] Waiting for the male judges to score her out of ten, 'Miss Garthamlock' imagines a cross-dressed version of the contest; her outrage at the ludicrousness unveiled by her fantasy fuels her rebellion. But she doesn't lead a 'bacchanalian Revenge of the Barbie Dolls', instead she makes a quiet, personal decision and 'snuck away oot o therr'.[57] Wrapping up her story with a moral, she announces that 'the theory of feminism's aw very well/but yiv got tae see it fur yirsel'.[58] Like La Corbie, she embodies a construction produced for the benefit of the constructor. Unlike La Corbie, the beauty queen has to do all the theatrical work of dismembering the construction by herself, and there is no room for the playful ambiguities and alienations that enrich the full-length drama. Miss Garthamlock has to do a lot of telling, whereas La Corbie has the luxury of showing. But their targets are cognate: to enable audience members to make up their own minds about the values inscribed in inherited cultural constructions of gender and nation. At the start of the beauty contest, Miss Garthamlock is tricked out in faux tartanry, 'I sashayed on in my harristweed heathermix onepiece', swimwear designed to reveal as much of her Scottishness as her body, but not exactly practical in either regard. Woman and Scotland are objectified as one, a union deftly evoked by the spontaneous rendition of the Alexander Brothers' nostalgic song 'For These Are My Mountains', which mixed with the wolf whistles to greet her display of 'nuclear missiles' (themselves a reference to Faslane naval base on Gare Loch).[59] Her name too, scrambles 'garter' and 'tartan' together with the English pronunciation of 'loch', the latter a fate which has been heard to befall Lochhead's own last name. This beauty queen is modelling the English gaze. Her restorative advice, apart from growing her 'oaxters' (armpits) back, '[r]eally rid and thick and hairy', is that '[e]very individual hus tae realize/[h]er hale fortune isnae in men's eyes'. The fate of the beauty queen, though not of the speaker, parallels that of La Corbie in the final tableau of the drama. The children of present-day Scotland, playing their dandelion game of 'Mary Queen of Scots Got Her Head Chopped Off', turn on La Corbie, now an innocent-seeming nurse maid, and rise up to throttle her.[60] They have understood her hoax. 'Away and get stuffed' is the parting shot of 'Almost Miss Scotland'.[61] These could also be the final words of the children to La Corbie.

Refracting Binaries: From the Colour of Black and White to Fugitive Colours

The injunction to 'see it fur yirsel' is reprised in *The Colour of Black and White*, the collection which follows *Bagpipe Muzak* and which interleaves new work with many of the recitations and poems from the earlier collection, including 'Almost Miss Scotland'.[62] Two poems almost give this 2003 collection its title; they are 'In the Black and White Era' and 'Black and White Allsorts'. In both poems the speaker of the poem, or the lyric 'I', has made a radical retreat, leaving the reader with no option but to see it for themselves. These two poems also almost form bookends to the collection: 'In the Black and White Era' is the third poem of Section I, while 'Black and White Allsorts' is the second poem of Section VIII, with which the volume closes. Lochhead's avoidance of symmetry in the organisation of the volume, and her refusal to match its title with a single poem, are aspects of the ironical way *The Colour of Black and White* playfully but consistently interrogates black and white habits of mind, teases us with our desire for clear either/or solutions and refuses binary thinking. The poems of this volume, individually and collectively, explore the interstices between black and white, the shading of gaps, the colour of uncertainty.

Yet, in their positioning and technique, there are quasi-symmetries between these two poems. One of the qualities they share is that they are both dedicated to poets who are Lochhead's friends and colleagues. The first is dedicated to Ian McMillan, the second to Jackie Kay: a northern white English man, and a mixed-race Scottish woman. In both cases the identity of the dedicatee, named in an extension of the title, informs the way these poems are interpreted, particularly in light of the absconded speaker. 'In the Black and White Era' tells a story which, given the father–son status of the internal narration, can be projected as a tale told by Ian McMillan to the poet.[63] It opens with inverted commas: '"Hitchcock,/there was a Hitchcock on," he said. "*Lifeboat*."' The reporting, lyric 'I' is present only in the 'he said'. This internal storytelling continues for the whole of the first stanza. The same voice speaks throughout the second stanza but it opens without inverted commas; the effect of this subtle control of punctuation is to remove ownership of the narrative. This creation of uncertainty about who is speaking coincides with uncertainty about what happened: 'What I remember, and I do remember/whatever my Mum says, and though Dad denies it'. Both the teller and the tale have become unreliable. The framing lyric 'I' never returns. As readers we can never be certain about the speaker's identity (is it Ian McMillan or are we imagining this?) nor the identity of the interrupting stranger; nor can we know whether these events took place at all. The poem denies closure, just as the internal speaker 'never saw the end' of *Lifeboat*. Both the intertextual reference to the Hitchcock film and the claimed identity of the stranger ('I was/on the same ship as you, Ark Royal, remember?') take the listener to the deeper past of the 'black and white era' of World War II, when there was, contemporary nostalgia dictates, clear demarcation between enemy and friend, home and away. These wartime certainties cling in the projected memory; neither speaker nor listener ever 'sees the end of it', as the telling cliché insists. Yet in the present time of the recollection, black and white thinking shades into grey, as moral, domestic and international boundaries are called into question.

Section VIII of the collection moves its subject matter assertively into the twenty-first century, opening with 'Year 2K email epistle to Carol Ann Duffy, Sister-poet & Friend of my Youth'.[64] Here the speaker's lyric voice is manifest even from the title and identifies itself with Liz Lochhead herself; the continuing presence of the poet and her 'sister-poet' in each other's lives, in the face of mortality, is a main strand of the poem, so that Lochhead's technically achieved personal presence carries thematic weight. The contrast with 'Black and White Allsorts' which follows, with its dedication to Jackie Kay, who was at the time Duffy's partner, could not be more stark; this is a poem made up of a list from which the lyric voice of the speaker is completely absent. The poem's title plays with the name of once-popular sweets, Liquorice Allsorts, glanced at in the 'liquorice bootlace' of the opening line.[65] Like 'In the Black and White Era', this poem appears to take its cue from the person to whom it is dedicated. Kay herself has often written about the racist prejudice she has encountered since childhood in her native Scotland. As a mixed-race woman Kay recounts the experience in her poetry of being treated as black and other in a predominantly white environment.

Lochhead's approach to this highly charged topic is to offer the reader a list which alternates black things with white things, all of them attractive or desirable except 'a black eye', those ominous words standing out in the last line of the first stanza. This poem creates another 'see it fur yirsel' situation, in which the reader is left alone with the material to draw their own conclusions. But there is some help in the way the list is composed: it works by creating contrasts, layering difference, black things and white things none of which are literally black or white; the list rhymes, with rhyme words placed both at the ends of lines and internally; the things listed are either gender-neutral or feminine; the last two lines are playfully local in their geographical reference, 'in Kelvingro-/ve park'. Finally, the language itself is seductive, an example of what Siobhan Redmond, who often performed Lochhead's revue pieces, describes as 'toothsome. It's a real pleasure to *say*. It's great when you have a huge long "chocolate éclair" of a phrase – in terms of the senses it's very gratifying to perform.'[66] The elaborate sequence of juxtapositions demonstrates how beauty and pleasure are intensified by contrast, while the intricate rhymes demonstrate how these oppositions are integrated with one another to create a mutually enhancing whole. The sense of necessary connection between opposites is embodied by splitting the word 'Kelvingrove' over the last two lines in order to complete the rhyme ('snow' with 'gro', 'dark' with 'park').[67] The specific West End of Glasgow location of this park delivers the complex whole to Lochhead's own doorstep, to emphasise the local and everyday nature of what is being saluted. As a critique of culture, this poem embraces the differences between black and white, shows their internally nuanced gradations and asserts an equality of otherness in their mutual relation.

Lochhead's manipulation of the retreat of the lyric 'I' predominates throughout Section VIII of *The Colour of Black and White*, which comprises recitations reprinted from *Bagpipe Muzak* together with new work written in the same style. The last poem, rich with irony in this context, is a riff on Frank Sinatra's song 'My Way', in which almost every line begins with the word 'I', creating a blank canvas onto which the reader projects their own subjectivity and their own narrative. This is poetry which speaks with a public voice; it assumes a collective identity and generates an audience which is both individuated and communal.

It sets the scene for her 2016 Makar collection, *Fugitive Colours*, in which Scotland is still negotiating with its closest neighbour, England, but is also positioned on an international stage. 'This is Scotland, this/our one small country in this great wide world', Lochhead reminds the Fellows of the Royal Incorporation of Architects in Scotland in the poem 'Grace', commissioned for their annual dinner in 2012.[68] While this is a poem written for a specific occasion, 'Grace' has a larger reach, evident in the two lines just quoted. Here, Scotland and the world are connected by the threefold repetition of 'this', pointing emphatically to both and yoking them together. Through the use of 'our' the speaker assumes a public position, to align herself with those who are addressed. The 'great wide world' is described in the next line as 'our . . . dear green place', a phrase which has particular resonance for Glaswegians since it is the epithet of the city itself. 'Glas' is the Gaelic word for blue/green, as both Clarke and Lochhead have pointed out in their poetry; it is also the first syllable of 'Glasgow'. By invoking the Gaelic etymology of 'Glasgow', Lochhead extends the literal and symbolic meaning of her home city's name to capture the whole earth. The commissioned poem 'Grace' views the world not in political terms as an assembly of nations, but as a green version of the blue planet, a place of nature rather than nations. The route into it, the poem asserts, is by viewing the whole as a locally cherished habitation. The stanza ends with a question, framed appropriately for architects but pitched for an audience at large: 'What shall we build of it, together/in this our one small time and space?' The poem addresses a 'fellowship' of architects, but it also posits a community of citizens who bear responsibility for the nurture and good governance of Scotland and its place in the world.

Fugitive Colours, like Lochhead's previous collections, is organised into separate parts, and 'Grace' is placed in the last section of poems: 'Makar Songs, Occassional [*sic*] and Performance Pieces Mainly'. The overriding principle of organisation within this section is the generation of communities through poetry. It opens with the poem Lochhead wrote for her appointment as Makar, 'Poets Need Not', which speaks for a community of poets. It closes with three performance pieces. What is striking about the arrangement is that it moves from poems with solemn, civic, ritual purpose, which all but erase the individuality of the poet, to recitations stamped with the zestful wit that has characterised Lochhead's iconoclastic work throughout her career. As a crescendo it asserts the presence of Lochhead the performer, artificer of both her public voice and her public. It also gives the volume a circular structure rather than a linear one, linking back to the opening section, 'Love and Grief, Elegies and Promises', in which one reviewer observed, 'Lochhead accesses the truly personal and particular and communicates with her readers at the level of the heart.'[69] More specifically, the songs evoked in the last poem of the collection, 'In Praise of Old Vinyl', return the reader to the 'Golden oldies' which accompany the lyric speaker and her late husband on their road trip out of Glasgow towards their 'Favourite Place' in the Highlands, the very first poem of the collection.[70]

Scotland's continuing negotiation with England is marked in the 'Makar Songs' section of the volume by the poem 'Open', written for the opening session of the Scottish Parliament in 2011, Lochhead's first year as Makar. Implicit in the poem is the notion that the devolved government of Scotland is newly formed, and the world lies all before it. Newness is invoked by the opening citation of Edwin Morgan's poem, 'Open the Doors', which he wrote for the parliament's inaugural session and which, in the event, Lochhead read aloud on his behalf. She describes her rehearsals with him for his '[f]our minutes of tongue-twisters', in the following poem, 'Spring 2010, and at His Desk by the Window is Eddie in a Red Shirt': '"Liz . . . you're not getting enough out of the/*not yet* . . .".'[71] The citation of Morgan's poem is not only an act of homage to her predecessor at a high point of the National Poet's purpose, it is also a declaration of continuity in the civic life represented by both poet and parliament. Lochhead ends her own poem with an exhortation to the assembled SMPs [Scottish Members of Parliament], which counts as much for politics as for performance poetry, 'But close the gap between what we say and what we do'.[72] It reiterates her conclusion to another ceremonial poem in the section, 'Connecting Cultures: for Commonwealth Day in Westminster Abbey, 2012', which ends, 'What we merely say says nothing –/All that matters is what we do.'[73] Representation, for Lochhead, whether in poetry or politics, must be performative, must be a form of enactment.

'*Art, art, what is it for?/ To bring into being what never existed before*': these words are the refrain of the performance poem 'Way Back in the Paleolithic',[74] which is placed in the collection as a pivot, midway through the volume as a whole, at the end of the third section, 'Ekphrasis, Etcetera'. This piece, not previously published in any of Lochhead's collections though delivered in performance, is another way of 'connecting cultures'. There is an implication that, even in the Paleolithic age, art played an important social role, so surely it should be more widely integrated in culture today. This assertion feeds into the way the piece articulates a fundamental impulse of *Fugitive Colours*, which is to insist on the value of the creative arts, and poetry in particular, for the generation of community and its ability to reach beyond itself. The poem declares that the '[a]rtistic vibe/. . . binds us together as part of the tribe'; furthermore, it projects, through the rhyme of 'dance' with 'trance', a cohesive and a visionary society.[75] The artist, so the recitation asserts, has occupied a continuous role since the days of prehistory, as one who builds communities and enables growth by a primal creative act. This includes the creation of the 'tribe' itself, the social and political grouping of individuals. For the Makar, spokes-poet for a nation, the high stakes are belied by the playful fun of the piece, which enables Lochhead to deliver her serious intent with a socially inclusive lightness of touch.

The dependence of the growth of community on the continuous and sustained work of its artists receives careful attention throughout *Fugitive Colours*. Many of the poems are dedicated to individual artists, or groups of artists, whose contributions are celebrated, drawing attention to thriving, diverse creativity within and beyond Scotland. Many are ekphrastic poems, which explore visual arts through language, translating in the case of 'In Alan Davie's Paintings' the colour of his palette into the colour of Scottish vowels: 'a braid and tappietourie swag o emerant/yallowchie/blae'.[76] Lochhead also draws attention to the continuity of her own career, not simply by demonstrating the vocal range that has characterised her work in lyric poetry, performance poetry, theatre-making poetry and ritual public poetry, but also by reprinting one poem from *The Colour of Black and White* next to its new sequel, the penultimately positioned 'Dirty Diva' poems.

Since the publication of *Dreaming Frankenstein* in 1984, each of Lochhead's successive collections have formed an interlinking daisy-chain of old and new work. For example, the rap 'What I'm Not' from *True Confessions and New Clichés* appears as the second half of 'The Complete Alternative History of the World, Part One' in *Bagpipe Muzak*, and the first half of this poem in turn was reprinted in *The Colour of Black and White* under the title 'In the Beginning'.[77] Other continuities are more obvious, such as the reprinting of 'Five Berlin Poems' from *Bagpipe Muzak* in *The Colour of Black and White*,[78] or the echo of *Dreaming Frankenstein* in 'Lucy's Diary' printed in both *Bagpipe Muzak* and *The Colour of Black and White*.[79] In a very literal way, these repetitions assert continuity across time. The poems' subject matter, or their social targets, still tug at the poet's attention; the address must be reiterated. It also allows readers who have followed Lochhead's career to recognise themselves, to create a personal and political narrative of what has changed and what has stayed the same, since their first encounters with these works. Cumulatively, these repetitions generate a sense of the interlinking of linear, progressive time with circular time. As such, they map on to the development of the nation for which, as Makar, Lochhead speaks. Scotland is both an ancient kingdom and a new democracy; the past needs to be carried into the future without rupture. The way in which Lochhead repeatedly weaves together old with new work affords an artistic example of continuity which sustains innovation, community which sustains diversity.

So, what about the 'Dirty Divas'? In the new poem, 'Another, Later, Song for That Same Dirty Diva', the Diva's recollections are captured by the speaker of the poem in the safe female space of the 'ladies john' of the 'Seniors Association of Greater Edmonton'.[80] They confirm that the complaints made by her youthful self in 'Song for a Dirty Diva' were a species of literary litotes, by which her 'mainstream addiction/to Hetero-sex' was never assuaged because all her male friends were 'friends of Dorothy' and her girlfriends were 'strictly Sapphic'.[81] The young Diva has a gargantuan sexual appetite, and her uninhibited articulation of it illustrates an important trend in women's progress towards self-understanding and self-determination. Yet, as so often in Lochhead's construction of female characters, progressive and regressive qualities are mixed together. Many of the sexual jokes are at the Diva's expense and might therefore undermine her; at the same time her heterosexual focus constructs homosexual men and women as nothing more than stereotypes who impede the satisfaction of her own desires. She thereby exposes and embodies the prejudices of a heteronormative culture which threaten to crush those who do not conform, just as surely as patriarchal structures had impoverished women of all sexual orientations and social classes.

The older Dirty Diva shows no signs of having led a sexually frustrated youth. Now a 'Senior', she recalls her sexual romp through the 1950s, '60s and '70s. On one level, the embedded narrative of Dirty Diva Senior affords a witty opportunity to contrast the changing social norms of then and now; for example, 'the complimentary condoms in the/Eighties, remember? Yes. Like . . . after dinner mints'.[82] On another level, both the Dirty Diva and her interlocutor assert acceptance of mortality alongside a *carpe diem* philosophy. The Diva is still outrageous and funny at her own expense, but she is also wise: '"Forget the nips and tucks, they are not the answers"'.[83] The answer, her actions show us, is to keep dancing, hobbling or not, and to embrace everything which facilitates that, even the 'free incontinence supplies' which so appal the speaker.[84]

More profoundly, the grouping of these 'Performance Pieces' in the same section as the formal 'Makar Songs' asks readers to remember that the past connects with the present, and that actions have consequences. By asserting continuity between Lochhead's earlier work and the work written during her role as Makar, it reaffirms her pioneering political likening of Scotland and woman. At the same time it redirects the simile away from an articulation of shared objectification and towards an assertion that both have now an unappeasable hunger for self-fulfilment. The section as a whole contends that while Scotland may have a new political identity following the devolution of government, it must not fall into the colonisers' trap of rewriting or erasing its own history. Like the Dirty Diva, Scotland must dance its embodied past into the future, no matter how unpalatable the past or what constraints the future brings.

Awarded the Queen's Gold Medal for Poetry in 2015, the year before she stepped down as Makar, Liz Lochhead was interviewed about her work in the *Guardian*. The journalist concluded: '[t]hrough her writing, Lochhead has twined herself into her country's history, both as a figure in it, in her role as national laureate, and an author of it.'[85] For all its entertainment of nostalgia, *Fugitive Colours* shows that while 'her country's history' captures the poet's attention, Lochhead's sights are set on what future will grow out of it.

Notes

1. Waters, 'The SRB Interview: Liz Lochhead'.
2. Duffy, 'Foreword', in Liz Lochhead, *A Choosing: Selected Poems* (Edinburgh: Polygon, 2011), p. ix.
3. Ibid. p. ix.
4. Clune, 'Hearing Voices, p. 89.
5. Ibid. p. 85.
6. Lochhead, 'Revelation', in *Memo for Spring*, p. 124.
7. McMillan, 'Choices: Poems 1972–2011', p. 26.
8. Lochhead, 'Hell for Poets', in *The Colour of Black and White*, p. 106.
9. Lochhead, 'On Midsummer Common', in *Dreaming Frankenstein*, p. 128.
10. Lochhead, 'Poem For Other Poor Fools', in *Dreaming Frankenstein*, p. 125.
11. Ibid. p. 125.
12. See Crawford, 'On "Something I'm Not"', for a fine close reading of this poem.
13. Lochhead, 'Outer', in *Islands*, p. 111.
14. Ibid., p. 112.
15. Ibid.
16. 'Inner', *Dreaming Frankenstein*, p. 112.
17. Ibid., p. 113.
18. Lochhead, 'George Square', in *Memo for Spring*, p. 148.
19. Lochhead, 'Outer', in *Islands*, p. 106.
20. Wilson and Somerville-Arjat (eds), *Sleeping with Monsters*, p. 11.
21. Ibid. pp. 10–11.
22. Ibid. p. 10.
23. González, '"Scotland, Whit Like?"', p. 364.
24. Wilson and Somerville-Arjat, *Sleeping with Monsters*, p. 11.
25. Craig, *Out of History*, p. 12.
26. Wilson and Somerville-Arjat, *Sleeping with Monsters*, p. 10.
27. Reizbaum, 'Canonical Double-Cross', p. 165.
28. Severin, '*The Colour of Black and White* and Scottish Identity', p. 37.
29. Lochhead, *Memo for Spring*, p. 142.
30. Clune, 'Hearing Voices', p. 78.
31. Boyd, 'The Voice of Revelation', p. 39.
32. Lochhead, *True Confessions*, pp. 20–2.
33. Laura Severin, 'Shapeshifting', in *Poetry off the Page*, p. 78. Severin expands upon this point in 'Distant Resonances'.
34. Severin, *Poetry off the Page*, p. 77.
35. Lochhead, *True Confessions*, p. 22.
36. Duffy, *Collected Poems*, p. 46.

37. Lochhead, *True Confessions*, p. 16.
38. Ibid. p. 17.
39. Ibid. p. 18.
40. Ibid. p. 90.
41. Ibid. p. 90.
42. Scullion, 'A Woman's Voice', p. 123.
43. Waters, 'The SRB Interview: Liz Lochhead'.
44. Ibid.
45. Lochhead, 'Bagpipe Muzak, Glasgow 1990', in *Bagpipe Muzak*, p. 26.
46. Clune, 'Hearing Voices', p. 88.
47. Lochhead, *Dreaming Frankenstein*, p. 70.
48. Reizbaum, 'Canonical Double-Cross', p. 183.
49. Wilson and Somerville-Arjat, *Sleeping with Monsters*, p. 12.
50. Nicholson, 'Knucklebones of Irony', p. 223.
51. Cunningham, 'Animal Rights Campaigner'.
52. For an account of masculinised Scottish nationalism see González, '"Scotland, Whit like?"', pp. 364–8.
53. Lochhead, *Mary Queen of Scots Got Her Head Chopped Off & Dracula*, p. 11.
54. Ibid. p. 12.
55. Lochhead, *Bagpipe Muzak*, pp. 3–6. This recitation and many of those published in *Bagpipe Muzak* were performed as *Nippy Sweeties*, by Elaine C. Smith, Angie Rew and Liz Lochhead, broadcast by STV in 1986: <https://www2.bfi.org.uk/films-tv-people/4ce2b74d44de9> (accessed 4 September 2020).
56. Lochhead, *Bagpipe Muzak*, p. 3.
57. Ibid. p. 5.
58. Ibid. p. 6.
59. Ibid. p. 3.
60. Lochhead, *Mary Queen of Scots Got Her Head Chopped Off & Dracula*, p. 67.
61. Lochhead, *Bagpipe Muzak*, p. 6.
62. Lochhead, *The Colour of Black and White*, pp. 108–11.
63. Ibid. pp. 6–7.
64. Ibid. p. 103.
65. Ibid. p. 104.
66. Clune, 'Hearing Voices', p. 81.
67. Lochhead, *The Colour of Black and White*, p. 105.
68. Lochhead, *Fugitive Colours*, p. 87.
69. Glaister, 'Picture This'.
70. Lochhead, 'Favourite Place', in *Fugitive Colours*, pp. 3–6.
71. Ibid. p. 81.

72. Lochhead, 'Open', in *Fugitive Colours*, p. 79.
73. Ibid. p. 76.
74. Ibid. pp. 60–2.
75. Ibid. p. 60; p. 62.
76. Ibid. p. 44.
77. Lochhead, 'What I'm Not', in *True Confessions*, pp. 55–6; 'The Complete Alternative History of the World, Part One', in *Bagpipe Muzak*, pp. 12–15; 'In the Beginning', in *The Colour of Black and White*, pp. 112–14.
78. Lochhead, 'Five Berlin Poems', in *Bagpipe Muzak*, pp. 77–84 and in *The Colour of Black and White*, pp. 75–83.
79. Lochhead, 'Lucy's Diary', in *Bagpipe Muzak*, pp. 60–2 and in *The Colour of Black and White*, pp. 67–9.
80. Lochhead, *Fugitive Colours*, pp. 113–15.
81. Ibid. pp. 111–12, and *The Colour of Black and White*, pp. 126–7.
82. Lochhead, *Fugitive Colours*, p. 115.
83. Ibid. p. 114.
84. Ibid. p. 115.
85. Crown, 'Liz Lochhead'.

6

Carol Ann Duffy: 'The edge has become the centre'

'The edge has become the centre'

At the outset of her laureateship, Carol Ann Duffy stated:

> Poetry has changed since the days of Larkin – he's a good poet, but poetry has changed for the better. It's not a bunch of similarly educated men – it's many voices, many styles. The edge has become the centre.[1]

Her appointment can be seen as the destination of a journey already mapped out by the moral imperative of her early poem 'Whoever She Was'. This was the poem she submitted anonymously and as an unknown poet to the National Poetry Competition twenty-six years earlier. A dramatic monologue spoken in the voice of a mother, 'Whoever She Was', won the National Poetry Prize in 1983. By winning, the trajectory of namelessness to name was launched, moving both the poet and her subjects from the margins towards the centre.

Carol Ann Duffy was twenty-seven in 1983 and the National Poetry Prize was in its fifth year, having been launched by the Poetry Society in 1978. Anonymised submissions, then as now, were judged by a panel of three poets. In 1983 Gillian Clarke was one of the judges, along with Vernon Scannell and Kevin Crossley Holland. 'Whoever She Was' followed fast on the heels of Clarke's exploration of the same theme, motherhood, in 'Letter from a Far Country' (1979/1982). While there is no similarity of treatment, since Clarke's poem ennobles maternal domesticity and Duffy's rages against it as a site of entrapment, nevertheless both poems attest to the validity of motherhood as a fit subject for poetry. 'Whoever She Was', and Clarke's part in its selection, consolidated the poetic legitimacy of this previously marginal material. The poem marks the beginning of Duffy's method of introducing what

Ian Gregson has characterised as 'shockingly "unpoetic" material into poetry', and puts a feminist agenda at its core.²

Twenty-eight years later, in 2011, Gillian Clarke, as National Poet of Wales, stood in Cardiff's redeveloped Old Library for the opening of the city's new heritage museum, The Cardiff Story. She read her commissioned poem, 'Whoever They Were', which, she stated, 'reflects the multiculturalism inherent in the city's foundations'.³ The echo between the titles of Duffy's 'Whoever She Was' and Clarke's 'Whoever They Were' may be subliminal, but it is unmistakable. Again, Clarke's tone and treatment, salutatory rather than enraged, are radically unlike those of Duffy's earlier poem, and there is no suggestion that the latter is a copy of the earlier original. But the echo is true in one important respect. Both poems announce the arrival in poetry of the representation of social identities and groups which had previously been culturally ignored, or silent, or unable to speak for themselves. Mothers and migrants are alike in that they have historically occupied positions of powerlessness within culture. They have been slow to move from namelessness, as the titles of these two poems suggest, to recognised individuality. Both poems make claims on social change; they call for new ethical perspectives and moral awareness. They also deliver these amplified sensibilities, thereby marking the generative aesthetic significance for poetry of the arrival of outsiders.

The dynamics between the two spaces, edge and centre, matter for a number of reasons, notwithstanding the fact that the terms 'edge' and 'centre' are undefined and even contentious. They can refer to physical geography, geopolitics, cultural geography, the psycho-social, gender identity or aesthetic practice, amongst other things, and their relative position depends on the perspective of the viewer. As Linden Peach asks, 'which margins? from whose perspective? . . . according to what criteria?'⁴ The answers are always a measure of the relative power, status, authority, respect or influence accorded to certain kinds of poet or certain kinds of poetry. The application of the terms is never far from the imperial origins of the metaphor, when London was the powerhouse of a global empire. But in the 2009 interview, Duffy defines the terms in which she understands the dichotomy, pitting 'similarly educated men' against 'many voices, many styles'. Through her chosen definition of edge and centre she reflects the battle for authority, both for herself and others, in which she has been engaged throughout her writing life.

Duffy's Laureate appointment in 2009 inevitably recalled the media attention she had received in 1999, when Andrew Motion became Poet Laureate. This was summarised at the time by Katharine Viner: 'the media set up an opposition between the Oxbridge-style poets who have the power: Motion, James Fenton, Craig Raine; and the "postmodern provincials" who'd been rejected yet again: Duffy, Don Paterson, Liz Lochhead, Simon Armitage. The decision was labelled "a disgrace", "an insult to the country's intelligence" and, infamously, "a bag o'shite".[5] Viner's denotation, 'postmodern provincials', allows both aesthetic practice and cultural geography to have played a part in picking the competing teams, but what really seems to have been decisive in 1999 was Duffy's perceived sexual orientation. In 2009 *The Irish Times* reported, 'Duffy (53) was regarded as runner-up to Andrew Motion 10 years ago but ruled out, according to some accounts, because Tony Blair feared her sexuality might not play well with "Middle England"';[6] or, as the *London Evening Standard* proclaimed, 'Ten years late, this lesbian icon is the right poet for the nation.'[7] Not her poetry but her personal identity had disqualified her in 1999 – an important indication of how weighty a part is played by identity politics, however manufactured they might be, in determining the agenda of which poetry and which poets are celebrated by the establishment. What had disqualified Duffy ten years earlier became her trump card in 2009, Jeanette Winterson claiming she was 'just the kind of Poet Laureate that Britain needs – not snobby, not class bound, not seeking personal advantage, political in that she wants to change things, still idealistic in that she believes she – and poetry – can change things. And, of course, she's a woman, she's a Celt, and she's gay.'[8]

Duffy described the profound sense of cultural alienation which she experienced in 1999 as a result of the way her sexual orientation became objectified, paraded and judged in the media: 'I think gay, straight, whatever, relationships are just a banal fact of life. They're just straight facts. I was very surprised: it made me see that the country I thought I lived in wasn't the one I lived in. It was appalling that sexuality could be written about in that kind of way.'[9] The context of the interview in which she stated this renewed experience of discovering herself in the cultural exterior was, ironically, occasioned by the Forward Prize shortlisting of *The World's Wife*. This collection fizzes with missing-person accounts by female characters drawn from myth, folk tale and popular culture. Through these dramatic monologues, Duffy writes women into the fabric of the cultural past from the perspective of the present. Anachronism is the technique that delivers much of the wit and political punch of these poems. As a method of exposing historic exclusions, it throws yet more light on the present when the poems are read against Duffy's exclusion from the quest for Poet Laureate to succeed Ted Hughes. These poems target the present, and Duffy's contemporaneous exclusion from the Laureate selection process on the grounds of her sexuality demonstrates the accuracy of their aim. The political agenda of *The World's Wife* continues the necessary work launched by 'Whoever She Was'. The popular success of *The World's Wife*, measured by its high sales and its appearance as a set text on A Level syllabuses, shows that despite official resistance there was nevertheless a public appetite for Duffy's agenda of inclusion. Running counter to her treatment by the political establishment and the media during 1999, this was already a familiar trope in the reception of her work; its capacity to represent the 'edge' in defiance of the 'centre', and fundamentally to destabilise those categories, had already been made conspicuous.

For instance, Caroline Gonda, writing in 1995, argues that Duffy's command of dislocation and displacement, based on her own migrant experience of moving from Scotland to England at an early age and on arrival experiencing herself as an outsider, is the very quality that marks her out as representative:

> Duffy's status as transplanted Scot and long-term resident in England places her on the boundary between assimilation and difference, belonging and exclusion, familiarity and alienation – paradoxically an ideal position for 'the representative poet of the present day'. For many of its natives, too, England in the '80s seemed increasingly an other country, a place of confusion, fear and loss.[10]

Gonda is herself quoting from Sean O'Brien's 1993 review of *Mean Time* in the *Sunday Times*, in which he claimed that '[Duffy] could well become the representative poet of the present day, much as Philip Larkin came to seem for the time between Attlee and Thatcher.'[11] These claims take the story of Duffy's place on the 'edge' and 'centre' spectrum back to the moment of her promotion as one of the New Generation poets in 1994, when grand designs were made by the Poetry Society on the disruption of these traditional positions.

The New Generation Poets were a group of twenty poets (eight women and twelve men) aged between thirty and fifty-four, selected by the Poetry Society in 1994 to represent the most promising contemporary poetry.[12] Their promotion was modelled on *Granta*'s first foregrounding of young novelists in 1993. It was designed to overturn the public perception of poetry as rarefied, difficult and remote, and at the same time to revitalise the poetry business for publishers and bookshops. Poetry by the NewGen was disseminated not only in print but also on radio, with poems being read hourly on Radio 1 during May 1994. Peter Forbes, editor of *The Poetry Review*, announced: '[t]his may prove that no-one should be frightened of poetry – none of these poets uses words that would not be spoken, there is very little "poetic" language here.'[13] Bill Swainson, of the Poetry Society, claimed, '[p]oetry now is not Oxbridge, it's not London. It's Glasgow and Birmingham. Poetry has gone regional. The only thing that every poet here has in common is confidence in his or her voice.'[14] Peter Marks, assessing celebrity culture of the 1990s, concludes, 'the new poets were unstuffy, energetic performers responsive to the vitality of the decade's mood and striving to connect to a new, young audience'.[15]

On the one hand, these constructions were designed not to contest the centre/edge status quo but to reinforce it by making it more visible. The poets themselves played into the polarisation. Sarah Maguire, for example, stated, '[t]he people who were considered marginal a decade ago have come to the fore, but their poetry is so much more relevant to most people's lives';[16] Don Paterson, '[i]t's . . . part of the new regionalism . . . Poetry has become more accessible, it's the working class takeover';[17] Robert Crawford, 'just because the centre ignores the margins, that doesn't mean the margins stop existing, or indeed writing'.[18] In each case the poets foreground what is for them the most salient point of their difference from the projected mainstream, whether this is gender, class or nation. On the other hand, Stan Smith, acknowledging that 'each poet writes from the recognised relativity and felt marginality of his or her own particular spot on the globe', argues that the effect of this was to unravel 'the centre–periphery binary which shapes so much modern thinking. Each carries out an assault on the idea either that *where-it's-at* is *here* (deposing "elsewhere"), or that things are *really* happening *somewhere else* (deposing the here and now).'[19] Carol Ann Duffy, regarded at the time as 'the biggest name on the list',[20] having just won the Forward Prize for *Mean Time*, held herself aloof even from the championed margin: her only reported media comment was that 'the whole thing "misses the point"'.[21] Nevertheless, whether the polarisation was strengthened or destabilised, as a marketing strategy it held good so that five years later, at the time of Andrew Motion's laureate appointment, Peter Forbes accounted for the antagonism between factions by stating 'the New Generation poets still think of themselves as outsiders'.[22]

The New Generation enterprise was itself riding on a critical wave which spread from the influential poetry anthology *The New Poetry*, edited by Michael Hulse, David Kennedy and David Morely in 1993. This volume presented itself as a deliberate act of counterculture to challenge the authority of *The Penguin Book of Contemporary British Poetry*, edited by Blake Morrison and Andrew Motion a decade earlier in 1982, containing the work of nineteen poets of whom just five were women. More expansive and building on poetry which had emerged during the intervening years, *The New Poetry* presented work by fifty-five poets (seventeen women, including Clarke, Duffy, Lochhead and Meehan, and thirty-eight men) arranged in order of age, with the oldest, Pauline Stainer, leading off and Simon Armitage, born in 1963, the youngest bringing up the rear. 'The new poetry', the editors announced, 'emphasises accessibility, democracy and responsiveness, humour and seriousness, and reaffirms the art's significance as public utterance.'[23] Pointing to their inclusion of Jackie Kay's work, they claimed that it offered 'an extreme example of what Terry Eagleton has termed "the marginal becoming central". A multicultural society challenges the very idea of a centre, and produces pluralism of poetic voice.'[24]

Ironically, though, the thrust of the anthologised extract 'Black Bottom' from Kay's *The Adoption Papers* is centripetal rather than centrifugal. The feelings explored in 'Black Bottom' revolve around all three speakers wanting to belong to the centre, to be unmarked, not different, not bullied or humiliated or set apart because of skin colour or hair. Indeed, the child's voice is Glaswegian, speaking in exactly the same locally inflected language as her aggressors and her parents. The consistency of voice between the child, her parents and her aggressors is a powerful index of the enormity of the persecution suffered by the child, and shows that the centre already contains the edge. Jo Gill argues of *The Adoption Papers* that the collection as a whole resists the clear demarcation of boundaries and generates new hybrid verse forms as one means of achieving this.[25] But this does not seem to be the 'pluralism of poetic voice' claimed by the editors of *The New Poetry* on the basis of their selection. Is it that the 'centre' has not been revealed to itself in this way before? Or are they suggesting that it is the poet's identity (objectified as black, working class, Scottish, female), rather than her poetry, that constitutes 'pluralism of poetic voice'? Stan Smith, appraising the claims of the editors' introduction, argues incisively that it 'offers a fantasy politics straight from the heart of a cultural elite that felt excluded'.[26]

Whatever agenda was being served, at every stage along the way of this edge/centre journey on which Duffy's poetry has been taken, the periphery has been defined according to the writer's personal identity or cultural belonging. Claims for representing the 'edge' have been based on the emergence of culturally diverse perspectives, and hitherto under-represented subject matters, powered by the identity of the poet. While this gives the poet an assured public authority which, as Eavan Boland and Gillian Clarke had argued and indeed demonstrated, women could not take for granted, the 'edge' has been presented entirely in terms of content and identity politics. Attention to aesthetic innovation of form or craft has been scant; Adam Thorpe was alone amongst journalists reporting on the New Generation to note that 'it's pretty well all mainstream modern literary poetry'.[27] Seen in this light, the edge has never really been very far from the centre, and any analysis of the poetic traditions within which Duffy herself works affirms this.

Fiona Sampson, for example, describes Duffy as 'the inheritor of a key English elegiac tradition running from Thomas Hardy by way of Philip Larkin'. Pointing as an example to the sonnet 'Prayer' from the end of *Mean Time*, Sampson notes how all three poets use 'the local and every-day to speak to society and the state of the world'.[28] Sampson observes, but does not elaborate, that it is 'noteworthy that the UK's first woman laureate is part of this masculine tradition'.[29] Alternatively, Marsha Bryant argues that Duffy's portrayal of social disaffection is achieved by the construction of 'perpetrators who function as media commodities', adopting heroic postures drawn from popular culture or using the language of headlines and advertising.[30] Bryant explores 'Psychopath', 'Education for Leisure' and 'Poet for our Times' to argue that Duffy deploys a 'mainstream extreme', critiquing capitalist consumerism by using its own methods against it. She contends that Duffy's use of the dramatic monologue form follows in the tradition of Robert Browning's gap-riddled technique rather than in the Romantics' cultivation of empathetic identification between speaker and reader which Victorian women poets carried forward.[31] For Bryant, Duffy successfully violates the codes of what is expected from a dramatic monologue written by a woman, as well as the codes of acceptable poetic language. Bryant concludes that these are 'tactics to assert [her] position as cultural insider, going to extremes in claiming the mainstream'.[32] Linda Kinnahan has made a lone attempt to characterise Duffy's work as exhibiting formal innovation belonging to an aesthetic avant-garde in *Lyric Interventions: Feminism, Experimental Poetry, and Contemporary Discourse*,[33] but this has been persuasively rejected by Redell Olsen, who regards such a positioning of Duffy's work as 'inexplicable'.[34]

What does being a 'cultural insider' mean? For Duffy, it means quite literally being inside culture, being present within a system of evolving artistic practice: 'For I am in love with you and this//is what it is like or what it is like in words'.[35] The craft of poetry, the reach for figurative language and form in which to cast or imagine experience, make up the culture which Duffy inhabits. As these lines from 'Words, Wide Night' suggest, her poetry transfigures experience and places it at an aesthetic distance yet provides it with a privileged means of articulation.[36] This, surely, is the missing point she noted in her one wry comment about the NewGen hype. Poetry was being overlooked in the rush to locate it in terms of gender, geography or class. That Duffy should feel suspicious of identity politics as guarantor of the value and validity of poetry matches the notoriously mercurial nature of her own personal identity. Born in Scotland to parents of Irish descent, raised in England from the age of six, she has no homogeneous national belonging; a woman, she is neither straightforwardly straight or gay, while as a mother she is neither conventionally partnered nor single; raised working class but moving into the middle class by education and profession, her class identity is mobile; raised Roman Catholic but living in a country where the Queen is head of the Anglican Church, and choosing not to believe in God while still espousing a spiritual dimension of experience, further complicate her self-hood. Only her poetic practice, her commitment to 'what it is like in words', which accommodates the divisions, histories and multiplications of her identity, provides her with insider status. 'Now, *Where do you come from?*/strangers ask. *Originally*? And I hesitate'.[37]

The metrical emphasis on 'Now' in this penultimate line of 'Originally', as well as its indeterminate reference and connection (when is 'now'? does it connect as 'now strangers ask', or 'now where do you come from'?) draws attention to the present as the only meaningful location of self. Jackie Kay's 'In My Country', which she describes as a poem about being Black and Scottish, ends with a similar assertion of the present and presence, configured as place rather than time: '*Where do you come from?*/"Here," I said, "Here. These parts."'[38] The speaker's 'here' unsettles by forcing the interlocutor (avatar for the reader) to look at their place with new eyes. Kay's 'here' mirrors Duffy's 'now'. Both are synchronic statements, indexes of the present moment. Yet what they point to is also mobile and diachronic, unfixed to literal time or place. It is a present which gathers into itself and contains the past, ranging across lived experience and delivering its traces in language. Both also point directly to the poems in which they are written, and as such are acts of self-reflection making the 'here and now' poetry itself, each poem a centre of self. Duffy asserts of her writing practice that it is 'where I put myself into – that's where I am fully present'.[39] Her commitment to the self-centring sufficiency of poetry looks directly forward to her post-laureate initiative and its punning title, 'WRITE where we are NOW', in which she facilitated responses by poets to the Covid-19 pandemic of 2020.[40]

But if Duffy adopts poetry as her homeplace, this too requires negotiation with its past and present inhabitants, most of whom are men and never more in evidence than at her appointment as Laureate, the 'first' woman. As readings of her poetry by Sampson and Bryant attest, her achievements are routinely measured against the masculine traditions in which she both necessarily and unhesitatingly works. Duffy flaunts the doubleness of voice which Alice Ostriker argues must afflict any woman writing in a masculine tradition, by accommodating the 'centre' within her 'edge'. Robert Browning provides the template for her dramatic monologues, Shakespeare her love sonnets and Larkin her lyric poetry. She thereby generates an aesthetic practice which is as fleet of foot as her own personal identity. It is no surprise that Duffy is drawn to the tradition which emanates from 'Anon', whom both she and Liz Lochhead personify and confidently claim as foremother. Duffy writes in the poem 'Anon', 'But I know best – how she passed on her pen',[41] and renews emphasis on the figure in *Sincerity*, where 'she' is directly invoked in the poems 'Anonymous' and 'How Death Comes', while implicitly present in others including 'Apostle' and 'The Creation of Adam and Eve'.[42] Lochhead celebrates the poetry which is handed down from anonymous foremothers in her poem 'Random' about the Scottish Poetry Library: 'dae mind *Anon,*/she's aye been baith *the real McCoy/*and your perfect contemporary'.[43] Cognate with the attraction of 'Anon' as a model for evading the centre/edge dichotomy is the great reservoir of legend, folk tale, myth and popular culture which Duffy, and indeed Lochhead, draw on so readily.

Narratives and motifs which are in public ownership, this body of material belongs to every individual teller of the tale. Feminist revision is well documented, and Duffy's contributions are widely discussed. 'Little Red-Cap', the opening dramatic monologue of *The World's Wife*, affords a manifesto for Duffy's method. The speaker serves a ten-year apprenticeship to the wolf, during which she is entranced by his library, 'a whole wall . . . aglow with books':

> Words, words were truly alive on the tongue, in the head,
> Warm, beating, frantic, winged: music and blood.

Erotically and viscerally embodied by Little Red-Cap, these living words lead her eventually to slaughter her captor and to exhume the 'glistening, virgin white of my grandmother's bones'. Her liberation:

> I filled his old belly with stones. I stitched him up.
> Out of the forest I come with my flowers, singing all alone.[44]

The image of the poet singing 'alone' as she leaves the dark wood, sylvan symbol of the pastoral tradition which Duffy here reconfigures to contain tumultuous sex and bloodshed, looks forward to the closing poem of the collection, 'Demeter'. Here the speaker's daughter emerges from her winter captivity, bringing 'all spring's flowers/to her mother's house.'[45] A female line is held open from Little Red-Cap's grandmother to Demeter's daughter, while the male line has been 'stitched up'. Asynchronous though this trajectory of poetry by women may be, it nevertheless provides a narrative by which female individuation assimilates male traditions and moves forward on its own terms. This in turn can be seen as a powerful example of the way in which 'many voices, many styles' prevail to outmode a centralising, homogenising story of poetry.

Sincerity

If the two major events in the domestic politics of the British Isles which took place during Duffy's tenure have exposed anything, it is that the choice between 'edge' and 'centre' is not a simple binary. Both the referendum on Scottish independence held in 2014 and the referendum on Brexit of 2016 asked citizens to choose between the competing claims of edge and centre. The outcomes in both cases fragmented the apparent clarity of binary choice, subjecting political futures to questions of degree rather than kind. A fragile union of nations within the UK, but how represented? Brexit, but on what terms? Duffy addressed both of these events in the collection which she published at the end of her laureate tenure, *Sincerity*. Adjusting the feminist slogan of the 1970s ('the personal is the political') which sought to enmesh what had been traditionally held apart, Duffy stated that the collection held her ambition 'to speak as myself both personally and as a citizen. I think the past two years with the twin evils of Brexit and Trump have been very stressful. Politics presses in on the personal, even if you're not writing political poems.'[46]

Sincerity is the third of the three collections of poetry which Duffy published during her laureateship. Like the first, *The Bees* (2011), it contains poems both personal and public, while it differs from *Ritual Lighting*, the second in the sequence, a volume dominated by her laureate voice. The title word, 'sincerity', resonates with current usage and etymological source:

> 'I like the word "sincerity",' she says. 'To speak and act out of one's beliefs, thoughts, feelings.' She was also drawn to its etymology, derived from the way in which 'dodgy sculptors' in ancient Greece and Rome would conceal mistakes or flaws by covering them with wax. So 'without wax' (*sine cera* in Latin), 'means genuine, not duplicitous,' she explains.[47]

In interview about this collection Duffy consistently makes two points. First, the aesthetic integrity of the whole added significance to its parts, achieved by careful sequencing of the poems so that they resonated with one another in an ordered arrangement. Secondly, the collection as a whole sounds alarm about the risks of the current political moment: 'I'm putting down markers for things that we can lose . . . civil society or a way of having grace in our public lives.'[48]

The collection is almost preternaturally alert to transience, loss and imminent loss. The grouping of the poems assures a cross-fertilisation between the articulation of personal grief and public mourning. These twinned perspectives are yoked in the dark wit of the poem 'Auden comes through at the séance', in which the phrase 'your mother' replaces the first words of the first lines of twenty-two poems ranging from Gray's 'Elegy in a Country Churchyard' through Arnold's 'Dover Beach', Hughes' 'Thought Fox', Dickinson's 'I heard a Fly buzz' and, hidden in stanza three, Auden's 'September 1, 1939'. Most of the inter-texts are elegiac or foreboding. A few document moments of joy, amongst them the closing line taken from Siegfried Sassoon, 'Your mother suddenly burst out singing', a statement of hope about what poetry can offer during political turbulence. Although this poem appears initially playful, it presents poetry which has entered public consciousness by making the personal or national mood known to itself. Duffy implicitly aligns her own work with these landmarks. The insistent presence of 'your mother' places women and family at the heart of the cultural past but also pivots between public and personal, gesturing towards the many intimate poems which *Sincerity* contains, and asserts the integration of personal and political.

In 2012 Duffy was awarded the Pen Pinter Prize, an honour which was named after Harold Pinter and which rewards literary contributions to freedom of expression. Pinter's widow, Dame Antonia Fraser, stated of Duffy's selection that '[s]he comments on contemporary events directly in a way we do not believe a Poet Laureate has done before.'[49] The uncompromised tone and subject matter of Duffy's earliest Laureate poems have often been noticed. Her first contribution was the broken sonnet 'Politics', about the MP's expenses scandal,[50] and her first Christmas poem, 'The Twelve Days of Christmas', presented a raft of unseasonal political topics including the war in Afghanistan, the financial crash, corrupt politicians, species extinction, immigrant detention centres and the Copenhagen conference on climate change.[51] At the time of this poem's publication she reaffirmed her decision to use the laureateship 'to prove that poetry can still be central to Britain's cultural life'.[52] As laureate, the oppositional public stance which she has taken throughout her career is placed on a platform, giving her voice more authority than it had previously. *Sincerity* is a resounding example of the way in which 'the edge has become the centre'; her unruly voice commands respect and generates possibility for debate by challenging the very figures who appointed her.

The anger which she directed against the Thatcher government and its legacy during the 1980s and 1990s, most notably in *The Other Country* (1990), flares again in the public poems of *Sincerity*, which speak to an era she considers 'much worse' than the 1980s.[53] The consistency of her perspective across the decades is a reassuring index of her ethical integrity, but it is also politically sobering. 'How do they suddenly appear fully formed as the same old bullshitters in suits we remember from Thatcher's era?' she asks, commenting on the sestina 'A Formal Complaint'.[54] The juxtaposition between the highly wrought complexity of this poetic form and the contemporary idioms of the six repeating words, 'arseholes', 'gatekeepers', 'chancers', 'tossers', 'bullshitters', 'patriots', makes a political point. Why should the sophisticated form of public life be degraded by these officials? Are we not shocked to see the grace of civic life brought low?

Its partner poem, 'Swearing In', with a similarly punning title, deploys the Old English poetic form of kennings to elaborate contempt for the 'swearing in' of Donald Trump to the American presidency. Apart from the final half-line of this nine-line poem, every word is a coined compound noun; the sheer density of fabricated vocabulary, let alone its meanings, forces attention to the generative impulse of language, affording a reality check on an election campaign based on slogans and lies.

Sincerity deploys time-honoured poetic forms in order to assert the dimension which poetry has traditionally brought to public debate. Alongside this, Duffy also references her own past body of work. 'Gorilla' and 'Io' both recall the shape-changing motifs of *The World's Wife*; 'The Ex-Ministers' resonates with the tone of *The Other Country*; the Shakespearian riffs 'CXVI' and 'Once' recall poems of desolation from *Mean Time* and *Rapture*; the surrealism of 'Blackbird' and 'Skirtful of Stones' revisits the method of *Feminine Gospels*; the bereavement poems 'The Rain' and 'Dark School' speak to their partners about mourning in *The Bees*; the dramatic monologues 'Stone Love' and 'Sleeping Place (What He Said)' link hands with Duffy's trademark form which announced itself in her first collection, *Standing Female Nude*.

But what stands out in *Sincerity* is the move of Duffy's ever-mobile first-person speaker away from the incarnation of characters who are strangers towards characters who are, as she puts it, 'masks or versions of myself'.[55] 'Vocation' is a key example, a dramatic monologue in which the first-person speaker and the subject matter, 'more my shadow than my shadow', seem to divide the self into speaker and riddling 'vocation'. Carol Rumens, in her delicately probing analysis of this poem, cautions against any simplistic identification between speaker, poet and author.[56] Yet the poem can be read as a meditation on the relationship between poet and Muse, 'So I am supplicant; alert at the lip/of wordlessness'. By changing the idea of the Muse to the idea of Vocation, the poem offers a sophisticated response to the trivialising patriarchal discussions of the 1970s about whether women poets could have Muses (and whether, therefore, they could be poets at all). It takes gender out of the discussion altogether, and focuses instead on a primal impulse to write. At the same time it is not afraid to invoke a male precursor as fellow journeyman, with its closing citation of Lafeu's line from *All's Well That Ends Well*, 'If its eyes smell onions, I shall weep anon'.[57] This line lays bare a spectrum of artifice-to-reality behind the recreation of emotion in poetry. The speaker will weep, but the shadow smells onions. The misquotation of the line, which Shakespeare wrote for the character to speak as 'Mine eyes smell onions . . .', indicates the divisions of an underlying self, an 'I' and 'eyes' fragmenting into speaker and vocation immersed in a synaesthesia of perception.

The poem links with 'Clerk of Hearts', which opens the collection, and 'Scarecrow', both meditating on the vocation of the poet; 'Apostle' presents the poet as bearer of witness, 'Anonymous' considers the poet's relationship with affairs of state, while 'Oval Map Sampler' maps out a female line of creativity in a dramatic monologue composed of haikus:

> Sew. I leave my mark,
> Like the maid or the monarch.
> Call it woman's work.[58]

These speakers bleed into the lyric 'I' of *Sincerity*, helping to construct a 360-degree image of a speaker who is biographically related to Duffy herself. As sequenced in the volume, these personal lyrics lead directly to poems which meditate on the human condition, such as 'Sincerity', the last poem of the collection. Dwelling explicitly on the word 'I' and its referent, this poem performs the speaker's final vanishing act. Consonant with Duffy's attention to aesthetic distance created by her medium, language, the speaker, 'I', is 'lost in translation'. Alternatively, 'I look up,/. . ./To see my breath/take its rightful place/with the stars,/with everyone else who breathes'.[59]

'In *Sincerity*, I wanted to explore myself,' Duffy asserts in interview.[60] This exploration enables her to scrutinise her vocation as well as to exercise it, to articulate a vulnerable, mortal self, and to end on a note of common humanity, holding an 'I' which is both particular and, more conventionally for the lyric mode, representative. Paradoxically, the exploration of self envisages an ultimate dissolution of self. Duffy's image of breath ascending to be 'with the stars' resonates with Paula Meehan's vision of stardust as the shared basis of earthly life, articulated for example in 'The Road to Agios Kirikos', in which ghost lovers listen to glow-worms singing 'the stardust of which they're made'.[61] Like Meehan's poem, 'Sincerity' presents a cosmic perspective in which all boundaries, of individuals and nations, are erased. Its position as the closing poem in a collection which dwells on a shared human condition is carefully chosen, just as the poem itself illustrates one of the guiding principles of her laureateship, that 'poetry is the music of being human'.[62]

Aphorisms and Authority

Eschewing prose, and writing only the briefest of introductions to the many anthologies she has edited or commissioned, Duffy's verbal medium is exclusively poetry. She has, however, been generous in giving press interviews. Scattered throughout these are pithy statements which capture her vision of the cultural value, place and purpose of poetry. They are couched as universal truths; authoritative and commanding, they announce confidence and compel assent. Considered together, they offer a commentary on how she views her art, and they constitute a compressed version of the critical essays which she never writes. While their frequency became more pronounced during her laureateship, perhaps because she was interviewed more often during this period than before it, her aphoristic statements about poetry are not exclusively a feature of her tenure. The selection offered here begins by drawing on material circulating in the press at the time of Andrew Motion's laureate appointment in 1999 and it continues through to her post-laureate statements made during the Covid-19 pandemic of 2020.

1999

'Poetry now is much more part of the fabric of people's lives than it was, say, 30 years ago. There weren't any women poets around then.'[63]

Poetry is 'trying to grow a past with words.'[64]

2002

'Childhood is like a long greenhouse where everything is growing, it's lush and steamy. It's where poems come from.'[65]

'When you've finished a book, you're standing in a different place; the landscape has changed.'[66]

2004

'A poem, if you like, is the attire of feeling: the literary form where words seem tailor-made for memory or desire.'[67]

2005

'In each poem, I'm trying to reveal a truth, so it can't have a fictional beginning.'[68]

'Poetry and prayer are very similar . . . I write quite a lot of sonnets and I think of them almost as prayers: short and memorable, something you can recite.'[69]

2007

'When I was young, there was a sense that if poetry wasn't written by dead men, then it had to be somehow difficult and have secrets. I've always been of the view that poetry is of the people and of our utterance.'[70]

'I still have a sense of a poem being a prayer in some way.'[71]

'Poetry was more of a vocation. It was a way of explaining the world through language to myself.'[72]

2009

'You can find poetry in your everyday life, your memory, in what people say on the bus, in the news, or just what's in your heart.'[73]

'The only way to write poetry is to read it.'[74]

'Poetry is all about looking at the ordinary and transforming it – the Midas touch.'[75]

[P]oetry [is] the place in language where everything that can be praised is praised, and where what needs to be called into question is so.[76]

[P]oetry, the music of being human, matters deeply to a huge and growing number of people in this country.[77]

'Poetry is our national art.'[78]

'Poetry isn't something outside of life; it is at the centre of life. We turn to poetry to help us to understand or cope with our most intense experiences.'[79]

'Poetry can't lie.'[80]

'Poetry is a way of being near something.'[81]

'Poetry selects its own occasions.'[82]

'Poetry is in your everyday life.'[83]

'Poetry takes us back to the human.'[84]

'[Poetry] is like a present.'[85]

2010

'Poetry has always been a journey for me – a journey I still feel I'm on.'[86]

2011

'The poem is a form of texting . . . it's the original text.'[87]

'[Poetry] is perfecting of a feeling in language – it's a way of saying more with less, just as texting is.'[88]

'[Poetry is] a kind of time capsule – it allows feelings and ideas to travel big distances in a very condensed form.'[89]

'The poem is *the* literary form of the 21st century ... It's able to connect young people in a deep way to language ... it's language as play.'[90]

'Poetry is a different way of seeing something, and seeing a subject in a different way is often a very good tool to better learning.'[91]

'Poetry can keep things in language, so although the person might be gone, you can use language as a kind of net and retain a little bit of their spirit.'[92]

'[Poetry is] how we explain ourselves, how we bear witness, how we tell the truth.'[93]

2014

'Poetry provides an important alternative voice to journalists or pundits or academics as a way of dealing with things that matter to us all.'[94]

2018

'I think poets should write not only from somewhere but from somewhen.'[95]

'Poetry should never be up its own arse.'[96]

'It's a question of trying to keep your finger on the pulse of what people might be interested in, or where the voice or the language of poetry might be worth adding to the kind of national babble and blether and jabber.'[97]

'Poetry comes out of silence.'[98]

'Politics presses in on the personal, even if you're not writing political poems.'[99]

'Poetry is the music of being human.'[100]

2020

'In our separate isolations, a poem is like the Tardis: bigger on the inside. Like spring – to recall T. S. Eliot – poetry mixes memory and desire.'[101]

'We need the voice of poetry in times of change and world-grief.'[102]

'A poem only seeks to add to the world and now seems the time to give.'[103]

'A poem can say in so few words something so precious and startling that it almost enters us.'[104]

'I don't think the whole world should read poetry because I'm a realist. It is our national art and part of our history, but not everyone is going to come to it. But then there are times in your life when you do come to poetry.'[105]

'Poetry must always change and will always change.'[106]

In the examples drawn from the period before her laureate appointment, Duffy's statements focus on her own relationship with poetry and writing, whereas from 2009 onwards they appear outward-facing and primarily concerned with the public agency of poetry. In 1999 she attributed the broadening presence of poetry in society to the advent of women poets, acknowledging that they diversified the matter and manner of poetry and thereby brought new readers to the field, building on methods practised by oppositional voices such as the Liverpool Beats as she herself had done. Her 2002 statement that each new collection changes the landscape was related to her own journey as a writer, but in the case of influential collections such as her own, her comment has a wider application. New collections do not only alter the starting point from which the author sets out to write again, but change the landscape of poetry at large, for writers and readers alike, by creating new horizons and new expectations. Her own debut collection, *Standing Female Nude* (1985), is a case in point, and so are collections by her fellow National Poets, such as Clarke's *Letter from a Far Country* (1982), Lochhead's *Dreaming Frankenstein* (1984) and Meehan's *Pillow Talk* (1994). All of these works reconfigure the cultural geography of contemporary poetry, charting new territories for women, as poets and readers, to explore and extend.

Duffy's preoccupation with poetry as a way of telling truth, which emerges here from 2005 onwards, invites philosophical inquiry into the relationship between ethics and aesthetic practice. By asserting that '[i]n each poem, I'm trying to reveal a truth, so it can't have a fictional beginning,'[107] she diverts readers away from the default critique of poetry by women, which assumes that biographical interpretation can adequately account for the poem's meaning and significance. By challenging readers to move beyond a non-fictional beginning towards an appreciation of the embodied or revealed 'truth' of a poem, Duffy deliberately steers interpretation away from the belittlements of private or therapeutic approaches which have enmeshed the work of many of her predecessors. She thereby contributes to the broadening of the critical field available to readers of poetry by women, and participates in debate which stretches from Plato, through the Romantics, to the present day.[108] Paula Meehan also explores the ways in which poetry and truth are intimately and variously connected in the first of her Ireland Chair of Poetry lectures, 'Imaginary Bonnets with Real Bees in Them'. The lecture title, and its discussion, plays with a phrase from Marianne Moore's *ars poetica*, her poem, 'Poetry': 'imaginary gardens with real toads in them'.[109] Duffy, too, invoked Moore's 'Poetry' as one of her landmark poems in 'Auden comes through at the séance', where she wrote, 'Your mother, too, dislikes it'.[110] Meehan, in that lecture, also takes time to offer a wry smile at the critical impulse to limit 'truth' to biographical interpretation when she relates the story of Moore's invention of a pet crow.[111]

Duffy's faith in the imagination as an instrument of divination, a way of making sense of the world and simultaneously expanding it, is self-referentially articulated, for example, in a poem which begins with the idiom of her mother's Scottish expression, 'away and see': 'Away and see the things that words give a name to, the flight'.[112] By using a phrase that is familiar from Duffy's childhood, this poem parades its personal source; at the same time the poem asserts that the language of poetry enables heightened perception, expanded vision. The truth value of poetry matters to Duffy because without it, as Jerome McGann has argued, poetry can have no social function, no public or political authority.[113] Duffy's commitment to poetry as a public good and an enhancement of lived experience, whether that be as prayer, play or politics, is foundational to her practice.

'Poetry must always change'

Duffy came in to her laureateship announcing that poetry had changed, and she leaves it confident that change will continue. The constant renewal of poetry is reflected not simply in poetic practice but also in the agencies and establishments which facilitate or promote it. These include the Poet Laureate role itself, which during Duffy's tenure became an agent of cultural evolution, not just a reflection of it. She has been prodigal with the channels in which she has chosen to work, writing drama and ballet for children as well as adults, curating a sometimes weekly 'Poetry Corner' for the *Daily Mirror* on poems of interest to women, engaging her fellow poets to write for numerous projects of cultural or social significance, undertaking a demanding series of reading tours across England, Wales and Scotland, and accepting commissions to write for charities and events of national significance such as the sonnet 'The Wound in Time' for Danny Boyle's 'Pages of the Sea' installation to mark the Armistice Day centenary in 2018.[114]

One means by which she chose actively to facilitate change was her inauguration of the Ted Hughes Award for New Work in Poetry. Administered by the Poetry Society and funded by Duffy's Laureate Honorarium, the prize was awarded annually during the ten years of her tenure.[115] It was used to reward and promote innovative work and to extend public understanding of the formal parameters of poetry. Winners include audio and multimedia works such as Lavinia Greenlaw's *Audio Obscura* (2011) and Maggie Sawkins' *Zones of Avoidance* (2013), performance and spoken word poetry such as Kate Tempest's *Brand New Ancients* (2012) and Hollie McNish's *Nobody Told Me* (2016). In its last two years the award was won by non-white poets: Raymond Antrobus' *The Perseverance* (2018) and Jay Bernard's *Surge: Side A* (2017). Bernard wrote about their work for the Poetry Book Society's support for Black Lives Matter, and the anniversary of the Grenfell Tower tragedy, in June 2020. *Surge: Side A* gives an account of the New Cross Massacre of 1981, read against Bernard's painful personal struggle for place and identity.[116] They conclude:

> Many questions emerged not only about memory and history, but about my place in Britain as a queer black person. This opened out into a final sense of coherence: I am from here, I am specific to this place, I am haunted by this history but I also haunt it back.[117]

Bernard's poetry articulates a painful, Black, recent history of Britain, and in so doing guarantees cultural renewal. When Duffy embarked on her tenure she stated, 'I believe that the continuance of the laureateship acknowledges that poetry is vital to the imagining of what Britain has been, what it is and what it might yet become.'[118] By creating a national poetry award which sought out work such as Jay Bernard's, Duffy created the conditions which would enable her ambitions for the place of poetry in Britain's cultural life to be fulfilled. The way in which she approached the administrative aspect of the laureateship enabled her to move its influence beyond the opportunities and limitations which her own identity and practice could deliver.

Duffy's pronouncement of 2009, that 'the edge has become the centre', reflects the long personal journey which her own career has taken. She began as the unknown winner of the National Poetry Competition in 1983, took her place in *The New Poetry* anthology in 1993, was selected as one of the 1994 New Generation Poets, then considered and dismissed for the laureateship in 1999. Despite the fact that all along the way she was winning national prizes for her work, successive media allocations of outsider status throughout the 1990s structured public perception of her practice and may indeed have conditioned her own view of her work. Even if her sense of self as an outsider remains, this is now an advantage given the shifts towards inclusivity and diversity which have taken place in British culture during the twenty-first century. The success of the NewGen project in overturning traditional ideas of whose voices resonate with audiences can be seen in the appointment not just of Carol Ann Duffy from this group of poets, but also her successor as Poet Laureate, Simon Armitage. The newly centred edge is well populated if not outright crowded, so that these old binaries become meaningless. One of Duffy's major achievements has been to work as an agent of this disruption.

Notes

1. Winterson, 'A Return to Simple Pleasures'.
2. Gregson, *Contemporary Poetry and Postmodernism*, p. 97.
3. Waldram, 'Cardiff gets dedicated poem'.
4. Peach, 'Paper margins', p. 102.
5. Viner, 'Metre Maid'.
6. Millar, 'Carol Ann Duffy becomes first female poet laureate of Britain'.
7. *London Evening Standard*, 'Ten years late'.
8. Winterson, 'A Return to Simple Pleasures'.
9. Viner, 'Metre Maid'.
10. Gonda, 'An Other Country?', p. 18.
11. Gonda gives the reference as 'Sean O'Brien, writing in *The Sunday Times*, quoted on back cover of Carol Ann Duffy, *Mean Time* (London, Anvil Press Poetry 1993)'. Gonda, 'An Other Country?', p. 23, n. 23.
12. The full list of poets was reported in Ellison, 'Birth of the Muse': 'The 20 whose work will be promoted in bookshops in May as New Generation Poets are: Moniza Alvi, *The Country at My Shoulder*; Simon Armitage, *Kid*; John Burnside, *The Myth of the Twin*; Robert Crawford, *Talkies*; David Dabydeen, *Turner*; Michael Donaghy, *Errata*; Carol Ann Duffy, *Mean Time*; Ian Duhig, *The Bradford Count*; Elizabeth Garrett, *The Rule of Three*; Lavinia Greenlaw, *Night Photograph*; W N Herbert, *Forked Tongue*; Michael Hofmann, *Corona, Corona*; Mick Imlah, *Birthmarks*; Kathleen Jamie, *The Queen of Sheba*; Sarah Maguire, *Spilt Milk*; Glyn Maxwell, *Out of the Rain*; Jamie McKendrick, *The Kiosk on the Brink*; Don Paterson, *Nil Nil*; Pauline Stainer, *Sighting the Slave Ship*; Susan Wicks, *Open Diagnosis*.'
13. Roberts, 'Hit parade of new poets'.
14. Lister, 'New generation of writers'.
15. Marks, *Literature of the 1990s*, p. 129.
16. Fowler, 'New generation reclaims poetry'.
17. Ellison, 'Birth of the Muse'.
18. Turner, 'The blank verse generation'.
19. Smith, 'The things that words give a name to', p. 312.
20. Thorpe, 'The candyfloss of attention'.
21. Ibid.
22. Lane, 'I think, therefore iamb'.
23. Michael Hulse et al. (eds), 'Introduction', in *The New Poetry*, p. 16.
24. Ibid. p. 18. The embedded quote is from Terry Eagleton, 'Comment', *Poetry Review*, 79:4 (1989/90), p. 46. Its validity is incisively tested by Peach, 'Paper margins'.
25. Gill, *Women's Poetry*, pp. 177–9.

26. Smith, 'Suburbs of Dissent', p. 537.
27. Thorpe, 'The candyfloss of attention'.
28. Sampson, *Lyric Cousins*, p. 178.
29. Ibid. p. 191, n. 9.
30. Bryant, *Women's Poetry and Popular Culture*, p. 150.
31. Ibid. p. 151. For a classic analysis of Duffy's dramatic monologues, see Deryn Rees-Jones, 'Masquerades', in *Carol Ann Duffy*, pp. 17–29.
32. Bryant, *Women's Poetry and Popular Culture*, p. 173.
33. Kinnahan, *Lyric Interventions*.
34. Olsen, 'Strategies of Critical Practice', p. 382.
35. Duffy, 'Words, Wide Night', in *The Other Country, Collected Poems*, p. 169.
36. This aspect of Duffy's work has been expertly explored by, for example: Michael Woods, '"What it is like in words": translation, reflection and refraction in the poetry of Carol Ann Duffy', in Michelis and Rowland (eds), *The Poetry of Carol Ann Duffy*, pp. 169–85; and Stan Smith, '"What like is it?" Carol Ann Duffy's Différance', in *Poetry and Displacement*, pp. 101–22.
37. Duffy, 'Originally', in *The Other Country, Collected Poems*, p. 127.
38. Kay, 'In My Country', in *Other Lovers*, p. 24.
39. Dougary, 'Poetry is the music of being human'.
40. Manchester Metropolitan University, 'Write Where We Are Now'.
41. Duffy, 'Anon', in *Feminine Gospels, Collected Poems*, p. 335.
42. Duffy, *Sincerity*, p. 16; p. 65; p. 55; p. 56.
43. Lochhead, 'Random. *For Robyn Marsack*', <http://www.scottishpoetrylibrary.org.uk/poem/random/> (accessed 9 July 2020).
44. Duffy, 'Little Red-Cap', in *The World's Wife, Collected Poems*, pp. 229–30.
45. Duffy, 'Demeter', in *The World's Wife, Collected Poems*, p. 300.
46. Major, 'The SRB Interview: Carol Ann Duffy'.
47. Allardice, 'Carol Ann Duffy: "With the evil twins of Trump and Brexit"'.
48. Ibid.
49. Rahim, 'Carol Ann Duffy wins Pen Pinter Prize'.
50. Duffy, 'Politics'.
51. Commissioned for the Christmas issue of the *Radio Times*, this poem was not included in her *Collected Poems*. The *Daily Mirror* was one of the few newspapers to print the whole poem; see Duffy, 'The 12 Days of Christmas'.
52. Thorpe, 'Laureate puts political spin on 12 days of Christmas'.
53. Allardice, 'Carol Ann Duffy: "With the evil twins of Trump and Brexit"'.
54. Major, 'The SRB Interview: Carol Ann Duffy'; Carol Ann Duffy, 'A Formal Complaint', in *Sincerity*, pp. 24–5.
55. Major, 'The SRB Interview: Carol Ann Duffy'.
56. Rumens, 'Poem of the Week'.

57. Lafeu's line is 'If mine eyes smell onions, I shall weep anon'. See Rumens, 'Poem of the Week'.
58. Duffy, 'Oval Map Sampler', in *Sincerity*, p. 6.
59. Duffy, 'Sincerity', in *Sincerity*, p. 75.
60. Major, 'The SRB Interview: Carol Ann Duffy'.
61. Meehan, 'The Road to Agios Kirikos', in *Geomantic*, p. 92.
62. Major, 'The SRB Interview: Carol Ann Duffy'.
63. Viner, 'Metre Maid'.
64. Ibid.
65. Forbes, 'Winning lines'.
66. Ibid.
67. Cited in Goring, 'This is a woman's world', from the preface to Carol Ann Duffy (ed.), *Out of Fashion: An Anthology of Poems* (London: Faber and Faber, 2004).
68. Anderson, 'Christmas Carol'.
69. Ibid.
70. Wroe, 'The great performer'.
71. Ibid.
72. Ibid.
73. *Daily Mirror*, 'Carol Ann Duffy'.
74. Ibid.
75. Millar, 'Carol Ann Duffy becomes first female poet laureate of Britain'.
76. Duffy, 'Sisters in Poetry'.
77. Ibid.
78. Winterson, 'A return to simple pleasures'.
79. Ibid.
80. Ibid.
81. Ibid.
82. Ibid.
83. Ibid.
84. Ibid.
85. Thorpe, 'Laureate puts political spin on 12 days of Christmas'.
86. Preston, 'Carol Ann Duffy interview'.
87. Moorhead, 'Carol Ann Duffy: Poems are a form of texting'.
88. Ibid.
89. Ibid.
90. Ibid.
91. Ibid.
92. Dougary, 'Poetry is the music of being human'.
93. Ibid.

94. Wroe, 'Carol Ann Duffy on five years as poet laureate'.
95. Allardice, 'Carol Ann Duffy: "With the evil twins of Trump and Brexit"'.
96. Ibid.
97. Ibid.
98. Ibid.
99. Major, 'The SRB Interview: Carol Ann Duffy'.
100. Ibid.
101. Duffy, 'Poems to get us through'.
102. Flood, 'Carol Ann Duffy leads British poets'.
103. Ibid.
104. *Manchester Metropolitan University Magazine*, 'The Music of Being Human'.
105. Ibid.
106. Ibid.
107. Anderson, 'Christmas Carol'.
108. See for example Ghosh (ed.), *Philosophy and Poetry*.
109. Meehan, *Imaginary Bonnets*, p. 6.
110. Duffy, 'Auden comes through at the séance', in *Sincerity*, p. 66.
111. Meehan, *Imaginary Bonnets*, p. 7.
112. Duffy, 'Away and See', in *Mean Time, Collected Poems*, p. 197.
113. McGann, 'Laura (Riding) Jackson and the Literal Truth', pp. 456–7.
114. Flood, 'Poet laureate writes sonnet'.
115. See <https://poetrysociety.org.uk/competitions/ted-hughes-award/> (accessed 30 July 2020).
116. See <https://poetrysociety.org.uk/competitions/ted-hughes-award/2017-2/> (accessed 30 July 2020).
117. See <https://www.poetrybooks.co.uk/blogs/news/meet-the-poets-jay-bernard> (accessed 30 July 2020).
118. Duffy, 'Sisters in Poetry'.

7

Answering Back: Poetry in Conversation with Wordsworth, Burns and Yeats

The imperative to interrogate poetic forms or subjects traditionally the preserve of men has been central to the undertakings of Clarke, Duffy, Lochhead and Meehan, as it has been to the majority of women poets writing during the later twentieth century. Vicki Bertram's groundbreaking festival of women's poetry, *Kicking Daffodils*, which took place at Brookes University, Oxford in 1994, and her subsequently edited collection of essays, testify to the wide-ranging nature of this enterprise.[1] In 1997 Eavan Boland lent her weight to the endeavour, publishing her 'Letter to a Young Woman Poet' in which she exhorted the woman poet of the future to revisit the site of her past exclusion, warning that 'if we do not change that past, it will change us'.[2] Her instructions give feminist urgency to T. S. Eliot's assertion, made in 'Tradition and the Individual Talent', that 'the past should be altered by the present as much as the present is directed by the past'.[3] Like Eliot, Boland envisages a dynamic relationship between past, present and future poetry; she argues that engagement with the past is the only way for women to inscribe themselves into tradition: '[i]f women go to the poetic past as I believe they should, if they engage responsibly with it and struggle to change it . . . then they will have the right to influence what is handed on in poetry, as well as the way it is handed on.'[4] The poets under scrutiny here have not been slow to generate dialogue with tradition, nor indeed to 'answer back', as Duffy put it in 2008 when she commissioned responses from contemporary poets to poems of the past.

All four were contributors to Duffy's anthology *Answering Back: Living poets reply to the poetry of the past* (2008),[5] a volume which presents forty-six contemporary responses to poems from the past. Duffy constructs scrupulous gender parity amongst the living poets, selecting twenty-three women and twenty-three men. Each was invited to select their own partner poem from the past, nine of which are by women (including two by Elizabeth Bishop), so that thirty-seven of the stimulus poems are by men. As can be seen from this preponderance of male poets, *Answering Back* was not about re-gendering tradition, but about creating dialogue. Duffy notes in her 'Foreword' that '[t]hroughout, there is a strong sense of the living and the dead poets' belief in the triumph of language over time ... Poetry', she concludes, 'is language as life; not only a baton-like passing on of tradition but a way of making the human immortal.'[6] Her focus on art and artifice, and her complete neglect of the gender of the past, suggests that during the decade which intervened between the publication of this anthology and the interventions by Bertram and Boland, the combative politics of feminist revision had moved on.

This chapter examines how Clarke, Duffy, Lochhead and Meehan have advanced their relationship with tradition by focusing in particular on their negotiation with three patriarchal poets of national standing and international reputation: William Wordsworth, Poet Laureate from 1843 to 1850; Robert Burns, popularly considered the national poet of Scotland; and W. B. Yeats, hailed in 2015, the 150th anniversary of his birth, as National Poet of Ireland. Just as aesthetic priorities for women poets may have changed between the last decade of the twentieth century and the first decade of the twenty-first, so too Clarke, Duffy, Meehan and Lochhead have, over the course of their careers, occupied shifting territory in relation to their male forebears. Initially, Wordsworth, Burns and Yeats might have stood for traditions which they needed to resist, while from their perspective as twenty-first-century laureates, these men may be peers rather than threats.

Duffy goes so far as to salute Wordsworth as a moderniser: a poet who invigorated poetry with the oral culture of his contemporaries, and a Laureate who renegotiated the terms of the office. Interviewed for the *Scottish Review of Books* in 2018, Duffy affirmed her agreement with T. S. Eliot's notion that 'the music of poetry must be a music latent in the common speech of your time'. She stated that the idea 'goes back ... to Wordsworth and Coleridge in the *Lyrical Ballads* ... with that sense of poetry coming out of the oral tradition ... Ordinary speech is one of the colours on the palette. I can't see why you wouldn't use it. I wouldn't know what else to do.' In the same interview she explained the artistic freedom of the Laureate, stating, '[t]here is no requirement to write anything. That came from when Wordsworth was appointed. He asked that if he were Laureate that it would be agreed he wouldn't have to write any poems.'[7] Through an exploration of examples considered in this chapter, we see Clarke, Duffy, Lochhead and Meehan addressing their predecessors through familiar strategies of feminist revision, such as appropriation, shifting emphasis or perspective, satire, and even blunt rejection. But, as suggested by

Duffy's 'Foreword' to *Answering Back*, we also find gender differences and identity politics falling away, while the language and ambition of poetry fly free.

Vicki Bertram explains that the title, *Kicking Daffodils*, of the 1994 festival of women's poetry was inspired by Grace Nichols' poem 'Spring':

> If the flower represents English poetic tradition (the colonial model), the poem is in no doubt of the enduring potence of that tradition: this is not a dead white patriarch's tradition but one that issues its own challenges to the contemporary post-colonial poet . . . It is the daffodil, symbol of English poetic tradition, that is doing the kicking; and it is not a vicious kick, but something more mischievous and goading.[8]

The poets considered here respond, like Nichols, to the thriving culture represented by Wordsworth's daffodils. They share with her a wary playfulness as well as a willingness to recognise, and appropriate, the vitality of the past, connecting themselves with tradition while turning its direction to their own ends.

Wordsworth

William Wordsworth is at the centre of Gillian Clarke's early poem 'Miracle on St David's Day',[9] composed after she delivered a poetry reading at a care home for the mentally ill. The poem is printed directly following the long narrative meditation 'Letter from a Far Country' in Clarke's groundbreaking second collection. 'Miracle' extends the tone of inwardness created by 'Letter from a Far Country', and it is prefaced by a quotation from Wordsworth's poem, '*They flash upon that inward eye/which is the bliss of solitude*' – "The Daffodils", Wordsworth'. Clarke's poem describes an extraordinary encounter with Wordsworth's lyric 'I wandered lonely as a cloud' (also known as 'The Daffodils'). St David is the patron saint of Wales and the daffodil is the national flower of Wales, reclaimed here from its appropriation by the 'English' lyric; flower and saint are united through the unexpected, alarming and revelatory recitation of Wordsworth's poem by a patient in the care home who previously 'has never spoken'.

The labourer, who had been trapped in silence, stands unbidden to recite, 'hoarse but word-perfect'. The poem's speaker and her audience listen. The environment and all within it are transfigured as even the daffodils blooming outside become part of the rapt audience. The past in which he learned the poem by rote is suddenly real and connected with the present through his physical embodiment of the speaking lyric. The daffodils of Wordsworth's poem are transplanted to a new, specifically Welsh, context but the miracle described in Clarke's poem transcends both nation and gender. The transformation of the present is achieved by language, in the condensed and memory-laden form of poetry. As a poet, Clarke is witness to the 'miracle', has perhaps facilitated it, and she records it. Wordsworth's poem itself is changed by the new associations she gives to it. Clarke explains on her website that '[a]ll you need to know about this poem is that it is a true story. It happened in the '70s, and it took me years to find a way to write the poem.'[10] But this does not preclude the possibility that the episode has a figurative significance in which the long-silent speaker is the woman poet herself, re-voicing the inherited lyric in a new context, bridging gaps between past and present, male and female poet, English and Welsh.

Dorothy Wordsworth's diary description of wild daffodils seen during a walk with her brother to Ullswater in 1802, and Wordsworth's recourse to it in 1804 for the composition of the famous 'Daffodils' lyric, are well known. The Wordsworth Trust notes that in 'her journal entry for 15 April 1802, Dorothy describes how the daffodils "tossed and reeled and danced, and seemed as if they verily laughed with the wind, that blew upon them over the lake"'.[11] As might be expected from the poet of *The World's Wife*, Carol Ann Duffy approaches the brother through the perspective of the sister when she addresses, in poetry, the legacy of William Wordsworth. Jeanette Winterson finds the ghost of Dorothy behind 'Mrs Darwin':

[h]idden behind this ditty in diary form is the shadow of Dorothy Wordsworth, endlessly walking, endlessly writing her Lake District journal so that William could use it for that 'emotion recollected in tranquillity' he liked a poem to be. The famous daffodils, we remember, were Dorothy's.[12]

Duffy helped to bring public attention to Dorothy Wordsworth's achievements by collaborating in 2010, as Laureate, with the Wordsworth Trust to establish a Festival of Women's Poetry for Grasmere. She stated, '[i]t seemed appropriate for us to do this in the name of Dorothy Wordsworth, a nurturing spirit behind William and herself an enormous talent. The Dorothy Wordsworth Festival of Women's Poetry is now a biennial event.'[13] At the second festival, in April 2012, Duffy gave readings alongside her fellow National Poets, Gillian Clarke and Liz Lochhead. In 2014 she again hosted an extensive series of readings, workshops and interviews, culminating in a reading in St Oswald's Church by Gillian Allnutt, Sinéad Morrissey and herself.[14] Then City Laureate of Belfast, Morrissey read from her recently published collection *Parallax*, opening with the poem '1801' written in the diarist's voice of Dorothy Wordsworth.[15]

Duffy also brought Dorothy out of the shadows on that occasion, reading what would become her Christmas Poem for 2014, 'Dorothy Wordsworth's Christmas Birthday', which was first published in the *Guardian* on 20 December 2014. The poem creates a matrix of references to poetry by both Coleridge and Wordsworth alongside the diaries of Dorothy Wordsworth, whose birthday was indeed the 25th of December (1771). The effect of Duffy's use of quotation, half-quotation, and local Lake District references is to show a complex environment of people and places in which no one individual stands isolated or supreme. Her emphasis on landscape, and her insistence that the poet is part of the landscape rather than separate from it, does away with the fetish of the solitary male genius. Instead, we find community, collaboration and process.

The poem opens by citing the title of Coleridge's poem 'Frost at Midnight', immediately turning, in the second line, to an embedded reference to Dorothy's diaries, 'First, frost at midnight –/Moon, Venus and Jupiter/named in their places'.[16] Duffy's inter-text is an entry in Dorothy Wordsworth's *Grasmere Journal* which draws particular attention to the position of Jupiter:

> When we returned many stars were out, the clouds were moveless, in the sky soft purple, the lake of Rydale calm, Jupiter behind. Jupiter at least *we* call him, but William says we always call the largest star Jupiter.[17]

In Duffy's third stanza, the poem's setting of time and place pauses over Dorothy's word 'moveless' ('the strange word moveless'), though it does so without quotation marks and without any indication that the 'strange word' is found in Dorothy's journal. It is simply part of the landscape of language which the poem configures. Several further elements of 'Frost at Midnight' also resurface in Duffy's ludic reprise: the owl as time keeper, the singing robin, peeling church bells, fire in the grate, ice, 'lakes and shores/And mountain crags'.[18] Both the word 'moveless' and the invocation of Coleridge's poem are apt for the scene setting. Its focus is on the mysteries of midnight as a moment of suspension and transition in which 'Dorothy Wordsworth ages/one year in an hour'.[19] This is a point from which the speaker of Duffy's poem can range freely across time, in which past and future fuse, drawing the poetry of the past into a transcendent present and asserting a vital connection with tradition.

Wordsworth does not enter the poem until its midpoint, stanza 19 of 37. He is pictured on the morning of Dorothy's birthday as she returns home from a walk with Coleridge, working in bed, 'rhyming *cloud* with *crowd*'.[20] It is a comically dismissive reference to his famous lyric, which is further undercut in the next stanza where the cat, keeping the solitary poet company, is 'rhyming *purr* with *purr*'. From there, Duffy weaves deft allusions to Wordsworth's poetry into the birthday narrative. The threesome walk to the frozen lake, where Wordsworth skates on the ice. The skating lyric from *The Prelude* Book I underwrites Duffy's description:

> And in the frosty season, when the sun
> Was set, and visible for many a mile
> The cottage windows through the twilight blaz'd,
> I heeded not the summons:—happy time
> It was, indeed, for all of us; to me
> It was a time of rapture . . . [21]

Duffy replays Wordsworth's description of the sunset, '[t]he orange sky of evening died away' with a more contemporary reference to Christmas fruit, 'a tangerine sun';[22] while his startling observation that he 'cut across the image of a star/That gleam'd upon the ice' had already found its allusive place in stanza two of Duffy's poem, where ice traps 'nervous stars' in the lake. Dorothy's perspective presides over the account of her birthday, always domestic in her view of her brother. The stanza which describes her own 'ecstatic . . . stare', jolts the reader, therefore, by its opening, 'Nowt to show more fair'.[23] Duffy makes it appear as though it were Dorothy's homely observation in 'local accent'[24] which gave Wordsworth the grandeur of the first line of the sonnet 'Westminster Bridge': 'Earth has not anything to show more fair'.[25] This juxtaposition of the vernacular phrase as Duffy's narrator puts it with its intertextual echo as Wordsworth used it, makes it seem as though he betrayed both his sister (by taking her words without acknowledgement) and his own poetic credo as stated in the 1800 preface to *Lyrical Ballads*, to 'use the language really spoken by men', which the standardised version of the phrase clearly is not. Yet the ambiguity surrounding the identity of the speaking voice of Duffy's quasi-ballad means that the phrase is simply a presence in the poem, like the landscape itself, something given, a gift to the reader. Ownership and competition are out of place in the context of this poem's enterprise, which undercuts Wordsworth's very definition of a 'Poet': 'a man speaking to men'.[26] More than 'a woman speaking', 'Dorothy Wordsworth's Christmas Birthday' is poetry speaking to poetry.

A chorus from the local carol singers moves the poem towards its conclusion. 'Miss Wordsworth and the poets' join in.[27] The picture is one of strong community and annual ritual until the last stanza brings in a bleak sense of mortal transience, the snows of yesteryear, and an echo of Wordsworth's own haunted sense of the earth's diurnal round. The day's celebrations are bound between the planets pictured at the beginning of the poem, 'Moon, Venus and Jupiter', and snow on Dorothy's tongue at the end. The cosmic framing of warmth and wassail, the backward glance to 1799, present a picture in which it is not only Dorothy who ages a year in an hour. Individual lives are speeded up, pass quickly. Life is short and art is long. 'Dorothy Wordsworth's Christmas Birthday' presents richly complex relationships, between writers and texts, between people and places, between past and present, in which all contribute to the constellation and none are preeminent. By its deft allusions to the work of all three writers, as by its almost-ballad form, the poem adjusts received tradition and inscribes woman into the 'illuminating . . . manuscript' of Romantic poetry.[28] At the same time, it reminds us that all are subject to mortality and poetry redeems all alike.

Lochhead's Makar poem 'How to Be the Perfect Romantic Poet' develops the theme of reshaping the reputation of the solitary male genius.[29] The how-to-be advice is given as a list of imperatives, as though instructing an actor on how to play a role. Satirical, brimming with zestful energy, Lochhead conjures up a composite character based on the lives and works of canonical Romantic poets. Her first instruction is 'Be born male', addressing head-on the gender imperative of this group of writers. Women play secondary roles in Lochhead's scenario: a maligned maid, a disappointed mother, a bossed-about sister, an unloved wife ('the wrong woman'), all of them opportunities for the poet's (female) Muse.

Wordsworth's poem 'To My Sister' is cited within Lochhead's poem as a generic example of how sisters, necessary props for the role, are to be treated:

> *Then come my Sister! Come, I pray,*
> *With speed put on your woodland dress;*
> *And bring no book: for this one day*
> *We'll give to idleness.*[30]

The ironising perspective of contemporary gender politics which Lochhead's poem brings to these lines exposes the extent to which the sister's life is controlled by the brother: how she spends her time, what she wears, her access to the world outside, the judgement of her moral conduct, when to work and when to be 'idle', all are in her brother's gift. It should be noted, however, that outwith the confines of Lochhead's poem, the aesthetic virtues of Wordsworth's 'To My Sister' find a powerful advocate in Eavan Boland, who has extolled the poem's attention to ordinary, intimate pleasures of the pastoral and its refusal of the Romantic sublime:

> he is absolutely writing, in that poem, in the spirit of his great preface [to *Lyrical Ballads*]: against ornament, against the sublime, against the

over-reaching meaning. If I could nominate a place, a text, a series of words as the river-mouth where are the beginnings of the wonderful, humane enterprise which early Romanticism was, it would be this poem, this morning in Somerset, this cloak hanging on a hook, and this refusal to make any of it less truthful than it was.[31]

The overall effect of 'How to Be the Perfect Romantic Poet' is to present the conduct and subject matter of Lochhead's would-be Romantic as driven by outdated fashions which settle eventually into cliché and are therefore as easy to copy as the sequence of injunctions suggests. What is not easy to imitate is the completion of the final instruction: '[m]iss all deadlines . . . in pursuit of the fugitive colours of the day'.[32] This gives, of course, the title to Lochhead's volume as a whole. Her irony therefore turns on itself by honouring the Romantics' poetic ambition and vaulting free of the poem's clichés. The quest to capture transience, to make poetry a form of divination, to be free of the punning term 'deadlines', are ways, as Duffy put it, by which poetry makes 'the human immortal'. The pursuit, Lochhead suggests in concluding the poem, is more important than the gender of the pursuer.

These three poems are literal examples of responses to Wordsworth, displaying familiar strategies of feminist revision: appropriation, shifting perspective on familiar narratives, and satire. But there are more deeply embedded and less literal modes of response too. Paula Meehan shares with Grace Nichols the previously colonised subject's suspicion of the English lyric tradition. She stated in 2009 that 'I wouldn't ever have allowed myself to write "nature poetry" because I would have associated it with a narrow, pastoral, English tradition I was wary of,' finding 'the pastoral to be a dead hand'.[33] Meehan's objections are twofold, political and aesthetic. On the one hand she refuses to reproduce a lyric tradition which voices an ownership of land that excludes her as a colonised subject; and on the other hand she rejects the premise of the egotistical sublime, which seeks to separate the observing poet from the natural world: 'I would have tried to find a way to write about nature that actually took into account the fact that I was part of it.'[34] More recently, during her tenure as Ireland Chair, she has acknowledged the pull of Wordsworth's vision, but presented it as now divorced from the priorities of lived experience:

> An awful lot of the experience in late-twentieth-century and early twenty-first-century poetry is of displacement. The poetry is of those who are not rooted, who are looking for a place to be citizens of, or places where they feel their spirit can be at rest. I think that is more the common experience

than lying on the couch and gazing upon 'that inward eye/Which is the bliss of solitude,' which we all crave, right?[35]

Despite her ideological differences with Wordsworthian tradition, Meehan's practice is not without kinship with the Romantics. Her search for direction in life, which she describes in her professorial lecture 'Planet Water' and which she solved, in 1978, by guidance from the elements, landscapes and seascapes around her on the Shetland island of Papa Stour, recall the questions which the young Wordsworth asked of 'Nature':

> The earth is all before me . . .
> I look about; and should the chosen guide
> Be nothing better than a wandering cloud,
> I cannot miss my way.[36]

At that time, Meehan invoked the *I Ching*, and she reaffirms in 2016 the opportunities given by that system to exercise a 'watchful mind' and practice '[d]ivination . . . a kind of mirroring, reading the self through external symbols or systems of symbolic coding'.[37] She continues to find solace and mystery in nature and to describe her feelings in terms shared with Wordsworth:

> To look down at your feet, at the grasses and vetches, at the scribble of the tideline on sand, is one kind of joyous encounter with the world; to look up into the vastness of the heavens prompts another kind of rapture.[38]

Her use of the word 'rapture' is a kind of vector that reaches across to Wordsworth's usage of that term, recalling, for example, his description of skating in Book 1 of *The Prelude* (already remembered by Duffy in 'Dorothy Wordsworth's Christmas Birthday'), summarised as '[i]t was a time of rapture'; alternatively, he recollects the 'dizzy raptures' of his youthful pleasure in nature in 'Tintern Abbey'. Meehan's sense of transporting marvel in the natural world chimes with that of Wordsworth as she brings into the present, and filters through her own philosophy, Wordsworth's sense of the natural sublime and the connected 'life of things'.[39]

It is an example of the 'sense of coherence and community between the living and the dead poets' which Duffy observed in *Answering Back*,[40] and in which Duffy's own sonnet 'Rapture' participates. In that poem the speaker considers how lovers' separation is overcome, '[h]uge skies connect us, joining here to there'.[41] The enraptured contemplation of nature by different perceiving subjects crosses distances in the present, as well as asserting interconnections with the poetic past. This poem further illustrates a fundamental technique of composition which Duffy traces back to Wordsworth. For all the intensely conveyed emotion of much of her poetry, it is often communicated from the distance of retrospect. Anthony Rowland has noticed, for example, how Duffy 'self-consciously echoes Wordsworth's "Daffodils" in the second part of "Two Small Poems of Desire"':[42] 'The way I prefer to play you back/is naked . . .//I am brought up sharp in a busy street,/staring inwards as you put down your drink'.[43] Rowland comments, 'when the amorous subject starts "staring inwards" in the midst of "a busy street" it is unclear whether the loved object is present, putting down a drink, or, as with the flowers in Wordsworth's lyric, poignantly absent'.[44] The specific ambiguities belong to this poem, but Duffy's method is consistent: 'I never write when I'm in any kind of mood, when I'm upset or feeling any strong emotions . . . It's the old Wordsworth cliché, emotion recollected in tranquillity. The original emotion has to be there as a homeopathic tincture, but it mustn't be the whole bottle.'[45]

Burns

Liz Lochhead's first official engagement as Makar was to open the Robert Burns Birthplace Museum in Alloway, Ayrshire, on 21 January 2011. It was a highly symbolic occasion as it marked out one of the Makar's primary duties, the promotion of Scottish poetry at home and abroad. On the one hand it could be seen as an apt first step, the new Makar saluting Scotland's Bard, whom she herself has described as 'Oor Rabbie, your Rabbie, a'body's Rabbie . . . impossible to think of merely as a poet, more a myth';[46] on the other hand, it could be seen as potentially compromising for a woman to promote the status of a man famed as much for his philandering as for his poetry, or famed for his philandering because of his poetry. Lochhead, as a poet, has always been clear that what she admires is Burns' lyricism: 'it's the lyrics that do it for me'.[47] In addition, she celebrates his Scots, stating,

> above all it's about the language he preserved and imparted. Because of all those words I would never know if I'd never, aged 10 or 11, learned him off by heart. To this day, every time I see a white hoar frost I think 'cranreuch cauld', remembering Burns's 'To a Mouse'.[48]

Burns' language fashions the world in Scots; it creates a uniquely Scottish sensibility, constructs a literary artefact of Scottishness and manufactures a linguistic inheritance that is alive and developing in the present. The poetry of Burns runs through daily life and annual ritual in Scotland, as Lochhead demonstrated and indeed satirised in her early monologue 'Mrs Abernethy: Burns the Hero'.[49] Crossing boundaries of class, region and religion, Burns' work forges a remarkable symbiosis between poetry and national culture.

In 2011, Carol Ann Duffy said that Burns was

> the first poet she encountered as a child and the only one ever quoted in the Duffy household.
>
> She said: 'Burns for me has always been one of the greatest love poets. In fact, the older I get, the greater his love poems seem – simple, memorable, lyrical, true and deeply human.
>
> 'My father, who fancied himself as a terrific singer, would often throw in a Burns song along with his Rat Pack medley and Flower of Scotland.'[50]

Burns then, as well as being truly popular, is also a poet's poet who opens a treasure house of language and expression. Yet this status requires a careful negotiation between Burns' work and his life, a negotiation upon which Lochhead, as Makar and as public artist, has been outspoken.

His personal conduct towards women, until recently euphemistically referred to as 'loving the lassies', came into sharp focus in 2018 when a boastful letter about his treatment of his soon-to-be wife, Jean Armour, was printed in the press. Lochhead created a media sensation by denouncing him as a 'sex-pest', the Harvey Weinstein of his day, and stated that she would no longer attend Burns Suppers or give talks about him at such celebrations. She insisted, however, then as in 2009 when Scotland celebrated the 250th anniversary of his birth, that 'he's not a role model, he's a great poet'.[51]

In fact, she had said the same in her poem 'From a Mouse' which she wrote to commission for the Scottish Poetry Library in 2009 as part of the 250th celebrations of Burns: 'he was an *awfy man*', says the mouse.[52] 'From a Mouse' is quite literally an 'answering back' to Burns' poem 'To a Mouse'. It is a dramatic monologue in the voice of the well-trained 'eponymous *Moose*', which speaks in Scots (mainly Glaswegian) and uses Burns' characteristic stanza form, known as Standard Habbie (six lines, rhyming aabcbc, or aaabab; four of the lines are in tetrametre, while lines 4 and 6 are in dimetre). Lochhead has said of this form, '[n]ow none but a parodist dare essay the Burns stanza';[53] her mouse is there to use the complexity of the form against what she identifies as falsehoods and false sentiments within Burns' poem, and which circulate in response to both the poem and the man himself. One mouse to another, one poem to another, one poet to another, Lochhead's female mouse dismantles the pretensions of the 'ploughman-poet' as well as the selective memory of his admirers. Burns denounced hypocrisy, and his mouse has learned her lessons well. But the *Moose* is also looking to the present and the future, updating the topicality of Burns' poem with the subject of climate emergency, ending her speech: 'As for Mother Nature? Whether yez get the message/Remains to be seen'.[54] So the 'Artefact' travels through time, changing time and itself on the way.

There is an implicit democracy about using the 'language really used by men' (women and mice included), crafting poetry in the demotic, as well as code-switching between Scots and English, high and low registers. Lochhead relishes the political opportunities that lie cradled in Burns' language, as well as in his more explicit statements of allegiance to Scotland (e.g. 'Scots wha hae') and his espousal of the revolutionary creeds of 'liberty, fraternity, equality'. She makes vibrant use of Burns' politics in her own craft as a poet and in her public discourse as Makar. In 2009 she contributed fifteen audio recordings of Burns' poems to the 716 recordings made for the BBC Burns' 250th celebrations.[55] More than half of those she selected to read are directly political, including 'Ode to the departed Regency bill 1789' and 'Ode [for General Washington's Birthday]'. In 2014 Lochhead composed a dramatic monologue in the voice of Burns for the National Theatre of Scotland's 'Dear Scotland' project, which brought to life twenty portraits in the National Portrait Gallery.[56] Lochhead's 'Burns' was a response to Alexander Nasmyth's portrait.[57] It spoke to present-day Scotland in light of the impending referendum on Scottish independence, which had been announced on 21 March 2013 and took place on 18 September 2014. The voice is very close to her own, and even the self-critical line that it is spoken by 'the sloganeer and not the poet' does not save its political method or intent. Lochhead repurposed this monologue for direct campaigning to support the Yes vote for Scottish independence, delivering it at 'Aye Talks' in July 2014 in Govan Old Parish Church, Glasgow.[58] The poem moves easily from the ostensibly disinterested environment of the National Portrait Gallery to the instrumental context of the 'Yes' campaign. Unlike the ironised and sophisticated voice of the 'eponymous *Moose*', Lochhead's 'Burns' speaks to her contemporaries with blunt single purpose.

Lochhead's technique here entails the risk that arguments are not fully made or carefully scrutinised, that the speaker deems it sufficiently persuasive to articulate his or her points in Scots, using the authority of a puppet called Burns as a kind of shorthand. To challenge them becomes tantamount to challenging Burns, and confusions compound. The very close alignment between the public statements of the Makar to bring the poetry of Burns to bear on the politics of Scottish independence makes it difficult to achieve a critical distance from any one of these on the topic of self-determination. However, the fact that Lochhead appropriates the voice of the Bard with such wit and flair to speak on the subject of national belonging indicates that the anxieties of exclusion which beset Eavan Boland in relation to the burden of tradition are not troubling here. As Lochhead stated in 'My Hero Robert Burns', 'above all it's about the language'; Lochhead is liberated, not held up, by the rhythms and vocabulary of his poetry.

Duffy also used the figure of Burns to comment on the Scottish referendum, publishing 'September 2014' in the *Guardian* on 23 September 2014.[59] The poem is cautiously equivocal, fitting for either outcome. Unlike Lochhead, Duffy does not take a public position on the topic. The 'roses' offered from 'our bloodied hands' are a token of love, apt gesture either for farewell or continued union. The emotion of love is stated in the Gaelic epigraph to the poem, '*Tha gaol agam ort*' ('I love you'). The rose is the emblem of England, and explicitly made so by its conjunctive contrast with the thistle of Scotland, both of which can 'draw blood'. Yet a rose in the context of love poetry must always evoke the connotation of Burns' lyric 'O my luve's like a red, red rose'.[60] In the case of Duffy's poem, the love token is red by association with blood. If the simile has been stolen from a Scottish poet and then offered back as a sign of consolation from the victor (who, after all, is 'our'? the laureate of the union, or England?), then the poem adds insult to injury. But if it is borrowed in homage like that figured in the lines about the relationship between Keats and Burns, 'where, somewhere, Rabbie Burns might swim,/or pilgrim Keats come walking/out of love for him', then the image is a mark of respect and mutual endeavour. The fact that the English rose and the Scottish rose are both in play is a sign of the poem's political equivocation.

Like Lochhead, Duffy also contributed to the 2009 Scottish Poetry Library Burns collection, but unlike Lochhead, she did not take it as an opportunity to speak of the politics of nationalism. Instead, Duffy responded to Burns as a love poet: her poem is 'Sung'.[61] Duffy's poem is a meditation on the transience of human life and love. Language, poetry, song and Burns' most famous simile of the 'red, red rose' outlast not simply the span of a life, the momentary intensity of experience, but also the writing on the beloved's tombstone. Even this monument, meant to bestow immortality, is by its very physicality subject to decay. The name inscribed in stone as pictured in the poem is worn and overgrown. It cannot be made out: 'MAR—ORIS—',[62] sending the reader on a futile crossword puzzle. Duffy echoes Burns' lyric 'Mary Morison', a song about desire, a lament for unattainable love grasped in one tantalising moment. Mary Morrison's real gravestone, in Mauchline, Scotland, states that she was 'the Poet's bonnie Mary Morrison who died 29th June 1791 aged 20'.[63] Burns' song of aching desire has lasted, though the singer and his subject who died so young are long gone. It is the language of poetry that Duffy foregrounds in 'Sung', as the only weapon against time. Whereas for her contribution to *Answering Back* she had chosen to make a facetious response to Kipling's great gamble in 'If', Duffy's answer to Burns is a melancholic adumbration of the spiritual reach of the poet's craft. 'Sung', even in the past tense of the title, embodies Duffy's idea that '[p]oetry is . . . language as life' which offers 'triumph over time'.[64] Shakespearean in its invocation of *ars longa vita brevis*, 'Sung' posits that it really does not matter who loved whom or what their genders were; what survives of them is song.

Gerard Carruthers points out that '[i]n the early twenty-first century it has become something of a rite of mid-career passage for Scottish writers formally to salute the totem that is Robert Burns . . . Robert Crawford, Andrew O'Hagan, Ian Rankin and Don Paterson . . . have produced anthologies of Scotland's "national bard".'[65] Conspicuously, these editors are all men; their method of salutation, as well as the outcomes of it, are markedly distinct from the techniques adopted by the women considered here, whose focus has not been on repackaging, but on active poetic dialogue.

Yeats

All four poets met in Sligo, in the Republic of Ireland, on 13 June 2015 at the 'Poet Laureate and National Poet' event to launch the start of a week-long Yeats Festival celebrating the 150th anniversary of his birth. Gillian Clarke viewed the event as an opportunity to be an ambassador for Wales on an international stage. She stated in her report to Literature Wales:

> More than ever I see the role of National Poet as a diplomatic opportunity, a chance to spread understanding of our bilingual culture. It can't be too often stressed that Wales/Cymru is the safe-keeper of Europe's oldest spoken and literary language. This should be a matter of pride to Britain, as well as Europe, and be cherished and given all the help it needs.[66]

Clarke's poetry has dealt extensively with the intertwined transmission of ancient Irish and Welsh bardic tradition in her treatment of the *Mabinogion* in *The King of Britain's Daughter*. She walks a Welsh path parallel with Yeats' Irish, to bring Celtic legend into the present. Alice Entwistle has illuminated the way in which Clarke draws out the woman's story from this legendary material. She argues that Clarke uses it to articulate her personal growth as a poet as well as to position a renewed cultural identity for Wales. Entwistle contends that 'as Branwen's intermediary, the starling, affords her voice and freedom, so Clarke's imaginative traversing of the gulf dividing Ireland from Wales might be argued to have helped free her into poetic articulacy'.[67] It is certainly the case that while Clarke does not directly address Yeats' body of work, she shares with him the ambition to redeploy ancient Celtic tradition to fashion revitalising narratives of sovereignty which bypass the fractures of colonisation.

Duffy, by contrast, responds directly to Yeats. She lists 'The Song of Wandering Aengus' as the first of her favourite poems, loved since childhood, on her blog posts for Pan Macmillan.[68] Yeats' poem carries forward traditions of the Muse and the *femme fatale*, and depicts the poet as subject to enchantment manifest in both the imagery and the musicality of the lyric. Yeats fills his Celtic Twilight with ghosts of the Romantics: his line 'And pluck till time and times are done' evokes the eternity of desire as expressed in Burns' line 'till all the seas gang dry' from 'A red, red rose'; the 'glimmering girl' offers a haunting glimpse of Keats' 'La Belle Dame sans Merci'.[69] Given the multiplicity of references channelled through Yeats' poem, to look for a literal response to 'The Song of Wandering Aengus' in Duffy's poetry would be, as Paula Meehan puts it, an act of 'climbing up the signpost instead of following the road'.[70] Yet in Duffy's collection *Rapture*, much of the imagery of nature, transfigured and transfiguring under powerful emotion, as well as the representation of an unattainable beloved who inhabits the imagination, find kinship with Yeats' quest for the eternally elusive 'glimmering girl'. Perhaps these features are most particularly prominent in Duffy's poem 'Give', in which the beloved steals away with her cosmic gifts of 'the gold/from the sun' and the 'silvery cold/of the moon',[71] echoing Yeats' 'silver apples of the moon' and 'golden apples of the sun'. Yet it is Duffy's internal rhyme of 'gold' with 'cold', and the assonance of 'sun' and 'moon', which reveal her more profound interest in Yeats' poetry. For Duffy, it is the lyricism of Yeats' work which engages her interest, just as it is this aspect of Burns' craft which she carries away.

For Paula Meehan the relationship with Yeats is more complex, and more conflicted, as it evolves over the course of her career. His work entered her bloodstream early. Writing for *The Irish Times* in 2015 for the 'Yeats 150' celebrations, Meehan selected 'Easter 1916' as her favourite Yeats poem, explaining how she and her classmates had responded to his work during an earlier anniversary:

> Miss Shannon's class, Central Model girls' school, Gardiner Street, 1966. The 50th anniversary of the Easter Rising. She beats out the metre with her stick. 'Who does the poet meet at close of day, girls?' 'Who knows what "motley" means?' 'Who can tell me what "vainglorious" means? Hands up!' I am 11 years of age. I live on a street named for one of the dead

heroes. I want to grow up and die for Ireland myself. They go in deep, these early poems. And this poem goes in deepest of all. Mesmeric and mysterious: 'what if excess of love/Bewildered them till they died?'[72]

The schoolgirl's simple ardour gave way to more complicated reactions as Meehan began to write. She started, she explains in conversation with Eavan Boland, by writing song lyrics, which were influenced by her 'readings in tradition, especially the Romantics, Shelley and Keats and Coleridge, and of course Yeats, who seemed a natural inheritor of their energies'.[73] But soon, as a young poet, she had to confront the towering significance of his work on two particular levels: its representation of Ireland to itself, and his use of the occult.

Anglo-Irish and consorting with the land-owning class, Yeats represented wealth and privilege, bought, the young Meehan believed, by impoverishing her own people. She expresses her hostility to both his class and his craft in an early poem, 'The Apprentice', stating baldly, 'You are no master of mine'.[74] Kathryn Kirkpatrick contends that here, 'she quarrels with the spectre of Yeats who looks out "from high Georgian windows" at a debased city poor, "clowns" in his "private review"'.[75] Meehan admits that, 'I was at times a very judgemental young poet and my judgements weren't necessarily literary.'[76] Her early resistance to Yeats comes from her need to speak up for her social class, to train her sights on the deprivations she witnessed and experienced: 'I had to believe that there was a home in poetry for the lives I saw about me.'[77] By the end of the collection in which 'The Apprentice' is published, *Return and No Blame*, the speaker seems as assured a 'spell maker' as her dancing male muse, more than ready to share territory with Yeats, to whose 'Among School Children' she alludes in the two-part poem 'Dancer'.[78] One way in which she achieves this in *Return and No Blame* is to respond to Yeats' Twilight cult with her own exploration of Celtic legend when she allows the seventh-century travelling woman poet Liadain to speak a brave lament in 'Liadain's Dream of Cuirtheoir'.[79] Like Clarke, Meehan finds a woman's perspective in indigenous legend, to counter tales of nation-building prowess extracted by Yeats.

At the same time, she salutes the 'sixty-year-old smiling public man',[80] acknowledging that Yeats' public poetry is a monument that enshrines national sensibility: 'his great poems of war, of the Civil War, and of the revolutionary rising – they're graven in. They were some of the most powerful utterances ever made in poetry on the island.'[81] It was not only the politics of Yeats' poems of the revolution that stirred Meehan; she was seduced too by the 'actual music' of his poetry, which she describes as '[a]n undersong . . . that hits the same visceral place that Dublin accent of my childhood hits'.[82] This is where the risk lay. His class politics were easy to dismiss, his national politics easy to admire, but his music created a controlling poetics from which Meehan struggled to free herself: Yeats 'so bedazzled the eye that the city you're walking around in becomes invisible to you. That the suffering of its people becomes invisible to you because you're walking around in a mythical Hazelwood. You're tying a berry to a thread to catch the glimmering trout.'[83] She confesses that she had to '"de-Yeats" myself, detox from him' in order to acquire an independent voice.[84]

Her self-awareness of the spell that Yeats once cast over her allows Meehan, in her maturity, to adopt his locutions without irony. His phrase 'the bee-loud glade', for example, from 'The Lake Isle of Innisfree', is woven into Meehan's idiolect, shaping the way she perceives her environment and communicates it.[85] Describing her favourite Greek island, Ikaria, in her lecture 'Imaginary Bonnets with Real Bees in Them', she relishes the 'bee-loud glades' which she finds there.[86] The last poem of her 2016 collection, *Geomantic*, is called 'The Island'; it begins with a deliberate invocation of Yeats and Innisfree, 'At home again on Ikaria/our own bee-loud glade'.[87] The superimposition of the imaginary and the real, Innisfree and Ikaria, not only deftly illustrates the topic of her 2014 lecture, but it also demonstrates the extent to which the poetry of Yeats continues to assert its shaping presence in Meehan's worldview.

The distance between the 'mythical Hazelwood' which once confined Meehan and the 'bee-loud glade' in which she embraces freedom encapsulates her career-long negotiation with Yeats. She has stated that 'the real journey is to find within yourself an identity of your pre-colonial being. You can do that through myth.'[88] As Pilar Villar-Argáiz contends, 'Meehan uses myth as a way of responding to official narratives.'[89] But what happens when the mythical material has itself become an 'official narrative'? Yeats' construction of a pre-colonial Ireland out of ancient Irish legend was so dominant, and yet so disconnected from what Meehan found most urgently in need of articulation, that in order to liberate her poetics from it she had first to turn to America and the work of Gary Snyder before she could turn homeward with a renewed sense of how to access and deploy myth within her own practice.

Meehan's formative engagement with Snyder's work also helped her to position her own inclination towards mystic or pre-rational forms of experience in relation to Yeats' predilection for occult knowledges. She asserts that 'the more mystic elements in his work and in his life spoke very clearly to me – his striving for self knowledge and arcane knowledge, his looking for soul experience'.[90] Meehan concludes her first Professorial lecture with an account of her developing relationship with Yeats. She is wryly amused at her young self and her friends, who planned to make a documentary film about Yeats living on Howth Hill that would turn, according to the synopsis, on stealing his tarot cards from the National Library in Dublin.[91] She notes how her fascination with Yeats' tarot prepared her for her encounter with Snyder's work: 'Yeats . . . believed in these practices, not a million miles from Gary Snyder's imperatives in "What You Should Know to Be a Poet".'[92] The confluence amplifies the value of both, and Meehan states, 'Yeats the dreamer is the one I love most. I prefer him to the man of action.'[93]

The lecture draws to a close with a quotation from Yeats' *Autobiographies*, his invocation to the bees 'to nest in the house of the stare' as he sought solace in nature at time of tumult, and his assertion that he 'began to smell honey in places where honey could not be'.[94] At the end of this quotation, Meehan announces, 'Sweet Yeats! His instinct, his intuition, his sixth sense, his watchful, elegant mind.' By describing Yeats in terms lifted from Snyder's poetic credo, Meehan equalises the status between these two mentors. All three poets become peers, participants in a shared endeavour.

Her accommodation of forbears as peers continues into the final paragraph of the lecture. The dead and the living, men and women, enter the space of her practice as equals:

> Dineen and the *Bechbretha*, Messrs Yeats and Snyder, Ms Moore and Ms Boland and Ms Duffy, the whole room buzzing, all the bees in my bonnet wide awake. The real and the imaginary worlds fitted one into the other in a glorious golden light.[95]

Figures from the past mix with her contemporaries, enabling and mutually enriching. There is no distinction between genders. It recalls the synergies between the living and the dead, noted by Duffy in her 'Foreword' to *Answering Back*.

While this chapter has explored a range of responses to Wordsworth, Burns and Yeats, in every case the prior poetry has been a catalyst for something new in the work of Clarke, Duffy, Lochhead and Meehan. Neither have their responses been static. They have evolved with their developing careers and all, in their maturity, salute the insights and craft they have learned. Yeats' public poetry has shaped the way the birth of the Republic occupies the national, and indeed the international, imagination for all four poets. His lyrical sense of constant renewal in the natural world, and the powerful non-human forces which shape it, provides a counterweight to the impassioned fractures of political struggle which Meehan, Duffy and Clarke have pursued through their own scrutiny of relationships between the inner and outer lives. Burns presents Lochhead with a reservoir of Scots, a living document of national belonging structured through language, which enables her to connect childhood experience with the ambition of adult politics and to push both, language and politics, forward in pursuit of a new Scotland. At the same time both Lochhead and Duffy carry forward the intensity of momentary emotion captured by his song, learning from his craft and sharing his vision of *ars longa vitae brevis*. Wordsworth opens a natural landscape in language, and his meditations on fully perceived nature for the individual subject have resonated with all four poets according to their own preferred philosophies.

Adrienne Rich's essay 'When We Dead Awaken: Writing as Revision', published in 1971, was a powerful rallying cry in Anglo-American feminism, and for the woman poet. Rich asserted:

> Re-vision, the act of looking back, of seeing with fresh eyes, of entering an old text from a new critical direction – is for women more than a chapter in cultural history: it is an act of survival. Until we can understand the assumptions in which we are drenched, we cannot know ourselves.[96]

In looking back at Wordsworth, Burns and Yeats, the four poets considered here have indeed entered old texts from new directions, refocusing their precursors' configurations of landscape, language and politics. They have connected with inherited feelings of national belonging and pride which their forbears have helped to generate for the present. Rather than rejecting the earlier work, Clarke, Duffy, Lochhead and Meehan have written themselves into tradition, adjusting its direction to their own ends. Above all, they have responded to the earlier work as poets, meeting practice with practice rather than with gender politics. Certainly some of their responses display the mischievous or combative 'glint' or 'edge' which Duffy observed amongst the poems of *Answering Back*, but the predominant response has been, as Duffy also noted of her anthology, to celebrate a community of poets.[97]

Notes

1. Bertram (ed.), *Kicking Daffodils*.
2. Boland, 'Letter to a Young Woman Poet', in *A Journey with Two Maps*, p. 251. First published in *PNR* 24.2 (1997).
3. Eliot, 'Tradition and the Individual Talent', in *The Sacred Wood*, p. 45.
4. Boland, 'Letter to a Young Woman Poet', p. 265.
5. Duffy (ed.), *Answering Back*. Clarke wrote 'Nettles' in answer to Edward Thomas' 'Tall Nettles', Lochhead 'Midwinter Song' to Donne's 'A Nocturnall Upon S Lucies Day', Meehan 'Quitting the Bars' to Elizabeth

Bishop's 'One Art', and Duffy herself contributed 'Kipling', in dialogue with Kipling's 'If'.
6. Duffy, 'Foreword', in *Answering Back*, pp. xi–xii.
7. Major, 'The SRB Interview: Carol Ann Duffy'.
8. Bertram, *Kicking Daffodils*, pp. 1–2.
9. Clarke, 'Miracle on St David's Day', in *Letter from a Far Country*, p. 19.
10. See <http://www.gillianclarke.co.uk/gc2017/miracle-on-st-davids-day/> (accessed 24 March 2020).
11. See <https://wordsworth.org.uk/wordsworth/daffodils-and-other-poems/wordsworths-daffodils/> (accessed 3 December 2019).
12. Winterson, 'On the poetry of Carol Ann Duffy'; Carol Ann Duffy, 'Mrs Darwin', in *The World's Wife*, *Collected Poems*, p. 246.
13. Mullen, 'Carol Ann Duffy leads the way'.
14. For more detail on the 2014 Festival, see <https://grasmerepoetry.wordpress.com/2014/04/24/the-dorothy-wordsworth-festival-2014-sinead-morrissey-gillian-allnutt-and-poet-laureate-carol-ann-duffy/> (accessed 7 April 2020).
15. Morrissey, '1801', in *Parallax*, p. 11.
16. Duffy, 'Dorothy Wordsworth's Christmas Birthday', in *Collected Poems*, p. 554.
17. Dorothy Wordsworth, 29 January 1802, in *The Grasmere and Alfoxden Journals*, p. 60. Cited in Trilling, 'The Wordsworths'.
18. Samuel Taylor Coleridge, 'Frost at Midnight', <https://www.poetryfoundation.org/poems/43986/frost-at-midnight> (accessed 24 March 2020), ll.58–9.
19. Duffy, *Collected Poems*, p. 554.
20. Ibid. p. 556.
21. William Wordsworth, *The Prelude*, Book I; see <https://www.poetryfoundation.org/poems/45542/the-prelude-book-1-childhood-and-school-time> (accessed 24 March 2020), stanza 7.
22. Duffy, *Collected Poems*, p. 557.
23. Ibid. p. 557. Wordsworth refers to Dorothy's 'wild eyes' in 'Lines Composed a Few Miles above Tintern Abbey, On Revisiting the Banks of the Wye during a Tour. July 13, 1798'.
24. Duffy, *Collected Poems*, p. 555.
25. William Wordsworth, 'Composed upon Westminster Bridge, September 3, 1802'; see <https://www.poetryfoundation.org/poems/45514/composed-upon-westminster-bridge-september-3-1802> (accessed 24 March 2020).
26. Wordsworth, 1800 Preface to *Lyrical Ballads*.
27. Duffy, *Collected Poems*, p. 558.

28. Ibid. p. 557.
29. Lochhead, 'How to Be the Perfect Romantic Poet', in *Fugitive Colours*, pp. 32–3.
30. Ibid. p. 32, and Wordsworth, 'To My Sister', *Lyrical Ballads* (2nd. ed., 1800).
31. Boland, 'Romantic readings: "To My Sister", by William Wordsworth'.
32. Lochhead, *Fugitive Colours*, p. 33.
33. Randolph, '*Painting Rain*', p. 49.
34. Ibid. p. 49.
35. Knittel and Meehan, '"Nature Doesn't Stop"', p. 79.
36. Wordsworth, Book I, *The Prelude*.
37. Meehan, 'Planet Water', p. 64.
38. Ibid. pp. 62–3.
39. William Wordsworth, 'Lines Composed a Few Miles above Tintern Abbey, On Revisiting the Banks of the Wye during a Tour. July 13, 1798'; see <https://www.poetryfoundation.org/poems/45527/lines-composed-a-few-miles-above-tintern-abbey-on-revisiting-the-banks-of-the-wye-during-a-tour-july-13-1798> (accessed 25 March 2020).
40. Duffy, 'Foreword', in *Answering Back*, p. xii.
41. Duffy, 'Rapture', in *Rapture, Collected Poems*, p. 384.
42. Rowland, 'Love and Masculinity', p. 210.
43. From Duffy, *The Other Country, Collected Poems*, p. 164.
44. Rowland, 'Love and Masculinity', p. 210.
45. Major, 'The SRB Interview: Carol Ann Duffy'.
46. Lochhead, 'My Hero Robert Burns'.
47. Gish, 'Shakespeare and the Invention of Language', p. 50.
48. Lochhead, 'My Hero Robert Burns'.
49. Lochhead, *True Confessions*, pp. 6–7.
50. Barry, 'Acclaimed writer Carol Ann Duffy on Rabbie Burns'.
51. Dugdale, 'Robert Burns'.
52. Lochhead, *Fugitive Colours*, p. 92.
53. Lochhead, 'My Hero Robert Burns'.
54. Lochhead, *Fugitive Colours*, p. 92.
55. See <http://www.bbc.co.uk/arts/robertburns/works/readers/liz_lochhead/> (accessed 26 March 2020).
56. 'Dear Scotland', March to April 2014, <https://www.nationaltheatrescotland.com/production/dear-scotland/> (accessed 26 March 2020).
57. See <https://www.nationalgalleries.org/art-and-artists/1962/robert-burns-1759-1796-poet.> (accessed 26 March 2020).
58. See 'Liz Lochhead', *YouTube*, <https://www.youtube.com/watch?v=7AHCoyIksR4> (from 8 minutes) (accessed 26 March 2020).

59. Duffy, 'September 2014'.
60. See <https://www.scottishpoetrylibrary.org.uk/poem/red-red-rose/> (accessed 26 March 2020).
61. See <https://www.scottishpoetrylibrary.org.uk/poem/mary-morison/> (accessed 26 March 2020).
62. Duffy, 'Sung', in *Collected Poems*, p. 494.
63. See <https://www.google.com/search?q=Mary+Morrison+Burns+Mauchline&source=lnms&tbm=isch&sa=X&ved=2ahUKEwin5JHIl7joAhV5QEEAHWGvCGEQ_AUoAnoECAsQBA&biw=1600&bih=789#imgrc=Tdrsnj03c-PukM> (accessed 26 March 2020).
64. Duffy, 'Foreword', in *Answering Back*, pp. xii; xi.
65. Carruthers, 'Scotland, Britain and the Elsewhere of Poetry', p. 85.
66. Clarke, 'National Poet of Wales/Bardd Genedlaethol Cymru. 1. Retrospective report: October 2014 – April 2015'.
67. Entwistle, 'Traverses: Gillian Clarke, Christine Evans, Catherine Fisher and Ireland/Wales', in *Poetry, Geography, Gender*, p. 124.
68. Duffy, 'Carol Ann Duffy's favourite poems'.
69. Yeats, 'The Song of Wandering Aengus', in *The Wind Among the Reeds* (1899), *Collected Poems*, pp. 66–7.
70. Meehan, 'Imaginary Bonnets with Real Bees in Them', in *Imaginary Bonnets*, p. 23.
71. Duffy, *Collected Poems*, p. 396.
72. Meehan, 'My favourite W. B. Yeats poem'.
73. Boland, 'Two Poets and a City: A Conversation', in *A Poet's Dublin*, pp. 99–100.
74. Meehan, *Return and No Blame*, p. 27.
75. Kirkpatrick, 'Between Country and City', p. 112.
76. Randolph, 'The Body Politic', p. 245.
77. Boland, *A Poet's Dublin*, p. 104.
78. Ibid. p. 57; Yeats, 'Among School Children', in *The Tower* (1928), *Collected Poems*, pp. 242–5. See in particular the last line of that poem, 'How can we know the dancer from the dance?', p. 245.
79. Meehan, *Return and No Blame*, p. 60.
80. Yeats, 'Among School Children', in *Collected Poems*, p. 243.
81. Randolph, 'The Body Politic', p. 244.
82. Ibid. p. 244.
83. Ibid. p. 244.
84. Ibid. p. 245.
85. Yeats, 'The Lake Isle of Innisfree', in *The Rose* (1893), *Collected Poems*, p. 44.

86. Meehan, 'Imaginary Bonnets', p. 16; p. 18.
87. Meehan, *Geomantic*, p. 95.
88. González-Arias, '"Playing with the ghosts of words"', p. 196. Cited in Villar-Argáiz, 'The Enchantment of Myth', p. 93.
89. Villar-Argáiz, 'The Enchantment of Myth', p. 96.
90. Randolph, 'Body Politic', p. 244.
91. Meehan, 'Imaginary Bonnets', pp. 24–5.
92. Ibid. p. 25.
93. Ibid. p. 25.
94. Ibid. p. 26.
95. Ibid. p. 26.
96. Rich, *Adrienne Rich's Poetry and Prose*, p. 167.
97. Duffy, 'Foreword', in *Answering Back*, pp. xi–xii.

8

National Poets and the National Curriculum

If Clarke, Duffy, Lochhead and Meehan have occupied premier positions within cultural establishments, their paths towards them began with the same initiation into public life shared by most of the British and Irish population: attendance at school. While relationships between individuals and institutions form important themes across these poets' work, salient examples amongst them being church and government, the individual's relationship with school stands out as primary. Furthermore, school is their only institutional topic embroiled in a thoroughgoing two-way conversation: all have found their work prescribed on school curricula. School leavers across the four nations of the UK, and in Ireland, are assessed on poetry by Clarke, Duffy, Lochhead and Meehan. Equally, all have made it part of their brief as laureates to engage with children and young people in school. This chapter brings the poets' representations of school into dialogue with the uses made of their work within educational curricula and prescribed syllabi. It explores emerging tensions, controversies and occasional political flashpoints.

Four Poems about School

The point of entry into the world beyond the private space of home is presented by Liz Lochhead's 2003 poem 'Kidspoem/Bairnsang'.[1] This poem explores a Scottish child's initiation into hierarchies of learned, imposed and indeed alien cultural norms first encountered at school. Its form facilitates the delivery of shock, warm humour, wit and biting social criticism in equal measure. The poem's assured yet troubling poise is achieved by its formal mimicry of the now old-fashioned playground circle song or round, such as 'There was an old man named Michael Finnegan . . . begin again'. Because such poems have infinite repetition built into their structure, the formal qualities of Lochhead's poem gesture towards the repetition of rote learning as well as the handing down of cultural expectations which school experience entails. Yet its playful disruptions, shifts in language, verb tense and time frame, and the name-calling slogan of the last line all suggest how a retrospective appraisal of the education acquired by the child can empower rather than diminish or entrap.

The primary repetition of the poem is paradoxically also a statement of difference. In Scots the speaker recalls the way her mother dressed her up against the cold for her first day at school. Halfway across the playground, halfway across a line ('and sent me aff across the playground'), the experience is recalled again, this time in Standard English. Scots is the language of home, English the language of not-home, and school is the place where that difference is learned. Indeed, school is the place that the child discovers not only that she is Scottish at all, but also inferior in every way according to the inflections of language, class, gender and nationality enshrined in the system she enters at the gate. As this bilingual poem see-saws between languages, the use of Standard English by a native Scots speaker is made to seem inauthentic and freighted with the burdens of colonisation and patriarchy. Using it, the speaker is compromised by these values, forced, however subtly, to capitulate with the coloniser. It is only through the collision of languages, enabled by the speaker's mature retrospective command of both, that an amplified understanding of constructed values and identity arrives. This is articulated in the last stanza of the poem, which breaks with the formal patterning of the circular song. The last word of the poem, 'dead', announces the speaker's release from outmoded impositions.

The mother's ceremonial dressing of her daughter is preparation for battle; the child's woollen coat is her armour, her protection against the symbolic cold of an alien culture. The language learned by the child from her mother is the language that must be forgotten in the new place. The playground represents the space of negotiation between private and public, the child's solitary walk across it is the individual's journey towards a politically constructed identity. It is also a journey away from truth. But, since the month is January, these events are presided over by the god Janus, enabling the two-way vision that permits comparison and evaluation so that truth and its mask are both exposed.

Lochhead asserts that 'Kidspoem/Bairnsang' is not autobiographical. She also points out that the child's first language resembles that spoken by her grandmother's generation rather that of her own mother.[2] The representative experience and the political fable do, however, recall her biographical account of school in her memoir 'A Protestant Girlhood':

Nothing in my Education had ever led me to believe that anything among my own real ordinary things had the right to be written down. What you wrote could not be the truth. It did not have the authority of English things, the things in books. Muffins and jam. I knew what they wanted you to write. My grown-up writer's fear is that this might still be so.[3]

As a writer her preoccupation, in both the poem and the memoir, is with the authenticity of expression, and as a political writer her concern is to reclaim the cultural status, the value, the literary 'authority' of her 'own real ordinary things'. These include the 'pixie' and the 'pawkies', the 'birling' and the 'scelp' of 'Kidspoem/Bairnsang'. In this context it is no surprise that the speaker of the much earlier poem 'In the Dreamschool' finds herself in an interminable history lesson, standing up in 'nothing but/a washed-in vest' to yammer her perpetually 'wrong answers'.[4] For the culturally colonised subject this is more than a familiar anxiety nightmare; it exposes the nakedness of the dreamer when the clothes of home have been removed and the new dress given out at school does not fit.

Paula Meehan's 'The Exact Moment I Became a Poet', published in *Dharmakaya* in 2000, also focuses on the speaker's encounter at school with language that carries alienating values.[5] Unlike 'Kidspoem/Bairnsang', Meehan's poem is autobiographical and the speaker's voice is closely aligned with her own. The 'exact moment', we are told in the first line, took place in 1963 when Meehan was nine years old and she was attending the Central Model Girls' School, Gardiner Street, Dublin, where her teacher was indeed Miss Shannon, who is named in the poem. 'The Exact Moment' is a first-person lyric which describes the memory of a transforming vision. It is set out in nine stanzas of three lines each. Stanza five forms the pivot between the classroom situation, which is documented over the first four stanzas, and its metaphorical interpretation, which extends over the last four stanzas. The poem describes how the child becomes suddenly aware of her social class, the way it shapes women's destiny, and how women of her class are belittled. The revelation is contained in the effect on the child of the teacher's use of the colloquial metaphor 'end up'.

The teacher exhorts her pupils to pay attention. Otherwise, she cautions, they will 'end up/in the sewing factory'. The listening child, whose family and friends work there, is transported by a vision of what 'ending up' in a factory means. Instead of a sewing factory she sees a chicken production line, on which the women, as birds, are trussed and plucked and stuffed, and she includes herself amongst them. Objectified and commodified, the child feels diminished, and indeed made alien to herself, by the social attitudes conveyed so casually in the teacher's expression. The poem concludes, 'Words could pluck you/leave you naked/your lovely shiny feathers all gone'. The child's destiny as a poet becomes apparent through her alert sensitivity to the power of language and its embedded meanings.

There are several points of comparison with Lochhead's 'Kidspoem/Bairnsang'. In both poems the speaking subject moves from a private, domestic understanding of self into a public, politicised self-appraisal which involves an 'othering' of self and new awareness of constructed social hierarchies. In both poems the speaker recalls events, and there is a juxtaposition not just of languages but of past and present, together with an awareness of how maturity places and articulates the experiences of childhood. For Lochhead this is expressed as learning 'to forget', a lesson which is explosively rejected in the final stanza which turns against being fashioned as 'posh, grown-up, male, English, and dead'.[6] Meehan juxtaposes the child's frightened vision, lyrically described, with the adult's 'back construction' of political anger, which pitches the idea that the teacher's words robbed 'labour' of its 'dignity'.[7] Both poems turn, ultimately, on the way in which the school system silences the identities the children brought from home into the classroom, and sends out a displaced version of themselves.

Gillian Clarke's poem 'Running Away to the Sea – 1955' (*Ice*, 2012) has a secondary rather than junior school setting and recalls an event from her last year at school when she was seventeen.[8] It focuses on the boundary of leaving rather than entering school, symbolised by its location on a sandy beach between hot dunes and the blue sea. The speaker, closely aligned with Clarke herself, and her friend have 'bunked off'. Heady with adolescence and summer heat, exhilarated by breaking the rules, the two girls 'dawdle' on the shore of adulthood. In this context, lessons seem unreal, a place of drowsing and 'daydreaming' where the Sister's voice is 'far away', and the geography of North Africa seems simply a list of biblical names that sounds like the underwater murmuring of rosary prayers.

In the last stanza the remembered time moves forward a year, to 1956. The innocent dreaming, delineated and protected by school rules, is gone. Not only has the speaker left school properly, rather than 'bunking off', but the tumultuous political events of the Suez Canal crisis and the USSR invasion of Hungary take place. A world that appeared whole begins to fragment, 'as empires loosened their grip'. The penultimate stanza of the poem is refocused by the last. To describe 'Egypt, the Red Sea, the Bitter Lakes, Suez' as 'A psalm of Biblical names called Geography' seems suddenly complacent, and the disconnection between school and the world beyond seems profound. In Clarke's poem, school is a place of soporific unreality, a charmed space in which to grow up; the awakening to real lessons takes place afterwards and elsewhere.

School is a frequent subject in Carol Ann Duffy's poetry (several poems on this subject are discussed by Jane Dowson)[9] but nowhere is her attention to it more sustained than in the narrative poem *The Laughter of Stafford Girls High*, published in *Feminine Gospels* (2002) and subsequently adapted for BBC Radio 4.[10] It is a poem which celebrates rule-breaking, the collective agency of women and the banishing of false consciousness.

We never find out what the literal joke was that 'Carolann Clare' wrote down and passed on at the start of the poem, but we know that it was an iconoclastic and subversive act.[11] She broke the school rules by passing a note in a lesson, and defied establishment norms of state and religion by tearing a page out of the King James Bible to use as paper. The girl was rewriting, or writing over, the Gospels, or, since the page was from the back of the Bible, she was making Revelations. Her transgression allows us to see the classroom situation itself as ridiculous, where laughter is an appropriate response: girls are sitting in silent rows learning by rote the alphabetically ordered names of English rivers. The names are meaningless, boredom is palpable, the politics embedded and taken for granted. The naming of rivers is underpinned by questions of authority and land ownership. Who has the power to name the river? Whose estates does it irrigate? The lesson conveys, however indirectly, masculine systems of government, and the girls are not just bored, they are also alienated by the patriarchy which it preaches. This is the first of many lists that occur across the poem: the Beaufort scale, Poets Laureate, the world's highest mountains, the monarchs of England, the names of the planets, Britain's largest lakes.[12] All of them speak of male authority and masculine ambition, as do the quotations from literature which are overheard from English lessons: from *Julius Caesar*, Mark Anthony addresses his 'countrymen'; from *The Merchant of Venice*, Portia has to dress as a man to deliver her courtroom speech about mercy; 'The Song of Wandering Aengus' celebrates a lover in search of his fairy Muse.[13]

The language which describes the first laughter that erupts in the face of these condensed images of masculine power is 'watery', like the lesson's rivers: 'a gurgle, a ripple, a dribble,/a babble, a gargle, a plash, a splash of a laugh'. The laughter is likened to an element that is ungendered and free, in contrast with the topic of the lesson which it interrupts. Their laughter defies, resists and eventually banishes the impositions of convention, providing ample illustration for the idea pursued by Jihyun Yun that Duffy uses wit, humour and laughter as instruments of feminist disruption.[14] Furthermore, once the laughter is released, the girls pass it on in ways that challenge feminine conduct, they 'kicked it', 'toed it', 'heeled it'.[15] The metaphors from the traditionally masculine game of football immediately expose the constructed nature of the obedient femininity to which the girls had hitherto adhered. The river of laughter challenges gender norms and carries the girls and their teachers to freedom and the sea. By the end of the poem the official curriculum has been abandoned, the school is empty and 'its desks the small coffins/of lessons, its blackboards the tombstones of learning'.[16] Pupils and teachers have made individual choices about their destinies, some of which challenge heteronormative expectations of women, such as mountaineering in the Himalayas, forming a lesbian relationship or leaving a husband. Only the Cambridge-educated and empire-decorated Headmistress, 'Clarice Maud Bream, MBE, DLitt' is unable to change.[17] Her fate is to be imprisoned by her ideology: 'In the hospital, a nurse brought some warm milk and a pill to the Head,/who stared through the bars at the blackened hulk of the school'.[18]

All four poets attest to the immense power held by the institution over the child, depicting school as a place where the child is interpellated and transformed. The poems imply that learning to negotiate, and retrospectively to resist, the values promulgated by school, are the main lessons of education, which prevail over any discipline content or skill a child might acquire. In this they uphold the notion, put forward by both Marxist and feminist educational theorists, that there is a 'covert curriculum' which conveys what Victoria Elliott recently summarises by citing Vallance as: 'the inculcation of values, political socialization, training in obedience and docility, the perpetuation of traditional class structure – functions that may be characterized generally as social control'.[19] In the poems considered here, with the exception of 'Kidspoem/Bairnsang', where there is no teacher but simply a system, it is noticeable that the agents of this social control, the teachers, as well as their pupils, are all female. The intergenerational handing-down of the norms of patriarchy are thereby foregrounded, and the ironies that a female teaching staff instructs a female body of students to follow rules which will marginalise and silence them, are made acute.

Poetry by Women in the Curriculum, and the Tortured Poem

School curricula in Ireland and the four nations of the UK have been under continuous review for decades, as successive governments seek to control education policy. In England, Wales and Northern Ireland the Education Reform Act (1988) introduced the national curriculum. Since then there have been five reforming statutory orders, requiring a total of six different GCSE curricula to be taught in thirty years. Following devolution in 1997, education policy was passed to each devolved administration, which resulted in further curriculum change in Wales and Northern Ireland. In Scotland, which has longstanding independence in education policy, the Curriculum for Excellence was introduced in 2010–11, first assessed in schools in 2014 when the previous Standard Grades were replaced by National Grades. In Ireland the English Literature syllabus of the Leaving Certificate underwent major reform in 1999, for first examination in 2001. These changes have all had an impact on the classroom presence (or absence) of poetry by Clarke, Duffy, Lochhead and Meehan.

Research by Victoria Elliott into the representation of gender (by author and protagonist) in the most recently reformed GCSE English Literature curricula which were first delivered in classrooms in England, Wales and Northern Ireland in 2015, and the National 5 English in Scotland (reformed in 2013), reveals that even in the second decade of the twenty-first century, 'the educational canon in the UK as represented by the set texts for examination in English literature at 16 is overwhelmingly male'.[20] Where poetry by Clarke, Duffy and Lochhead is prescribed, it is therefore placed in a minority. Elliott's research is complemented by Julie Blake's specific investigation of how poetry fares in the national curriculum since 1988. Blake's scrutiny of the relationship between the poets named in successive statutory orders and poets named in the syllabi of English examination boards/awarding bodies shows that poetry exhibits a similar gender imbalance to that found by Elliott across all genres of the English Literature curriculum. Blake finds that women make up 23 per cent of the statutory order poet lists, while awarding body poetry prescriptions actually increase this percentage to '37 per cent'.[21] Even so, poetry by women forms a minority within a minority for study in the current English Literature GCSE in England.

The imbalance did not go unnoticed in the British print media. When the most recent curriculum was unveiled by the Department for Education (DfE), it was greeted in the *Independent* with the headline 'Pupils face literary diet of "dead white men"', reflecting how the profession responded to the reforms, voiced by English teacher Iain Yeoman.[22] The revisions introduced in 2013–14 by Education Secretary Michael Gove to the English Literature curriculum were the most far-reaching and politically conservative since the 1995 introduction of a curriculum more explicitly weighted towards literary heritage than its first iteration. The 1995 reforms were delivered under Education Secretary John Patten, having been initiated by his predecessor Kenneth Clarke and influenced by the Dearing Report. The 1995 statutory order announced that GCSE pupils' 'reading should include . . . poems of high quality by four major poets with well established critical reputations, whose works were published after 1900, *eg T. S. Eliot, Seamus Heaney, Thomas Hardy, Ted Hughes, Philip Larkin,*

R. S. Thomas, W. B. Yeats' (emphasis original).²³ As a stipulation it falls short of actually prescribing these poets by using the formulation 'eg', but as a list of exclusively male poets it suggests either that women did not write poetry after 1900, or if they did, their poetry did not carry a sufficiently 'well established critical reputation' to be worthy of study. It should therefore come as no surprise that the 2013 headline in the *Independent* echoes the teaching profession's response to the 1995 curriculum, reported by Peter Benton:

> 'Teaching Wordsworth to GCSE pupils reinforces the stereotypes I'm trying to tackle,' says a teacher who had earlier remarked the difficulty of disabusing his pupils of the idea that poetry was written only 'by dead, white males in frilly shirts'.²⁴

Both professional responses unerringly recall the final line of Lochhead's 'Kidspoem/Bairnsang', together with its emotional affront at the requirement to conform with the 'posh, grown-up, male, English, and dead'.

It is therefore against the grain that Clarke, Duffy and Lochhead have been studied at GCSE since 1988.²⁵ Their presence fluctuates throughout the six successive curriculum variations issued by the DES/DFEE/DfE since and including 1988. Julie Blake presents the dates during which these six different GCSE series of curriculi obtained in England: series 1, 1988–93; series 2, 1994–97; series 3, 1998–2003; series 4, 2004–11; series 5, 2012–16; series 6, 2017 ff. She has identified which poets were named in statutory orders for study at GCSE throughout all six series. From her research it can be seen that Gillian Clarke and Liz Lochhead were named in series 4 (2004–11) and 5 (2012–16), while Duffy was only named in series 5 (2012–16).²⁶ Turning to the texts set by awarding bodies as they interpreted the statutory orders for classroom practice and assessment, Blake discovered there was 'no simple overlay between the national curriculum name lists and the poet selections made by the GCSE awarding bodies'.²⁷ She ascribes this variation to resistance against the prescriptions by government within the teaching profession and awarding bodies. The presence of Clarke, Duffy and Lochhead in awarding body anthologies are examples of such variance, since their work has been set for study even when they have not been named in policy documents. Poems by Clarke and Duffy have been set texts in all six series of GCSE, and poems by Lochhead have been set in all but series 4 and 5 which were, paradoxically, exactly the series in which she was listed in the DfEE/DfE statutory orders.

Blake further demonstrates that there has been a profound decline in the number of poets available for study at GCSE, from '1,039 poets in 1988, before the national curriculum for key stage 4 English was established, to 73 poets in the series examined from 2017'.[28] This, therefore, establishes a context in which prescribed poems by Clarke, Duffy and Lochhead, while representing a minority within the global corpus of GCSE poetry, nevertheless acquire much greater prominence than they would have had prior to 1988. The foregrounding of their poetry is brought about by the listing of poets in statutory orders and further lists of set texts by awarding bodies. Lists, dominant in Duffy's astute satire *The Laughter of Stafford Girls High*, are powerful instruments of education policy, and in Duffy's poem, no less than in the DES/DfEE/DfE documents, their function is to form a canon. In *The Laughter of Stafford Girls High*, the canonical lists are gleefully trashed, but as they feature in the pages of the statutory orders they are all too powerful a means to create a hierarchy of values, by exclusion no less than inclusion. It is, for example, conspicuous that Paula Meehan has never been named in any English statutory order, nor has her work been selected for study by any English awarding body. This may be one reason why her work is relatively little known in mainland Britain, and demonstrates the power of the list beyond the classroom.

The situation in England could hardly find a starker contrast than that evident in Ireland when the new English Literature syllabus was ushered in for the new millennium. Niall MacMonagle – who edited an anthology, *Poetry Now* (Celtic Press, 1999), for the revised Leaving Certificate, taught English at Wesley College, Dublin, and went on to found the island of Ireland poetry speaking contest, Poetry Aloud, in 2006 – announced the coming changes in the *Irish Times* (26 June 1999):

> The old Leaving Cert had many dead white males, some nineteenth-century women novelists, one woman poet, three living dramatists, one living poet . . . [O]ver the coming years, new poets will be introduced. Adrienne Rich, Derek Walcott, Paula Meehan, Carol Ann Duffy, W. B. Yeats, Derek Mahon, Kerry Hardie, Wordsworth, Hopkins, Kavanagh, Donne, Brendan Kennelly, Denise Levertov and dozens more will come on board in a series of revolving lists.

The notion of 'revolving lists' heralds plenitude. It gives structure without stasis, and builds evolution and contingency into the canon.

In England, however, we can only observe the cultural impoverishment enacted by the state on GCSE pupils since 1988, and consider the hazards for the few prescribed poems left standing. Sue Dymoke's investigation of teacher response to the 1997/8 Northern Examination and Assessment Board (NEAB) Anthology documents one teacher who was worried about '"the fate of some wonderful poems" within a system where students are "taught by enthusiastic teachers but at the end of the day Carol Ann Duffy's that woman we had to do for GCSE'".[29] Dymoke summarises the then prevailing professional view of the set texts: 'no matter how brilliant a poet she is, there may be more to poetry than torturing five poems by Carol Ann Duffy'.[30] Paradoxically, therefore, the prominence given to Duffy's work and her fellow National Poets by awarding body syllabi may militate against the deeper appreciation of their poetry, and poetry in general, in school and therefore potentially also in students' later life.

The 'torturing' of poetry at school has been confronted by the poets themselves, directly and obliquely, within and outwith the period of their National Poet service. Amongst Duffy's early poems, several of which, as Jane Dowson notes, 'satirize or undermine the voices of education',[31] is her 1985 poem 'Head of English', in which the teacher exhorts her students: 'Remember/the lesson on assonance, for not all poems,/Sadly, rhyme these days'.[32] 'The Head of English' anticipates the way in which assessment objectives, introduced with the national curriculum, force attention to the technical aspects of poetry. The consequences have been widely denounced by poets, teachers and educationalists. As outgoing Poet Laureate, Andrew Motion objected to this aspect of the way poetry is taught,[33] and Peter Benton compiles evidence to show that '[w]e are in danger of transforming pupils into trainspotting fanatics eagerly looking for assonance, sibilance, similes, etc. and ignoring the taste of it.'[34] These teaching methods mean that the assessed response to the poem itself falls somewhere between taxonomy and summary, with significance and aesthetic integrity altogether lost.

Lochhead used the authority of her Makar role to fuel her outrage. In an interview for *The Nation* (29 June 2015) she too rounded on the 'over-analytical and technical approach' required by the examination methods of the Scottish Qualifications Authority: '[i]t's clear that even teachers think poetry is a code. I have been asked by a boy . . . "when you wrote that poem about the bull, what did you really want to say?" His education had allowed him to get the misapprehension that a poem is a code trying to get a message across.' The effect of current teaching and assessment methods was, Lochhead stated, 'to make you hate poetry for the rest of your life'.[35] One means of countering such cultural depletion adopted by Lochhead was to give her Makar support to the Scottish launch of the schools extracurricular poetry recitation competition Poetry by Heart, trialled at the Scottish Poetry Library in 2014 before its full launch in 2015. Gillian Clarke has taken yet another approach, dedicating a page on her personal website 'For Students' which includes 'Exam Tips: My 10 Tips on How to Get a Good Grade'. Her advice runs completely counter to the technical focus which dominates the classroom, beginning with: 'Relax. You and the poet are human and you both speak English.'[36]

Gillian Clarke and Carol Ann Duffy in the AQA Syllabus 2004–2011 (Series 4)

Following the post-1997 devolution of educational policy to the four nations of the United Kingdom, the DfEE reset national curriculum policy for England. In 2000 the Westminster parliament enacted the *Education (National Curriculum) (Attainment Targets and Programmes of Study in English) (England) Order 2000*. The revised curriculum came into force on 1 August 2000 and the new suite of GCSEs (Series 4) was first examined in 2004. For GCSE English Literature this included the stipulation that students should study in detail the work of four poets published after 1914, naming amongst possible examples Clarke and Lochhead. The AQA (reformed from the NEAB in 2000) selected Seamus Heaney, Gillian Clarke, Carol Ann Duffy and Simon Armitage as their four representatives of 'recent and contemporary poetry'. By choosing poets born in Northern Ireland, Wales, Scotland and England, these make an exemplary covert declaration that while this might represent a curriculum for study in England (albeit also available in Wales and Northern Ireland), 'English' literature crosses the borders of the four nations. A more cynical interpretation might be that this represented the AQA's bid to retain its market leadership by making itself attractive to schools in Wales and Northern Ireland as well as in England. Whatever governed the selection, it had the additional virtue of comprising two women and two men, thereby seeming to secure gender parity.

The way in which the four poets are introduced to students in the *AQA Literature Anthology* (2004), issued free by the AQA to every student in subscribing English Departments, confirms a relatively even-handed treatment. The only significant difference in the 'About the poet' introductions are found in the fuller family details given about the women. Of Seamus Heaney we learn that he married Marie Devlin in 1965, but there is no mention that he has three children; of Simon Armitage there is no mention of his partnership, nor of his daughter born in 2000. This absence of personal information about the men contrasts with:

> Gillian Clarke has a daughter (about whom she writes in 'Catrin') and two sons. She lives with her architect husband on a smallholding in Talgarreg, in West Wales. Here they raise a small flock of sheep, and look after the land on organic principles.[37]

And,

> [Carol Ann Duffy] has a daughter, Ella (born in 1995) and lives in Manchester with her partner, the novelist Jackie Kay. Carol Ann Duffy was awarded an OBE in 1995, and a CBE in 2002.[38]

In the case of Gillian Clarke, information has to some extent been selected to frame the prescribed poems; this is not the case for the domestic information given about Duffy.

Scrutiny of the student handbook *Seamus Heaney and Gillian Clarke: Working with the Literature Anthology for AQA A 2004–2006*, published by Heinemann in 2004 to support the *AQA Literature Anthology*, reveals more significant perpetuation of gender stereotypes within the superficial parity.[39] The introduction to Heaney's poems prints brief bullet points about his life above a bolded headline: 'What are the main influences on Seamus Heaney's writing?' The answer begins: 'Heaney draws strongly on his Irish background. In 1982 he wrote a few lines explaining his objection to being included in *The Penguin Book of Contemporary British Poetry*: "Be advised, my passport's green/No glass of ours was ever raised/to toast the Queen."'[40] The reader is immediately presented with a poet who is well integrated in cultural tradition, who asserts a confident identity and distinct political affiliation. So far, so good.

The introduction to Clarke's poems also prints biographical bullet points, above the bolded headline, 'How did Gillian Clarke become known as a poet?'[41] The answer begins at a slant angle to the question: 'Having raised her family, Gillian now spends her time on an organic farm in Cardigan, West Wales, and pursuing her career as a writer.' The next paragraph develops the biographical approach: 'She didn't originally think her poems were good enough to publish. Her first poems were published in *Poetry Wales* when her former husband sent them off without her knowledge.' The first impression on the reader is of a person, referred to in an infantilising and over-familiar way by her first name, who is primarily domestic in her concerns, remote from cultural tradition, under-confident in her craft, who has children and has been married at least twice. The headline question thereby acquires a subtext that it is surprising that she has been heard of at all, and that her place in cultural tradition has been acquired by chance rather than literary authority. The introduction to Seamus Heaney's work never refers to him as 'Seamus', never refers to his marital status and never mentions his three children. Family, however, is just as important a theme in the set poems by Heaney as it is in Clarke's, yet gender stereotypes are clearly constructed in the Heinemann handbook along binary and hierarchical lines. The man, whose professional career takes precedence over all aspects of his life, is independent, authoritative and strong, whereas the woman, whose family takes precedence over her profession, is dependent, subservient and uncertain.

A similar pattern is observed in the same authors' companion handbook, *Carol Ann Duffy and Simon Armitage: Working with the Literature Anthology for AQA A 2004–2006*. Brief bullet points of autobiographical information are printed above the bolded headline question 'Who is Carol Ann Duffy?'.[42]

> Carol Ann Duffy started writing poetry when she was at school. Her English teacher encouraged her and helped her to get some of her poems published. She has gone on to achieve fame as a poet . . . In 1995, the year her daughter Ella was born, she was awarded the OBE for services to poetry.

While school is presented as a creative environment, the help given to Duffy by her teacher is emphasised and the gratuitous reference to her maternity is set in contrast with her OBE as though these two features of her life were in some kind of remarkable opposition (unlike the factual way this was handled in the *AQA Literature Anthology*). We can also note that the Heinemann handbook stresses her maternity but elides the information about her same-sex partnership given in the *AQA Literature Anthology*.

The introduction to Simon Armitage begins with the bolded headline 'Who is Simon Armitage?' The answer takes a different form:

> When speaking about his reasons for becoming a professional writer, Armitage has said: *I suppose everybody's looking for a way to engage with the world. They want to express themselves. I think that's universally true and it turned out that poetry was my way of engagement. I tried it, it seemed to work. I'd tried lots of other things, they'd all failed – so I stuck with poetry and it stuck with me.*[43]

The male writer is allowed to speak for himself, modest yet confident enough to make a pronouncement of universal truth. The next two paragraphs build on this authority, with the headlines 'The power' and 'The glory'. Again, Armitage is referred to by his last name while Duffy is given her full name (at least not just her first names, as was the case with Clarke), and he is granted a grand status by the headings of the concluding paragraphs, with their references to the Lord's Prayer. The fact that he became a father in 2000 is not mentioned. In both volumes, therefore, the reader is guided into an unconscious bias to respond to these poets' works in contrasting ways, to prioritise different features of their biographies and once again to recognise the man as singular and powerful, the woman as enmeshed in personal connections and surprising in her cultural authority.

There is a sense, therefore, in which this clear if submerged 'othering' of Clarke and Duffy within a syllabus that ostensibly represents them as holding equal status with their male counterparts adds complexity to the injunction, introduced to the statutory order of 1995, that GCSE students should 'read texts from other cultures and traditions that represent their distinctive voices and forms, and offer varied perspectives and subject matter'.[44] This was the same document which, as Blake argues, defined 'the English literary heritage' against '"texts from other cultures and traditions" . . . to strengthen the idea that this was a unique and distinctive tradition of native English greatness'.[45] While this stipulation was hugely controversial within the teaching profession[46] – and the wording 'other' was moderated to 'different' in the statutory order of 2000, which obtained in the jurisdiction under which the AQA selected Armitage, Clarke, Duffy and Heaney as their post-1914 poets – it is nevertheless the case that the way the Heinemann authors present Clarke and Duffy places them as different from the normative tradition embodied by Armitage and Heaney. Clarke and Duffy seem therefore to represent alternative perspectives, given by gender rather than race.

In the context of recognising that there is an implicit othering by gender even within the 'recent and contemporary poetry' content of the AQA syllabus, it is important to notice the deselection of Liz Lochhead in all awarding body syllabi of 2004, despite the fact that she was named in the 2000 statutory order as a poet whose work could represent the post-1914 curriculum and the NEAB had previously included her poem 'Rapunzstilskin' in their syllabus for GCSE Series 3.[47] To represent Scotland beyond the gender-inflected status of Duffy, the AQA set Tom Leonard's 'The nine o'clock news' from 'Unrelated Incidents' in Cluster 2 of the poems selected to fulfil the requirement to study poetry from 'different cultures and traditions'.[48] Leonard is the only white poet on that list, thereby grouping working-class white Scots with world literature, ethnic minority and migrant traditions. The commentary in the *AQA Literature Anthology* compounds the issue:

> A Scot may find it easier to follow than a reader from London, say . . . The most important idea in the poem is that of truth – a word which appears (as 'trooth') three times, as well as one 'troo'. The speaker in the poem (with whom the poet seems to sympathize) suggests that listeners or viewers trust a speaker with an RP (Received Pronunciation) or 'BBC' accent. He claims that viewers would be mistrustful of a newsreader with a regional accent, especially one like Glaswegian Scots, which has working-class or even

(unfairly) criminal associations in the minds of some people . . . Leonard may be a little naïve in his argument, however: RP gives credibility to people in authority or to newsreaders, because it shows them not to favour one area or region – it is meant to be neutral . . .[49]

Leonard, like Lochhead in her autobiographical statement about her school experience, is concerned to note the discrepancies between RP 'truth' and Glaswegian 'trooth',[50] but the commentator for AQA is deaf to the distinction, treating the language of the poem as a comic turn, devaluing all the sociolinguistic markers inscribed there and judging them 'from London, say'. The cumulative evidence of the gendered inflections of the way Duffy is presented in the Heinemann revision guide, the absence of Lochhead from all awarding body syllabi, and the alienation of Leonard by the *AQA Literature Anthology* indicates that Scottish identity is pushed well beyond the pale of the English-centric culture of the 2004–11 AQA syllabus.

This hierarchy of values, this ranking of national identity, gender and class, inscribed within the English Literature syllabus and its delivery, points towards the continuing pertinence of Ivor Goodson's claim that the imposition of a national curriculum is a political rescue package for a 'nation at risk'.[51] In 1990, when Goodson interrogated the politics that underpinned the 1988 introduction of the national curriculum, he argued that the major risk factor to the British economy and to British identity perceived by Thatcher's government was the impending integration of the UK with the EU in 1992:

> Symbolically the Channel Tunnel will connect UK life with that in Europe. The 'island nation' will quite literally be opened up to subterranean entry. The fear of the nation being at risk no doubt explains the hysteria behind so much of the Thatcher government's response to European integration. Pervasive in this response is the sense of a loss of control, a loss of national destiny and identity. The school curriculum provide [*sic*] one arena for reasserting control and for re-establishing national identity.[52]

At Goodson's time of writing, the post-1997 realities of national devolution had not been foreseen, nor indeed had the post-2016 impact of impending withdrawal from the EU, the rhetoric of which Goodson so uncannily foreshadows. But both of these dramatic changes to the geopolitical landscape are reflected in subsequent legislative decisions to determine the content of the English Literature curriculum. The nation-building project of a national curriculum, presented so incisively by Goodson in 1990, retains its potency, and not simply from the English side of the border.

Curriculum Interventions by Lochhead and Duffy

In 2012 the Scottish Government (a Scottish National Party government) announced that for the very first time it would legislate to prescribe texts for study and assessment at the National 5 exams in English. Prior to this, the awarding body in Scotland, the Scottish Qualifications Authority (SQA), had been free from government interference to set its own curriculum and syllabus. The legislation introduced the compulsory assessment for all students at school leaving age on a text of Scottish literature, selected from a list recommended by the Scottish Studies Working Group. Texts are grouped by genre of drama, fiction and poetry. Carol Ann Duffy is one of the four prescribed poets. The others are Robert Burns, Norman MacCaig and Jackie Kay.

Duffy's appearance on the list throws into disarray the neatly drawn boundaries of national identity which it seems to have been the purpose of the innovation to entrench. First, we have the question: what qualifies Duffy's poetry as Scottish? Is it by national identity of the author? By theme? By language? By place in tradition? All of these possibilities, well established in the larger debate about what makes a text Scottish, are held in play, but none of them can be answered simply.[53] Dorothy McMillan described Duffy in 1997 as 'not uncomplicatedly characterisable as a Scottish poet'.[54] She also stated that 'questions of . . . national belonging depend on where one is looking from'.[55] The view from which Duffy's national belonging is judged became evident in the way headlines on either side of the border announced her laureateship. In England, the *Guardian* announced 'Carol Ann Duffy becomes first female poet laureate' (1 May 2009); in Scotland, the *Herald* announced 'Scot is made first female laureate' (2 May 2009). These perspectives are brought together in the description of Duffy on the SQA resources page of the Scottish Poetry Library website: '[t]he first female, Scottish Poet Laureate in the role's 400 year history'. The Scottish identity of her poems is further affirmed in the selection of those set, two of which, 'The Way My Mother Speaks' and 'Originally', speak directly of Duffy's Scottish roots.[56]

The second topic of national belonging raised by Duffy's appearance on the Scottish list is a problematising of the way 'English' as a discipline so easily elides with understanding of 'Englishness'. The editors of *The Challenge of English in the National Curriculum* (1995) draw on the work of Brian Cox to make this point:

> controlling English is seen as one way of controlling society. Professor Cox has rightly said that 'a National Curriculum in English is intimately involved with questions about our national identity, indeed with the whole future ethos of British society. The teaching of English . . . affects the individual and social identity of us all.'[57]

Duffy's prior and extensive appearance in the AQA syllabus for GCSE Series 4 had seemed to position both herself and her poetry as an aspect of 'Englishness'. But neither English nor Englishness are static, nor, despite the ambitions of the national curriculum to enforce a cohesive national identity, are they ever unitary. Robert Crawford argued in 1992 that because Scotland lacked political independence, 'Scottish writing in English . . . is particularly vulnerable to being subsumed within the English literary tradition.'[58] In the political landscape of post-devolution Britain, the new education policy of the Scottish administration resists such vulnerability, putting pressure on the aspect of Englishness contained with English as a discipline. Yet, the prescription of Duffy's work on both sides of the border destabilises the very certainties embraced by any nationalising drive to the curriculum.

Liz Lochhead served on the Scottish Studies Working Group that made the list recommendations to government, and her voice as Makar was carefully orchestrated with that of the Education Minister Michael Russell to make the government press statement, issued strategically on Burns Day 2012. Lochhead stated:

> In common with just about every English teacher, academic, and certainly every fellow writer that I've consulted informally for their opinion, I am delighted that Scotland seeks to ensure that some Scottish texts are included in the literature taught in our schools. And that it will be a requirement to answer an examination question on at least one of these.
>
> Remembering that such texts may be in English, Scots-English, Scots, or any mixture of these, may come from any historical period, including the present, and are certainly not required to reflect a chauvinistic or uncritical view of Scottish society, it can only benefit our future citizens to so engage with their own culture.[59]

The SNP government's intervention was immediately contested by Scottish Conservatives, who inferred a Scottish independence agenda within this legislation. Liz Smith MSP, Scottish Conservative Education Spokesman [sic], commented:

> Overtly prescriptive recommendations which are, in effect, forcing schools to use more Scottish texts and subject materials could be construed as having an unfortunate political undertone and they are also completely against the spirit of Curriculum for Excellence.[60]

In June 2012 teachers at the annual conference of the Educational Institute of Scotland rejected the legislation and petitioned the Education Secretary to lift the 'diktat'.[61] In November 2012 the Scottish Secondary Teachers Association criticised the restrictive nature of the list of prescribed texts. Alan McKenzie, acting general secretary, stated, '[w]hatever we may think of the Scottish requirement, surely in the climate of the new curriculum the concept of a narrow list is wrong. We believe this list mentality runs contrary to curriculum philosophy and consider that many seminal texts are ignored.'[62] Victoria Elliott noted more informal professional resistance to the list, citing a teacher who blogged in March 2013: 'this is what happens when politicians (and, while we're at it, authors) are allowed to get involved in decisions which should always be made by teachers'.[63]

The teacher's parenthetical remark is clearly aimed at Lochhead. It seems that while the role of Makar was specifically designed to promote poetry and to be an ambassador for Scottish culture, as soon as these functions actually affect practice, they are not so welcome. The Makar's transition from cultural politics to real politics was disconcerting, though the prescribed selection of her poetry for study at the Higher level went uncontested. Lochhead's work was a legitimate object of study, but she was not a legitimate agent of change. And while on the one hand, the popular authority of her voice was politicised by government to ease the acceptance of its new legislation, an alternative working group co-opted her membership precisely in order, it claimed, to depoliticise the message. Andrew Denholm, in the *Herald* on 19 March 2012, reported:

> Leading academics, artists, writers and poets have united to fight depressing attempts to politicise the teaching of Scottish studies in secondary schools.
> The group which . . . includes . . . National Makar Liz Lochhead wants to see cross-party support for Scottish studies . . . Professor Murray Pittock, . . . convener of the new group, urged politicians to take a united approach.

The promotion of Scottish Studies was, in the event, scaled back so that the only innovation to the curriculum was the introduction of the required Scottish text for study at both National 5 and Higher English. Nevertheless, for all the protestation that this move in itself was not an aspect of the politics of an independent Scotland, Victoria Elliott proposes:

> The timing is intrinsically linked with the referendum on devolution but can hardly be expected to raise a sense of proud nationalism in time for September 2014, no matter the extension of the franchise to 16 year olds and 17 year olds . . . – the very people who will be first studying these texts.[64]

Throughout the referendum campaign Lochhead spoke for Scottish independence and in November 2014, following defeat, she joined the SNP. While criticism of her part in endorsing the compulsory study of Scottish Literature in schools had been refracted into criticism of government policy and professional resistance to list-making, this time the attacks were personal:

> In vain did some point out that certain past poet laureates of the UK have held party cards, and made no secret of it. No, came the reply, this is too divisive; Liz Lochhead is no longer the Makar for the 55 per cent who voted No, and so she should resign.[65]

Liz Smith argued that 'Liz Lochhead is an esteemed poet and playwright and she is absolutely entitled to join any political party she likes. But as Makar, and someone in receipt of Creative Scotland funding, she has a duty to reflect all of Scotland.'[66] Lochhead defended her rights as a private citizen, and asserted, 'My job is to project my job as poetry Makar as best I can, and that is nothing to do with my political views.'[67] The role was, however, political in its inception, and as we have seen from Lochhead's joint press release with Michael Russell on 25 January 2012, she did not shy away from this aspect of its deployment.

Without the heightened strength of feeling left in the wake of the 2014 independence referendum, the full political impact of her statement in support of prescribed Scottish texts went unscrutinised. What did she mean by her assertion that 'it can only benefit our future citizens to so engage with their own culture'? Victoria Elliott has queried, what exactly was the 'benefit' to consist in? Elliot suggests, in line with the type of claims made by Michael Gove for English Literature on the English national curriculum, that Lochhead may have meant that students will gain 'moral, or cultural capital'; Elliot also moots that the envisaged benefit could be 'personal investment in the national Scottish enterprise'.[68] These are all reasonable suggestions and likely to be accommodated by Lochhead's phrase. But, if we recall Lochhead's regret about the way her own induction into the values embedded in her Standard English schooling led her to an inauthenticity of expression and an alienated sense of self, it is most likely that the 'benefit' she foresaw was the straightforward ability of younger generations to tell and recognise the truth in their own language (Tom Leonard's 'trooth') and not to feel diminished by 'the authority of English things'. Of course, this is a moral benefit, but it is not the same kind of moral benefit as that meant by Michael Gove when he promoted the English literary heritage: 'Whether it is Austen's understanding of personal morality, Dickens' righteous indignation, Hardy's stern pagan virtue, all of these authors have something right to teach us which no other experience, other than intimate connection with their novels can possibly match.'[69] Gove's rhetoric assumes that all pupils start in the same moral, religious and social place, that all will be equally fortified by their 'intimate connection' with these authors' works, and that a morally vitalised, homogenised society will emerge. Such views are profoundly at odds with the individualised, localised subjects Lochhead's work seeks to empower.

Gove's speeches as Education Minister from 2010 provide clear answers to the rhetorical question asked by Goodson of the national curriculum in 1990: '[t]he styling of the curriculum as 'national' begs a number of questions about which nation is being referred to, for the UK is a nation sharply divided by social class.'[70] Educationalists have since added social divisions of ethnicity, faith and gender to Goodson's primary claim that it is social class which divides the UK, just as Lochhead has added national identity, but these observations only serve to support Goodson's argument that the national curriculum privileges the middle class and further disadvantages poorer members of society. He establishes this by demonstrating that the national curriculum rehabilitates '"traditional" (i.e. grammar school) subjects' (with its 'core' subjects of English, Science and Maths) which serve the professional and already wealth-creating classes while achieving little to prepare pupils for alternative kinds of future employment.[71] The result, Goodson asserts, is that 'a preferred segment of the nation has therefore been reinstated and prioritized, and legislated as "national"'.[72] It is the moral and social discipline of this group which fashions the homogenising, and excluding, standard for all.

These factors bring a new focus to the extraordinary censorship of Carol Ann Duffy's poem 'Education for Leisure' by the AQA from its GCSE syllabus. This action was taken in September 2008 on the basis of just three individual complaints. One of these had been made in 2004 about the poem's reference to flushing a goldfish down the toilet, while two made in 2008 claimed that the poem glorified knife crime. Of these, the complaint by Pat Schofield, a sixty-eight-year-old invigilator (or external examiner; press reports vary) for Lutterworth College, was escalated by her MP, Andrew Robathan, Conservative for South Leicestershire and Opposition Deputy Chief Whip (2005–10). Robathan petitioned the Director General of the AQA, Mike Cresswell, who took personal responsibility for the decision to remove the poem from its syllabus. Robathan's argument, reported in the *TES* on 5 September 2008, was:

> Carrying knives is distressingly common in our schools, in our cities and elsewhere . . . I don't think the poem glorifies carrying a knife, but it does make it seem normal and acceptable. I'm certainly not in favour of

censorship, but I thought it was a pretty poor poem, although that is a subjective judgement.[73]

The AQA's justification was, 'We had to make a decision in the current climate of knife crime and murders. We must treat these social issues sensitively – a lot of thought went into this decision.'[74]

Robathan's hand was strengthened by the context of prolonged parliamentary anxiety about a perceived rise in knife crime. On 30 April 2008 the House of Commons held a debate on teenage knife crime during which Diane Abbott asserted that '[t]he route from educational failure and exclusion to life on the streets, gang culture, knives, crime and prison is direct.'[75] The following year the Labour Government raised the age at which it was legal to buy a knife from sixteen to eighteen; national government and local councils introduced knife crime schemes and a youth crime action plan; there was an knife amnesty agreed during the Commons Knife Crime Debate on 9 June 2009. This political context for the ban was invoked by one journalist, reporting for the *Nottingham Evening Post*: '[w]e're finally tackling one of the root causes of knife crime. Poetry. Together we can stamp this sick filth out, one stanza at a time.'[76] The apparently arbitrary justification for the decision becomes even clearer when it is remembered that the *AQA Literature Anthology* which contained 'Education for Leisure' also contained two dramatic monologues by Simon Armitage which articulated violence and class anger: 'Hitcher' and 'Those bastards in their mansions'. Is it possible that the female gender of the poet made the threats posed in 'Education for Leisure' seem more unacceptable than those expressed by a male poet?

Those who condemned the poem were a small minority, but they spoke from the heart of the ideology that fashioned the national curriculum. They were opposed by teachers, Duffy's agent Peter Strauss, Michael Rosen (then Children's Laureate), and many journalists who reported the events. All were vociferous in the poem's defence and ready to explain the misreading on which the decision was based. Strauss stated, '[i]t's a pro-education, anti-violence poem written in the mid-1980s when Thatcher was in power and there were rising social problems and crime. It was written as a plea for education.'[77] And that was exactly the point. The poem articulates feelings of alienation and disenfranchisement experienced by the social class which the national curriculum was designed to deprioritise, and furthermore points the finger of blame directly at the heritage curriculum: 'I squash a fly against the window with my thumb./We did that at school. Shakespeare. It was in/another language. Now the fly is in another language.'[78] The superficial justification given for the censorship was that the poem promoted knife violence. The deeper and more compelling reason was that the poem confronted the political architects and middle-class beneficiaries of the national curriculum with the unacceptable consequences of their own education policy. Knife crime, linked directly to educational failure by Diane Abbott, provided a convenient opportunity to suppress the representation of social division which had widened since the poem's first publication in *Standing Female Nude*, three years before the Education Reform Act (1988) brought in the national curriculum.

The speaker of 'Education for Leisure' recalls 'doing' *King Lear* at school. The play represents a fragmenting nation and the precision of Duffy's invocation offers a moving commentary about those who are socially dispossessed by the process of division. The speaker conjures with lines spoken by the blinded Duke of Gloucester as he wanders on the heath: 'As flies to wanton boys are we to the gods;/They kill us for their sport' (4.1, 37–8). After the reference to these lines, the speaker asserts that his or her school experience of Shakespeare 'was in another language'. This metaphor resonates with Lochhead's depiction in 'Kidspoem/Bairnsang' of the way school alienates the child from itself by imposing another language, the terms of its social superiors. Both poets suggest that pupils encounter ideology at school which exacerbates division, whether of nation or class.

Duffy's only response to the controversy was to publish in the *Guardian*, on the day when the news broke, a sonnet: 'Mrs Schofield's GCSE'.[79] Written ironically in the form most closely associated with love poetry since Shakespeare's sonnet cycle, and addressed to the Muse, Duffy presents Pat Schofield with a series of quasi exam questions about the plays of Shakespeare. All the questions focus on violence represented in the plays, and all the quotations from Shakespeare encode a message from the poet to her Muse. 'You must prepare your bosom for his knife'; 'Something wicked this way comes'; 'Is this a dagger which I see?'; 'Et tu?'; 'Something is rotten in the state of Denmark'; 'Nothing will come of nothing:/Speak again'. Duffy disguises herself as the 'Scots witch', the aggressor reaching for her weapon, and the philosopher ready to give her antagonist a second chance. The fundamental irony, that all these plays are prescribed GCSE texts, was noted by the *Nottingham Evening Post*: 'apparently, as long as the person packing the blade is in doublet and hose, it's ok.'[80]

'Mrs Schofield's GCSE' won immediate and lasting public approval. A German translation was published in *Der Spiegel* on 15 September 2008 as part of a bemused report on the ban, and a mural of the poem designed by Stephen Raw was commissioned for the library of Leeds West Academy, unveiled in 2011. The Principal Teacher asserted '[w]e know the poem – like the rest of [Duffy's] work – will be an inspiration to students for years to come.'[81] It was published in *The Bees* (2011). Liz Lochhead, reviewing that collection for the

Guardian, plucks a line from this poem to summarise her admiration for the volume as a whole:

> Even 'Mrs Schofield's GCSE', a piece of old-style Duffy ventriloquism in the voice of the cloth-eared and irony-deficient English teacher whose objection to another Duffy monologue had it banned from the curriculum for glorifying violence, takes flight and asks the examinee to do the impossible, and 'explain how poetry/pursues the human like the smitten moon/ above the weeping, laughing earth'.[82]

For Lochhead, as for Duffy, the poet's most effective political weapon is poetry itself.

Questioning Cultural Consensus

One note emerges as consistent throughout this investigation of dynamics between these poets' work and what is taught in the English Literature classroom. It is, namely, that their poems' identification of ideology concealed within the discipline-led curriculum holds true. And where the professional agency of teachers or awarding bodies has sought to intervene by setting poems which by their form, content or authorship might challenge or mitigate that ideology, these poems have been made to seem 'other' or 'different'. In the case of 'Education for Leisure', they have been suppressed altogether. Jane Coles investigates the pedagogical consequences for teachers as they seek to deliver '[t]he curricular imposition of an authorised version of culture . . . in an attempt to engage students with subject matter completely disconnected from their everyday lives'. Coles draws on 'Bourdieu's analysis of the key role of the school system in creating an illusory "cultural consensus" . . . by ignoring the particular cultural histories of the participants' in order to assess the dysfunctional relationship between students and curriculum.[83]

Clarke, Duffy, Lochhead and Meehan position themselves for most of their careers as cultural outsiders, looking in; their poems about the experience of attending school uphold this. Their status as women poets means that their peripheral location has not only been chosen by them, but has also been conferred upon them, until the first decade of the twenty-first century. In all four cases, their service as laureates has overlapped only briefly with their prescribed presence in the classroom, ensuring that their predominantly marginal status was a feature of what students could have encountered in their work at school. Their poetry, after all, contests unitary culture and exposes the illusion of 'cultural consensus'. They are powerful voices of individuation, whether by nation, class or gender. But to be effective within a mass education programme their work has to be taught, not tortured, and presented without bias. It is an enduring indictment of the levelling strictures of prescription and assessment that, in the classroom at least, their work does not meet students on these terms, and that as a result, each poet has sought to distance herself from the methods of teaching and assessing poetry in school.

Notes

1. Lochhead, *The Colour of Black & White*, pp. 19–20.
2. See 'Liz Lochhead: "Kidspoem/Bairnsang"', *YouTube*, <https://www.youtube.com/watch?v=L2PfrDrAIR0> (accessed 13 November 2019).
3. Royle (ed.), *Jock Tamson's Bairns*, p. 121.
4. Lochhead, *Dreaming Frankenstein*, p. 57.
5. Meehan, *Dharmakaya*, p. 24.
6. Lochhead, *The Colour of Black & White*, p. 20.
7. Meehan, *Dharmakaya*, p. 24.
8. Clarke, *Ice*, p. 50.
9. Dowson, *Carol Ann Duffy*, pp. 194–6.
10. See <https://www.mixcloud.com/e2e/the-laughter-of-stafford-girls-high-by-carol-ann-duffy-starring-joanna-lumley-bbc-radio-4/> (accessed 13 November 2019).
11. Duffy, 'The Laughter of Stafford Girls High', in *Feminine Gospels, Collected Poems*, pp. 336–55; p. 336.
12. Ibid. p. 338; p. 339; p. 343; p. 344; p. 349; p. 353.
13. Ibid. p. 339; p. 350; p. 348.
14. Yun, 'The Power of Women's Laughter.
15. Duffy, *Collected Poems*, p. 337.
16. Ibid. p. 354.
17. Ibid. p. 345.
18. Ibid. p. 355.
19. Elliott, 'Gender and the contemporary educational canon', p. 45. Embedded citation of E. Vallance, 'Hiding the hidden curriculum: An interpretation of the language of justification in nineteenth-century educational reform', *Curriculum Theory Network*, 4.1 (1974), pp. 5–22; p. 5.
20. Elliott, 'Gender and the contemporary educational canon', p. 57.
21. Blake, *What Did the National Curriculum Do for Poetry?*, p. 142.
22. Richard Garner, *Independent*, 26 February 2013, cited in Blake, *What Did the National Curriculum Do for Poetry?*, p. 88.
23. DfE and Welsh Office, *English in the National Curriculum*, p. 20.

24. Benton, 'The Conveyor Belt Curriculum?', p. 85.
25. No doubt their work had also been studied previously, though Blake points out that the data here is harder to collate. Blake identifies poetry anthologies which typically resourced school English Departments in 1988, prior to the introduction of the National Curriculum, and these contain work by Clarke, Duffy and Lochhead: *The Faber Book of Twentieth Century Women's Poetry* and *The Penguin Book of Women Poets*. See Blake, *What Did the National Curriculum Do for Poetry?*, pp. 68–9.
26. Blake, *What Did the National Curriculum Do for Poetry?*, pp. 140–1.
27. Ibid. p. 142.
28. Ibid. p. 136.
29. Dymoke, 'The Dead Hand of the Exam', p. 90.
30. Ibid. p. 92.
31. Dowson, *Carol Ann Duffy*, p. 125.
32. Published in Duffy, *Standing Female Nude*; see Duffy, *Collected Poems*, pp. 9–10.
33. Simpson, 'National Curriculum Stifling Creativity'.
34. Benton, 'Unweaving the rainbow', p. 530. Both Benton and Motion are cited in Doug, 'The British schools' National Curriculum', p. 451.
35. John Gordon, also seeking to counter over-emphasis on poetry as densely coded printed text, used Lochhead's poem 'Men Talk' (*True Confessions*, pp. 134–5) as an object lesson in the exploration of the oral/aural qualities of poetry with GCSE students, presented in Gordon, 'Sound[']s right'.
36. See <http://www.gillianclarke.co.uk/gc2017/exam-tips/> (accessed 8 November 2019).
37. See <http://universalteacher.org.uk/anthology/gillianclarke.htm> (accessed 14 November 2019).
38. See <http://universalteacher.org.uk/anthology/carolannduffy.htm> (accessed 14 November 2019).
39. Draper et al., *Seamus Heaney and Gillian Clarke*. Poems by Heaney are 'Storm on the Island', 'Perch', 'Blackberry-Picking', 'Death of a Naturalist', 'Digging', 'Mid-Term Break', 'Follower', 'At a Potato Digging'. Poems by Clarke are 'Catrin', 'Baby-sitting', 'Mali', 'A Difficult Birth, Easter 1998', 'The Field-Mouse', 'October', 'On the Train', 'Cold Knap Lake'.
40. Draper et al., *Seamus Heaney and Gillian Clarke*, p. 6.
41. Ibid. p. 45.
42. Draper et al., *Carol Ann Duffy and Simon Armitage*, p. 6. Set poems are: 'Havisham', 'Elvis's Twin Sister', 'Anne Hathaway', 'Salome', 'Before You Were Mine', 'We Remember Your Childhood Well', 'Education for Leisure', 'Stealing'.

43. Draper et al., *Carol Ann Duffy and Simon Armitage*, p. 48. Set poems are: 'Mother, any distance greater than a single span', 'My father thought it bloody queer', 'Homecoming', 'November', 'Kid', 'Those bastards in their mansions', 'I've made out a will; I'm leaving myself', 'Hitcher'.
44. Draper et al., *Carol Ann Duffy and Simon Armitage*, p. 19.
45. Blake, *What Did the National Curriculum Do for Poetry?*, p. 76.
46. For example, see Dawson, 'Re-visioning the National Curriculum', pp. 193–201; and Rogers, 'Crossing "other cultures"?'
47. Childs, *Revise the NEAB Anthology*, p. 50.
48. See Dawson, 'Re-visioning the National Curriculum', p. 194, for the full list of Clusters 1 and 2 prescribed by the AQA under the 'different cultures' rubric.
49. See <http://universalteacher.org.uk/anthology/differentcultures.htm#unrelatedincidents> (accessed 15 November 2019).
50. As evidence of Lochhead's own regard for Leonard (her husband's favourite poet), she dedicated *The Colour of Black & White* to both men.
51. Goodson, '"Nations at risk"', p. 219.
52. Ibid. p. 220.
53. For a summary of this debate in general see Elliott, 'The treasure house of a nation?', pp. 286–7. For its specific relation to Duffy see Dowson, *Carol Ann Duffy*, p. 28 and pp. 171–3.
54. McMillan, 'Twentieth-century Poetry II: The Last Twenty-five Years', p. 550.
55. Ibid. p. 555.
56. See <https://www.scottishpoetrylibrary.org.uk/learning/sqa-set-texts/> (accessed 1 November 2019). The other poems prescribed for study in National 5 English are 'War Photographer', 'Valentine', 'Mrs Midas' and 'In Mrs Tilscher's Class'.
57. Protherough and King, 'Introduction: Whose curriculum?', in *The Challenge of English in the National Curriculum*, p. 4; citing Brian Cox, 'Editorial', *Critical Quarterly*, 32.4 (1990), p. 2.
58. Crawford, *Devolving English Literature*, p. 8.
59. *Scotsman*, 'Scots literature to be made compulsory'.
60. See <http://www.scottishconservatives.com/2012/03/no-need-for-scottish-studies-in-curriculum/> (accessed 1 November 2019).
61. *Herald* (Glasgow), 'Teachers slam SNP "diktat"'.
62. Denholm, 'Teachers criticise limited list'.
63. Elliott, 'The treasure house of a nation?', pp. 292–93.
64. Ibid., p. 294.
65. *Scotsman*, 'We're bigger than the referendum'.

66. Wade, 'Resign call is bonkers'.
67. Ibid.
68. Elliott, 'The treasure house of a nation?', p. 287.
69. Michael Gove, 'A liberal education', speech presented at Cambridge University; cited in Elliott, 'The treasure house of a nation?', p. 284.
70. Goodson, '"Nations at risk"', p. 222.
71. Ibid. p. 226.
72. Ibid.
73. Shaw, 'Board ditches knife poem'.
74. Ouseby, 'GSCE exam poem'.
75. Hansard vol. 475, Col. 83WH.
76. Mcfarlane, 'Knife crime and poetry'.
77. Curtis, 'Top exam board asks schools to destroy book'.
78. Duffy, 'Education for Leisure', in *Collected poems*, p. 13.
79. Duffy, 'Mrs Schofield's GCSE', *Guardian*, 6 September 2008, and *Collected Poems*, p. 445.
80. Mcfarlane, 'Knife crime and poetry'.
81. Flood, 'Leeds academy unveils mural'.
82. Lochhead, 'Review of *The Bees*'.
83. Coles, '"Every child's birthright"?', pp. 55–6. Her citation of P. Bourdieu is from 'Systems of education and systems of thought', in R. Dale, G. Esland, and M. MacDonald (eds), *Schooling and capitalism: A sociological reader* (London and Henley: Routledge Kegan Paul/Open University Press, 1976), pp. 192–200; p. 193.

9

Brexit and Britannia

On 2 July 2016 the Scots Makar, Jackie Kay, addressed the opening of the fifth session of the Scottish Parliament. Both the Makar and the Members of Scottish Parliament [MSPs] were newly elected. The poem Kay read was entitled 'Threshold'.[1] Commissioned for the occasion, like Edwin Morgan's 'Open the Doors' and Liz Lochhead's 'Open', Jackie Kay's delivery of 'Threshold' was the first duty required of the new Makar. The launch, therefore, was double. 'Threshold' inaugurated both Kay's five-year term of office and the five-year span of the Scottish Parliament serving from 2016 to 2021 under the Scottish National Party leader and First Minister Nicola Sturgeon.

Like its precursor poems, 'Threshold' explores the metaphor of the door, and Kay deliberately summons her Makar predecessors in her opening line, 'Let's blether about doors'.[2] Continuity within poetic tradition is an important constituent of national self-understanding, and Kay's poem articulates both tradition and self-understanding at a moment of acute political need. Just one week previously, on 23 June 2016, the United Kingdom had voted in the Brexit referendum to leave the European Union. Scotland, however, did not. With 62 per cent of Scottish voters declaring for Remain, Scotland was more assertively pro-European than any other country or region of the UK (including London, where Remain voters numbered 60 per cent).[3] Scotland's departure from UK policy became thereby not only cultural but also quantifiable.

The successful Vote Leave campaign, based on the slogan 'Take Back Control', had conveyed messages of the glory of British sovereignty. It was isolationist and anti-immigration. Kay's poem 'Threshold' is a defiant statement of resistance against these values, spoken to the representatives of a people who had also rejected them: '[o]ur strength is our difference'. By 'difference' Kay does not simply mean difference from the British majority, but also, and more overtly, she is referring to the internal diversity of the Scottish population. As a mixed-race poet, the embodied presence of her personal identity in the parliament chamber powerfully reinforces the endorsement of inclusion and diversity which is core to 'Threshold'. She explicitly invokes her own identity as an example of 'Scotland's changing faces – look at me!!' Scotland, Kay asserts, is on the brink of a new identity politics. Her poem heralds the opportunity to reflect on new directions: 'picture yourself on the threshold,/The exact moment when you might begin again'.

Kay's avatar for difference is not skin colour but language. The poem asserts that 'one language is never enough', and this is enacted through the extraordinary second part of 'Threshold'. Here Kay offers a refrain of 'welcome' and 'come in' in some fifty-seven world languages, ranging from Catalan to Tamil. The poem opens Scotland's door to the world, in aspiration as well as in description of the languages already spoken there, concluding, 'come join our brilliant gathering'. In performance, the repetition of greetings in world languages was delivered by two young, ethnically diverse speakers, although they did not include the full range of languages present in the printed form of the poem. Even so, the performance of 'Threshold' to the assembled parliament lasted for an audacious seven minutes and more, making it impossible for her audience to avoid confrontation with otherness and diversity. The poem's celebration of languages points both to Scotland's integration with the world and to its parliamentary democracy, the collaboration of many voices in debate. Carol Ann Duffy commented on watching the live broadcast of Kay's performance, 'I feel . . . pride for Scotland, the only country on mainland Britain with its arms open and its head held high.'[4]

Yet globalisation and democracy had been placed in mutual opposition by national populist movements sweeping both Europe and America in the period leading up to the Brexit referendum. As Akos Rona-Tas contends,

> [c]ountries hold elections. Political elites gain the levers of the nation state. Nation states buffeted by global forces do not have the power to deliver on political promises and expectations. Democracy does not seem to work, electorates become both disillusioned and radicalized and soon see regaining national sovereignty as the only remedy.[5]

Kay's ambition for an inclusive, global Scotland takes its place alongside awareness of the fragility of democracy in this climate. She warns the assembled MSPs, 'Democracy is in its infancy: guard her//Like you would a small daughter'. The feminisation of democracy in the context of the young Scottish Parliament is a gendering choice which highlights the fact that both she as Makar and the First Minister are women, leaders elected against the grain of masculine tradition in government as in poetry. Kay speaks, moreover, in front of another female presence, the Queen. As head of state, the monarch signals clearly that Scotland is not a nation state, that it has no sovereignty within the United Kingdom. The presence of the Queen therefore entails an element of foreboding, since the outcome of the Brexit referendum exposed as never before the instability of the union, and prior to the outcome Sturgeon had already stated that a Leave result could trigger a second referendum on Scottish independence.

'Threshold' concentrates attention on the manifold and contradictory forces which meet in this, and perhaps any, democratic parliament. It illuminates the almost uncanny moment of pause in the immediate aftermath of the Brexit referendum and speaks into the liminal space of transition, the borderland into which all four nations of the United Kingdom had stepped on 24 June 2016 and which they would occupy until the end of 2020. While 'Threshold' reflects on the moment of passage from one state of being to another and is built around the conceit of the open door, later on that same day, 2 July 2016, Kay travelled to St Andrews to read her poem 'Extinction', which is constructed in obverse fashion around the metaphor of the closed border: 'We closed the borders, folks, we nailed it./No trees, no plants, no immigrants'.[6] Whether the door is opening or closing, public attention during the Brexit movement is focused on borders.

Kay's reading of 'Extinction' in St Andrews that evening was part of the final event in Carol Ann Duffy's reading tour of Britain, 'Shore to Shore', which had set out to celebrate independent bookshops but found itself engulfed in Brexit politics.[7] Duffy's companions for the fifteen reading stops between Falmouth and St Andrews, crossing borders between England and Wales and between England and Scotland, were the outgoing National Poet of Wales, Gillian Clarke; Jackie Kay as incoming Makar; and Imtiaz Dharker, whom Duffy had pronounced 'world laureate'. Their collective public offices therefore drew maximum attention to national belonging and relationships between nations at a time when these were topics of intense political scrutiny on which every voter had to take a stand. The tour itself gave the travelling poets a unique opportunity, as Kay asserted, 'to take the political temperature of the country'.[8] Duffy reflected on the tumultuous political change which had come about during the two short weeks of their tour: '[w]e started . . . in a chorus of celebration, but the key has changed from major to minor and we end in a psalm of consolation – poetry as the music of being human . . . Home will be different when we get there.'[9]

Home would be particularly changed for Carol Ann Duffy, because her personal Remain politics were now explicitly misaligned with the public politics of the United Kingdom. She was among the first to note that the outcome of the referendum would threaten the union of the four nations, closing her 'Shore to Shore' diary entry for 24 June 2016 with a sombre warning: 'it's approaching 6am and JK Rowling has tweeted that Cameron's legacy will be the breaking of two unions. His unleashed genie has indeed given us our country back – torn in two like a bad poem.'[10] Having started her career as an outsider, this was at least familiar territory, though hardly ground on which the Poet Laureate might expect to find herself. Duffy's ambition on accepting the role in 2009, 'to prove that poetry can still be central to Britain's cultural life',[11] would now show its mettle.

Her first move, in the months following, was to collaborate with the Director of the National Theatre in London, Rufus Norris, in the composition of a verbatim drama, *My Country: A Work in Progress in the words of people across the UK and Carol Ann Duffy*.[12] The play formalises the kinds of conversation which Duffy and her companions encountered during the Shore to Shore tour and documented in their online diary. As members of the liberal, cosmopolitan elite, the poets and their self-selecting audiences were firmly pro-European. But this was not the case for many of the people they met in the towns and cities of the tour outside their performance venues. On the day of voting, 23 June 2016, Jackie Kay recorded the chat from the market stalls in Monmouth on the Welsh border: 'the man I buy my French loaf from at the bakery stand is a definite out and lists his reasons confidently. "It is not just about immigration," he says, eyeing my skin colour. "It's about being handed down decrees from Brussels when what do they know about us?"'[13]

My Country opened at the National Theatre, London, on 28 February 2017, before touring until June 2017. It was 'built from extracts of 70 long interviews', Norris explained, aiming 'to capture the anger and shock of the summer of 2016 and to shed some light on how we got to this point'.[14] The personified central character, Britannia, calls 'the gathering of the family of Britannia in the year 2017'.[15] She invites Caledonia, Cymru and Northern Ireland, together with the English regions, East Midlands, North-East and South-West. Britannia announces that she will speak 'the words of the leadership at Westminster', while her guests name fifty-four individuals from their countries and regions in whose words they will speak.[16] The purpose, Britannia announces, is 'not to agree', but to listen to one another. This is to be a 'Sacrament of Listening', a process without outcome other than that contained in Britannia's uncompleted simile, 'as the song of birds/reveals the light'.[17]

Having set the scene, the play arranges extracts from the verbatim accounts according to theme. In the first section, 'The Six Arias', each of Britannia's guests delivers a long narrative speech in a character placed by country or region, gender and social class, to build a picture of the population's cultural diversity. These are followed by sections on attitudes to 'Europe', 'Patriotism', 'Hardship' and 'Immigration'. Next is 'Listening and Leadership', quoting from speeches by David Cameron, Michael Gove, Boris Johnson and Nigel Farage, and cross-cutting these with citizens' comments. In a staged lack of listening, which goes some way to justify the enterprise of the drama itself, the effect of this collage is to emphasise the gulfs between the political leaders and those they purport to represent, as well as the competitive divisions between all sectors.

This section concludes with a dramatic monologue by Britannia, the only character who appears to have been listening at all. 'I am your memory, your dialects, your cathedrals,/your mosques and markets,' she begins.[18] Yet her offering of an all-encompassing matrix of ancient and contemporary Britishness tilts into potential self-aggrandisement – 'Who else but me can praise your ancient, living language as a jewel?' It comes to rest with a deliberate echo of Jo Cox's Maiden Speech, made in the House of Commons in June 2015: 'we . . . have far more in common than that which divides us'. These words became tragically ironic when Cox was murdered during her campaigning for the Remain vote in June 2016; Britannia's appropriation of Cox's phrase heightens the play's moral imperative to honour sources of national concord.[19] This monologue serves as an emotional climax of the play, and it was picked out by theatre reviewer Sarah Crompton as an intervention by 'Duffy herself . . . to reveal Britannia's weariness'.[20] As a moment of reflective exhaustion it may also signal Britannia's own outmodedness in relation to the centrifugal energies of her guests. There is irony in this, given that the play is driven by the desire to tease out the reasons for the Brexit decision, which was itself designed to shore up the ruins of a supposedly EU-ravaged Britain.

However, Britannia is saved from her world-weariness and commitment to due process by the very unruliness of her guests. Although she ends her monologue by calling for the 'vote', this is delayed and displaced by her guests' collective demands for a feast, bringing saturnalia to the stage and even the discovery of a common figure of fun in the shape of Donald Trump. Crompton observes that what begins as a 'celebration of difference – a feast where each constituent part of the land offers its own produce, its own dances', turns into a celebration of each as 'part of a whole'.[21] Britannia's status and relevance seem to be restored. Business is resumed, and after 'The Feast' comes 'The Vote'. Inevitably, Leave votes predominate and every Remain vote is a surprise, given the emphasis on anti-EU feeling which had been hitherto represented. The lack of Remain representation in the script was noted by both Michael Billington, reviewing for the *Guardian*, and Susannah Clapp in the *Observer*.[22] For Rufus Norris, this bias arose from anxiety about how the 'National' Theatre could represent the 'nation'.

Interviewed by Amelia Gentleman, who states that 'the completed script has more leave voices (more than the 52% of votes to leave), in recognition of the fact that more of the audience will come from a remain position', Norris elaborates, 'we have been incredibly diligent, making sure that what will inevitably be perceived as our pro-remain bias is properly balanced. We push it further the other way because you understand that the majority of people who will come to see it are likely to be on the remain side, because theatres are seen as a liberal echo chamber.'[23] This may be so, but as Norris also states, the entire enterprise was motivated by a desire to assuage the 'anger and shock' of the outcome, feelings not shared by the 52 per cent of leave voters. Although Norris states that '[t]he challenge is to keep our own personal politics out of it; the point is to give a voice to other people,' his vocabulary betrays a continuing sense of division by othering the very people he sought to welcome to the stage. Duffy's Britannia may be trapped by the bad faith of the institution, the 'National Theatre', and even by the lost cohesion of the 'Nation' she is designed to represent.

The ending of the play is prolonged, with 'The Vote' followed by three sections, 'Post-Vote', 'Aftermath' and 'The Leave-Taking', replicating the aftershocks felt by all sectors of British society. Finally Britannia is alone on stage with her closing question, 'Do I hear you listening?'[24] Her words echo the purpose of the gathering which she had set out in the opening scene, the 'Sacrament of Listening', but they also reach back to the conceptual beginnings of the project as described by one of the researchers, or 'gatherers':

> It was called *The Listening Project* at first, because the main emphasis was that people weren't being listened to. We hear a lot of noise from Westminster, the Scottish government, the Welsh government and the European parliament but we wanted to find out what people in the street think and feel.[25]

Amongst the voices Duffy and Norris crafted into the play, Duffy's own poetry is heard at three points of the drama, each time spoken by Britannia: at the end of the opening scene to establish the 'Sacrament of Listening'; at the end of the 'Listening and Leadership' section; and at the end of the play. On each occasion the act of listening is emphasised. Invoked at the beginning, listening is presented as a means to enlightenment, achieved through reciprocated attention: 'listen to me and let me hear your words'.[26] The line endings of these six lines of poetry carry meaning-bearing rhyme, as well as incantatory alliterations and assonances to generate a receptiveness that may go beyond the literal meaning of words: 'words', 'birds', 'light', 'lessening', 'loosening', 'listening'.[27] Only 'light' stands apart; enlightenment, after all, is the destination of the enterprise. Britannia's monologue at the end of the 'Listening and Leadership' section is a demonstration of listening as a route to creative omniscience and a way of taking the past and the present into the body, a way of embodying time: 'I have breathed you in, like air'.[28] Britannia's last speech, which is a direct address to the audience delivered in prose poetry, is both a warning and an exhortation about listening. The sacramental listening which Britannia sought to orchestrate does not, she asserts, provide the listener with moral authority: 'we cannot stand in judgement on each other's lives'.[29] It does, however, open the possibility of finding 'good leadership',[30] since mutual understanding of needs and interests, so absent from the verbatim evidence of the play, begins with listening which is active and multi-directional. It is also a personal responsibility and an intimate relationship: 'Do I hear you listening?'[31]

What Duffy brings to the collected material, therefore, is a means of articulating its value, not in terms of content, but in terms of how it can be received as a form of agency for finding political direction and ensuring personal growth. Britannia's poetic utterances contrast with the verbatim speeches by her guests; they are solemn and formal, respectful and responsive, in high contrast to the raging, fractious and deeply disenfranchised voices she hosts. There is a sense in which the play as a whole takes forward the ambitions of Jackie Kay's poem 'Threshold' by demonstrating that in order for many voices to be constructively represented, a formal, parliamentary environment, augured by Britannia's monologues, is necessary. Poetry and theatre can point the way, but they cannot replace; the National Theatre is not a debating chamber, though the Poet Laureate in the guise of Britannia can form a bridge between the houses of culture and the houses of parliament.

Duffy's Britannia could hardly strike a greater contrast with the Britannia who had appeared some twenty years earlier in Lochhead's drama *Elizabeth* in 1998, in a double bill with *Shanghaied* (1982), under the title *Britannia Rules* at the Royal Lyceum Theatre, Edinburgh. Lochhead's Britannia is performed by a cross-dressed man, almost a pantomime dame. Played by actor Billy Boyd, Britannia is a costume part for a float in the Coronation Parade to celebrate the ascent of Elizabeth II to the throne in 1953. Britannia's chariot is an upturned table, '*perhaps mounted on bogey wheels*':

> *As the chariot is finally revealed, side on we see two flat impressively painted cutouts graphically copied from Britannia's incarnation on coinage which fit against the outside of the legs of the upturned table and a chair inside to sit on. It looks both home made – and also rather splendid.*[32]

The character who chooses to dress up as Britannia is the most vulnerable within the plays' narrative: Hughie, mocked and left out as a child, gay as an adult, he radiates laughter and joy in the costume of Britannia. He holds a trident made from a broom, his helmet is crested with a paintbrush over a blonde wig, his skirt is a drape of fringed curtains and his shield is a piece of painted cardboard.[33] What does this confluence of character and iconography mean? Commissioned and produced the year after the 1997 referendum on devolution which heralded the establishment of the Scottish Parliament, Hughie as Britannia represents acceptance on his own terms of himself and by others. He takes part in the Coronation Parade, just as Scotland remains in the Union (for the time being), and in this costume he no longer has to hide his sexual orientation or apologise for his difference, just as Scotland's proper identity is affirmed within the United Kingdom by devolution. At the same time there is irony, mischief and subversion of the imperial British pieties, cut down to size with a broom and a cheeky laugh.

Although the two parts of *Britannia Rules* were written decades before Brexit was heard of, the plays scrutinise and find wanting the histories and ideas which came to form significant elements of Leave campaign rhetoric: the Second World War, British sovereignty and attitudes to foreigners.[34] Just as the travelling poets of Duffy's 'Shore to Shore' tour changed their sets to incorporate poems which had been composed for other political circumstances after 23 June 2016, in order to lament and diagnose the Brexit referendum outcome, so too Lochhead's *Britannia Rules* affords a proleptic commentary on the events of 2016. The first part of the double bill, *Shanghaied*, is about children evacuated during WW2 from the city to the country, from Glasgow to Argyll. The play, Lochhead asserts, 'was all about relationships: the moment-to-moment dance of shifting alliances as they bonded together or realigned themselves under new pressures'.[35] The children are polarised by social class, family allegiances, gender, age and religion, their differences marked by language use. By the end of *Shanghaied* the children have bonded deeply and are fluent in each other's speech patterns, speaking a hybrid of high and low registers, street and country. What these hybrid speech patterns reveal is that despite their rivalries and polarisations, they have nevertheless, as Duffy's Britannia would require, been listening to one another and found mutual respect, even things to copy and adopt. Fourteen years later, however, their hard-won social cohesion is shown to be nothing better than a figment of nostalgia, its substance crushed under the conservative pressures of 1950s Britain. Posh Emily, entering the inner-city environment of her childhood friends, fruitlessly seeks recognition from the now communist activist Billy. 'Emily,' he says, 'there was a war on . . . we were your war effort.'[36] Coronation Day seen from inner-city Glasgow forces the grown-up characters to take a stand in relation to the era of re-entrenched cultural divisions. One result is social fragmentation. Posh Emily is rejected by her childhood friends and Morag decides to emigrate to the town of Elizabeth in New Jersey, for a life she imagines free of the constraints placed on women in 1950s Scotland. Another means of resisting the imposition of heteronormative expectations is by subversion, embodied by Hughie's impersonation of Britannia, granting himself license to follow his own rules: 'Do you know what? I'm just going to go home like this, and my Da can just like it or lump it.'[37] Unlike Duffy's Britannia in *My Country*, Lochhead's Britannia is not burdened by memory, but instead embraces a future that will be of his own making. The transformed Britain of a devolved four nations is on the horizon.

When Duffy speaks in her own poetry, however, and without the inhibitions of an imperial avatar, she is as articulate about her disgust at the failures of political process which led to the Brexit outcome as she was clear about the disenfranchisements of 1980s Britain in *The Other Country* (1990). 'Britannia' is the title of one of five poems published in her last laureate collection, *Sincerity* (2018), which delineate her view of contemporary politics and public life. The companion poems of 'Britannia' are 'The Ex-Ministers', 'Gorilla', 'Swearing In' and 'A Formal Complaint'. Two of these, 'Gorilla' and 'Swearing In', are about the 2016 election of Donald Trump as American president. They are enfolded in the sequence by the three poems about British politics and public life, to demonstrate Duffy's view of the close alignment between British and American populism and the concomitant degradation of political integrity.

'Britannia' is a short, four-stanza poem spoken in Duffy's own voice which blends her experience of witnessing on television the 'national disasters' of Aberfan (1966) and Grenfell (2017).[38] Together these events claimed the lives of over 216 people, deaths caused by the neglect or wilful profiteering of responsible authorities. They are losses which afflict the nation, but also seem to be caused by values which the nation allows to prevail. The figure of Britannia is therefore deeply ambiguous. She makes an oblique entrance, conjured by the coins which the speaker remembers being asked to bring to her school's 'special assembly' after Aberfan, 'a sixpence, a shilling, a florin'. The antiquity of these coins from pre-decimalisation (1971) points not only to the time when Britannia figured on the back of pennies and halfpennies, but also tells the decades between these two disasters during which nothing has improved for citizens who could expect to be shielded rather than sacrificed by the state which Britannia represents. Throughout this time, the profile of the monarch, Queen Elizabeth II, has been printed on the face of all British coinage; as a female heraldic figure, the image of the Queen is easily elided with Britannia. The last line of the poem, grammatically incomplete though printed as a sentence, records this fusion and completes the observed disjunction between public and private, heraldic and experienced, the state and her people: 'The constant, dutiful Queen'. The monarch is powerless to do more than bear witness to disasters which bring shame on a nation.

The anger of the poem 'Britannia' is modulated by sorrow, and as such it stands apart from its companions in which anger is inflected by contempt and expressed through satire. Preceding 'Britannia' in the sequence, and facing it across the page, is the poem 'The Ex-Ministers', about self-serving greed and complacency amongst recent British Cabinet Ministers of all political persuasions. This was the poem which Duffy chose to publish as her contribution to the *Guardian*'s '11 Odes to Europe' on 9 December 2019, poems published 'as Britain braces itself for the Brexit endgame, [when] leading poets . . . take the pulse of our fragmenting world'.[39] Positioned in *Sincerity* opposite 'Britannia', 'The Ex-Ministers' expresses more than contempt for former politicians cavorting in the playground of the international rich and culpably divorced from the population they have exploited; it becomes rather a statement of accusation. The blood of 'Britannia', on the facing page, is on their hands. In the *Guardian*, flanked by poems about the social rifts exposed by Brexit and scrutinising the prejudices legitimated by it, 'The Ex-Ministers' emphasises flagrant neglect of duty by politicians charged with leadership.

Amongst Britannia's citizens most disenfranchised by the failures of political leadership are the Northern Irish (Hibernia's children). In *My Country* this is articulated bluntly by the character Northern Ireland, speaking in the voice of 'Richard': 'Britain doesn't want us. Who does want us? Nobody wants us. They've only held on to us because they know no one else wants us. If they cut us adrift there'd be a few pound more in their pockets. We've nothing to give apart from history of troubles.'[40] Northern Ireland voted predominantly to remain in the EU, tallying 55.8 per cent remain and 44.2 per cent leave in the referendum. As was the case for Scotland, therefore, the removal of Northern Ireland from the EU is against the majority will of its people.

The voicelessness of the citizens of Northern Ireland within the political processes of the United Kingdom extends to a lack of institutionalised representation by a 'national' poet, and Carol Ann Duffy as UK Poet Laureate rarely visited the country for readings during her tenure. She did, however, make one notable visit in 2014, to read in Belfast alongside the outgoing Belfast City Poet Laureate, Sinéad Morrissey.[41] Interviewed about Brexit in March 2019 on the eve of one of several deadlines by which UK membership of the EU would cease, Morrissey affirmed Northern Ireland's absence from British self-understanding: 'for most people in Britain, Northern Ireland may as well be the moon, and the Troubles a grainy flickering on a TV screen from decades ago, (mostly) unfolding somewhere else'.[42] For all Morrissey's dismay at the UK decision to quit Europe, and her foreboding at the inevitable destabilisation of her country's borders and internal security, the collection she published in the immediate aftermath of the referendum suggests her abiding faith in human ingenuity, particularly women's, to solve problems and engineer positive futures.

The collection is named *On Balance* (2017) and it explores extraordinary feats of imagination and skill, probing resilient creativity. It also sites much of this activity in Northern Ireland. 'The Mayfly', for example, describes the imaginative daring of Lilian Bland from County Antrim, the first woman ever to design, build and fly an aeroplane, 'may-fly,//may-not fly'.[43] The scale of her achievement is graphically described in the closing stanza, 'your footprint missing on earth for the span/of a furlong, as if a giant had lifted its boot/and then set it down'.[44] Yet not all of the poems are so uplifting; alongside hope there is also warning. The volume itself opens with 'The Millihelen', a poem about the precarious launch of the *Titanic* into the Belfast Lough, its ironic last line, 'in fact everything regains its equilibrium'.[45] *On Balance*, alert to the unbalancing political forces of the era, sounds caution at the over-reaching ambition of the Brexiteers. Morrissey is acutely aware of the particular vulnerability of Northern Ireland in this context, arguing that '[i]f Brexit allows British people to stabilise their own borders, to "take back control" . . . this only refers to some of its borders . . . That Brexit does not allow greater control over Britain's most westerly border, but instead radically destabilises it, is irrelevant.'[46]

The departure of the UK from the EU put pressure on the border between Northern Ireland and the Republic of Ireland because the security of this border was safeguarded by the European Convention on Human Rights under the terms of 1998 Good Friday Agreement.[47] This was the international treaty which brought about a ceasefire in Northern Ireland and set out terms for the establishment of the Northern Ireland Assembly. For the EU to uphold the security of these arrangements, both Northern Ireland and the Republic were required by the treaty to be European Union members. With the secession of UK membership, this border became, as Morrissey states, radically destabilised. Therefore 2016 marked the year in which Brexit forced attention to the way in which the UK and the EU would or could safely manage their only mutual land border. The sense of significance was compounded in Northern Ireland by the fact that 2016 was the centenary of the 1916 Easter Rising, a movement which led eventually to the partition of the island of Ireland into two separate jurisdictions, the six counties of Northern Ireland and the foundation of the Irish Republic. Eavan Boland commemorates the centenary with her poem 'Statue 2016'.[48] It salutes the campaigns of Constance Markievicz, urges acceptance that 'reason and faith are at odds' and grieves for the unnecessary loss of life in the course of decolonisation. The confluence of political forces and memories channelled into 2016 forms the subject of Medbh McGuckian's poem 'Kepler 452B', published in April 2017.[49]

Kepler 452B is the name of a planet which may have the conditions for life in the solar system of the star Kepler 452, some 1,402 light years distant from earth. The planet Kepler 452B, discovered by NASA in 2015, is also known as 'Earth 2.0', a good place, perhaps, for the Brexiteers' economic plan for 'Empire 2.0' – the term which emerged in Whitehall in March 2017 to describe the UK's global trading ambition – to unfold.[50] The title of McGuckian's poem announces that, as Morrissey points out, 'Northern Ireland may as well be the moon,' or certainly that as far as Westminster is concerned, it exists in a parallel universe. Yet, the speaker insists in the first stanza, 'There is only/One universe at a time', and it is to this 'one real world' that the reader's attention is compelled. Angry, fearless and grieving, the first-person speaker shifts her shape to project a nightmare vision of the present, 'now every thing breathes 2016'. The speaker is sometimes the moon, or a bonfire, a writer, a witness, or Ireland herself: 'I had ridden/Wrapped up in a Union Jack to protect me//From the sun, and when I rolled out of it,/I felt that I was born'. The poem overlays memories of Belfast during the Troubles with Dublin during the Rising, and notes how little has changed over the century, 'kicking the tight-/Laced city moodily behind me, step by step,/Yet not advancing an inch'. The plea of the final stanza is 'to re-think the river/Of the world-otherwise story before it/Comes home'.

Listening, as the Britannia of *My Country* exhorted, these poems tell a consistent story: Britannia no longer protects her citizens, no longer shields them with collective strength. She is on the way out, a herald of the past with little purchase on the future. These poems articulate fissures exposed by the Brexit debates, between the home nations as between social classes. For McGuckian, new life will come on departure from the 'Union Jack' ('Kepler 452B'), and anyway, 'Britain doesn't want us' (*My Country*). For Duffy, Britannia hosts '*murderers*' and buries her children under 'slurry' ('Britannia'). For Lochhead, if Britannia is to have a future it must be on new terms and 'and my Da can just like it or lump it' (*Britannia Rules*). Indeed, as Kay's poem 'Threshold' augurs, constructive energy radiates from the 'brilliant gathering' of many voices, not from the diktats of one. Morrissey's poem 'The Millihelen' suggests that an entity the size of the *Titanic* has to be broken before 'equilibrium' can be re-established, but her faith in human creativity assures that balance will be found.

Gillian Clarke was interviewed shortly after the signing of the European Union's foundational Maastricht Treaty in 1992; she stated, '[n]ow, I don't feel British at all. I'm Welsh and European. I may live out on the western fringe of Europe, but I feel extremely involved in it'.[51] Poetry is no respecter of borders, but a common and enriching currency across cultures.

Together, these poets shine fierce light on how the politics of Brexit exposed the impoverishments of 'home', and require Britannia to be reimagined for the future.

Notes

1. See Kay's performance at <https://www.youtube.com/watch?v=rmLxjUNVtQU&feature=emb_logo> ('Poet Jackie Kay recites . . .', *YouTube*, accessed 22 November 2020).
2. 'Threshold' is published on the Scottish Poetry Library website, <https://www.scottishpoetrylibrary.org.uk/poem/threshold/> (accessed 12 November 2020).
3. Patrick Le Galès, 'Brexit: UK as an exception or the banal avant garde of the disintegration of the EU?', in O'Reilly et al., 'Discussion Forum. Brexit', p. 852.
4. Duffy, 'Poets' tour: reaching the "unsure shore"'.
5. Akos Rona-Tas, 'Brexit: the conflict of globalization and democracy', in O'Reilly et al., 'Discussion Forum. Brexit', p. 846.
6. Kay's Shore to Shore performance of 'Extinction' is available on *YouTube*: <https://www.youtube.com/watch?v=OYZyrVmBeOc> (accessed 1 May 2018).
7. For an account of the tour and its significance, see Varty, 'National Poets on Tour'.
8. Goring, 'Makar Jackie Kay says Brexit vote could force her to quit Manchester'.
9. Duffy, 'Poets' tour: reaching the "unsure shore"'.
10. Duffy, 'Poets' tour: "UK has been torn in two like a bad poem"'.
11. Thorpe, 'Laureate puts political spin on 12 days of Christmas'.
12. See <https://www.nationaltheatre.org.uk/shows/my-country-uk-tour> (accessed 22 November 2020).
13. Kay, 'Poets' tour: in and out with lettuce and lardy cake'.
14. Gentleman, 'Rufus Norris'.
15. Duffy and Norris, *My Country*, p. 7.
16. Ibid. pp. 7–10.
17. Ibid. p. 11; p. 10.
18. Ibid. p. 38.
19. Ibid. pp. 38–9.
20. Crompton, 'Review: *My Country*'.
21. Ibid.

22. Billington, 'My Country: A Work in Progress review'; Clapp, 'My Country: A Work in Progress review'.
23. Gentleman, 'Rufus Norris'.
24. Duffy and Norris, *My Country*, p. 58.
25. Lawrie, 'How they created the NT's Brexit play *My Country*'.
26. Duffy and Norris, *My Country*, p. 10.
27. Ibid. pp. 10–11.
28. Ibid. p. 38.
29. Ibid. p. 58.
30. Ibid. p. 58.
31. Ibid. p. 58.
32. Lochhead, *Elizabeth*, in *Britannia Rules*, p. 111.
33. See <https://lyceum.org.uk/fiftieth-anniversary/entry/britannia-rules-1998> (accessed 22 December 2020).
34. For an account of how these topics were deployed during the Brexit campaign, see Eaglestone, 'Cruel Nostalgia and the Memory of the Second World War'.
35. Lochhead, 'Introduction', in *Britannia Rules*, p. 3.
36. Lochhead, *Elizabeth*, in *Britannia Rules*, p. 105.
37. Ibid. p. 98.
38. Duffy as quoted in Allardice, 'Carol Ann Duffy'.
39. 'Sometimes the world goes feral – 11 odes to Europe'.
40. Duffy and Norris, *My Country*, p. 19.
41. Savage, 'Poets in the City'.
42. Doyle, 'Brexit is aggressive'.
43. Morrissey, 'The Mayfly', in *On Balance*, p. 33.
44. Ibid. p. 35.
45. Ibid. p. 9.
46. Doyle, 'Brexit is aggressive'.
47. Belfast Agreement, 10 April 1998.
48. Boland, 'Statue 2016', in *The Historians*, pp. 49–50.
49. McGuckian, 'Kepler 452B'.
50. Andrews, 'Building Brexit on the myth of empire ignores our brutal history'.
51. 'Interview with Gillian Clarke', in Lloyd, *The Urgency of Identity*, p. 25.

10

Postscript for the Future

Writing in 1989, when Ted Hughes was Poet Laureate, Gillian Clarke observed that '[e]ven the Poets Laureate of England have not much used their role to keep the people's journal.'[1] She contrasts this with the case in Wales, where, she claims, poets are seen as 'social equals' with readers and considered 'ordinary', simply workers in a craft. The result, Clarke asserts, is that a poet in Wales navigates, as a matter of course, between intimate and public, between local and national.

Clarke, Duffy, Lochhead and Meehan have all reached the national, whether 'national' is considered in career terms or subject matter, by starting from the local, and in their leadership roles they have strengthened rather than abandoned their attention to the stuff of daily life. The imperative to open dialogue between ordinary citizens and the country they inhabit was one of Clarke's stated ambitions on her appointment. 'Poetry is for everyone. I think there is a misconception that poetry is for people with posh voices . . . What I hope is that through my role as National Poet of Wales I will be able to reach out to people who have never read poetry.'[2] While this is an ambition to extend the reach of poetry, it is pre-eminently driven by faith in the inclusive nature of the art and the communities it speaks for. The conviction that poetry is not something 'posh', speaking from somewhere else and about another place, is foundational for Clarke's practice and grows out of her gendered subjectivity. It also underwrites Duffy's ambition to revitalise the place of poetry in British cultural life. For all four women laureates, belonging and access to public platforms were hard won. Trained by experience never to take their own authority for granted, they have brought energy and focus to their laureate responsibilities. The cumulative effect of their laureate tenures has been to legitimate experience of the ordinary as a way of understanding a larger framework and the individual's place within it. Carol Ann Duffy's means of celebrating the Queen's Diamond Jubilee is a case in point. The poems she commissioned to mark each year of the monarch's reign create together a 'people's journal' of the era, commemorating intimate experience alongside national and world events, fusing the two, refusing the difference. *Jubilee Lines*, its punning title recalling the London Underground train line, suggests a direction of national travel in which individual experience is a constitutive part of a national life and essential to it.[3] The twitching of a net curtain is no longer a marker of exclusion ('Mrs Skinner, North Street'),[4] but a symptom of life as it is lived, and as requiring of attention as any grand state ceremonial. The effect of these poets' journeys towards laureateship has been both to democratise poetry and to democratise national self-understanding.

They leave behind a radically altered cultural landscape, mapped out in part by their own careers, which set new horizons of ambition for women poets. Despite Deryn Rees-Jones' 2013 observation that 'women poets are reviewed less than men poets, and in different ways; they win fewer prizes; fewer women send to magazines; fewer appear in prestigious literary publications', there is evidence in the grassroots of poetry to support optimism.[5] Statistical evidence for the agency of women as poets, editors and critics has been compiled by the Ledbury Poetry Critics.[6] In 2020 their research shows a steady rise in the number of poems published by women or non-binary poets in thirty UK magazines and newspapers surveyed, rising from 36.7 per cent in 2009 to 49.6 per cent in 2018.[7] Looking beyond numbers, it is also important to consider individual cases and to remember that whereas in the 1970s Gillian Clarke was the only women to edit a poetry journal of national standing, in 2021 there are a number of women in such roles. *Poetry Ireland* is edited by Colette Bryce, *Poetry Review* by Emily Berry, *Poetry London* by Martha Sprackland, and *PN Review* is joined by contributing editors Vahni Capildeo and Sasha Dugdale. New poetry journals, both print and online, are also edited by women, e.g. *Poetry Birmingham Literary Journal* is edited by Suna Afshan and Naush Sabah, while *bath magg* is co-edited by Mariah Whelan. The T. S. Eliot Prize in 2021 was chaired by Lavinia Greenlaw and awarded to Bhanu Kapil for *How to Wash a Heart*, edited by Deryn Rees-Jones at Pavilion Press. In 2020 all the Eric Gregory Awards for emerging poets were won by women – Amina Jama, Kadish Morris, Natalie Linh Bolderston, Roseanne Watt and Susannah Dickey.

Obviously, there is still work to do. Women remain significantly underrepresented as editors-in-chief at major poetry publishing houses. In 2021 the poetry lists of Bloodaxe, Cape, Carcanet, Faber, Penguin and Picador are all edited by men. Bucking this trend are Granta, where since 2020 Rachel Allen edits their new poetry list, and smaller independent presses such as Nine Arches Press, edited by Jane Commane.

Equally as important as the new horizons set for women poets is the fact that the concurrent laureate service of these once outsiders embodies hope that cultural establishments can embrace diversity, whether of gender, race, social class or religion. Their tenures have set a pace for change, and demonstrate that the perspective of the cosmopolitan elite need no longer prevail. A case in point is the enterprise of the Ledbury Emerging Critics, established in 2017 by poets Sandeep Parmar and Sarah Howe to analyse and increase the diversity of poetry reviewing by Black, Asian and Minority Ethnic (BAME) critics. If the four nations of the UK are to feel at ease with themselves there is urgent need for the 12.9 per cent of the UK population identifying as BAME in the 2011 census, set to rise in 2021, to be proportionately represented in cultural conversation and leadership roles. Only when there is sustained parity of representation can a new equilibrium be found, and the binary thinking (us/them, male/female, BAME/not BAME) that is a necessary instrument in the achievement of socio-economic and cultural equality be left behind. Only then will the literal numbers and percentages of representation cease to be significant. The need for these changes to take place is made more urgent by the Black Lives Matter campaigns of 2020 and the reverses to both gender and race equality in the UK brought about or exposed by the Covid-19 pandemic.

At the same time, the poets at the heart of this study have, throughout their writing lives, resisted the disempowerments of hierarchical binary thought. The margin, which was once a place in which to be female, poor, Scottish, and overlooked, has become in their work simply a place in which to be human. By writing away from London-centric cosmopolitanism, as indeed their latterly achieved appointments demand, each of these poets has transformed the significance and value of what was once a negatively feminised space. Eavan Boland, amongst the first to find her poetry dismissed for its preoccupation with experience at the edges of masculine power and tradition, reclaims the space and expands its metaphoric resonance. She finds there a picture of Ireland: 'Our island that was once/Settled and removed on the edge/Of Europe',[8] and ultimately a metaphor for the human condition. Her poetry, her language, she writes in the late poem 'Margin', has been a way of making a place for herself where 'I could stand if only for one moment/on its margin'.[9]

Gillian Clarke conceives of poetry itself as a liminal space where the mortal can be touched by immortality, where movement and stasis connect. In 'The Presence' she observes that a 'living thing once seen' will 'never be gone'; instead, its breath lingers 'between field and lawn. There. Not there'.[10] The creature inhabits a border between wild and cultivated, between being and not being, an ever-shifting boundary which marks out the path that Clarke's poetry treads. Paula Meehan celebrates the interstices of the liminal, the interpenetration of being and not being, presence and absence, memorialised in 'Death of a Field' and the orchestrated breath of its mantra, 'The end of dandelion is the start of Flash'.[11] The purpose of poetry to capture the transient is articulated too by Liz Lochhead's avowal that the poet pursues the 'fugitive colours of the day'.[12] Carol Ann Duffy finds in transience a shared humanity, reaching beyond the boundaries of nation to the precarious contingence of life itself, watching the night sky as her own breath seeks 'its rightful place/with the stars,/with everyone else who breathes.'[13]

The conditions of edge, liminality and transience, once imposed on female gender, have been expanded through these poets' works to encompass the relative positioning of nations, and are ultimately tuned to enrich understanding of being mortal, as destination and as point of departure.

Notes

1. Clarke, 'Voice of the Tribe', in *At the Source*, p. 61.
2. Richards, 'Poetry not just for the posh'.
3. Duffy (ed.), *Jubilee Lines*.
4. Duffy, 'Mrs Skinner, North Street', in *The Other Country*, *Collected Poems*, p. 133.
5. Rees-Jones, 'A Dog's Chance', p. 152.
6. See <https://www.liverpool.ac.uk/new-and-international-writing/emerging-critics/ledbury-poetry-critics,2020-annual-report/> (accessed 29 January 2021).
7. See <https://www.liverpool.ac.uk/media/livacuk/schoolofthearts/documents/english/State,of,Poetry,and,Poetry,Reviewing,2020,Ledbury,Critics,Report,-,final.pdf> (accessed 29 January 2021).
8. Boland, 'Our Future Will Become The Past of Other Women', in *The Historians*, p. 66.
9. Boland, 'Margin', in *The Historians*, p. 59.
10. Clarke, 'The Presence', in *Zoology*, p. 13.
11. Meehan, 'Death of a Field', in *Painting Rain*, p. 13.
12. Lochhead, 'How to Be the Perfect Romantic Poet', in *Fugitive Colours*, p. 33.
13. Duffy, 'Sincerity', in *Sincerity*, p. 75.

Works Cited

Books, Articles and Documents

Academi, 'National Poet of Wales 2010–2011. Contract between Gillian Clarke, National Poet of Wales, and Academi for the period from 1 April 2010 to 31 March 2011'.

Allardice, Lisa, 'Carol Ann Duffy: "With the evil twins of Trump and Brexit"', *Guardian*, 27 October 2018.

Anderson, Hephzibah, 'Christmas Carol', *Guardian*, 4 December 2005.

Andrews, Kehinde, 'Building Brexit on the myth of empire ignores our brutal history', *Guardian*, 7 March 2017.

Anglo-Welsh Review, 64 (1979); 65 (1979); 69 (1981); 72 (1982); 75 (1984); 78 (1984).

Anonymous, 'The English Poet Laureate and his love of retirement', *The Albion: A Journal of News, Politics and Literature*, 51.1 (1873), p. 12.

Anonymous, 'The New Laureate at Work', *Current Literature*, 19.2 (1896), p. 94.

Anonymous, 'Speech and the Radio', *The Youth's Companion*, 100.17 (29 April 1926), p. 328.

Auerbach, Nina, 'Introduction: Women and Nations', *Tulsa Studies in Women's Literature*, 6.2 (1987), pp. 181–8.

Bakhtin, M. M., 'Response to a Question for the *Novy Mir* Editorial Staff', in Caryl Emerson and Michael Holquist (eds), *Speech Genres and Other Late Essays* (Austin: University of Texas Press, 1986), p. 6.

Barry, Maggie, 'Acclaimed writer Carol Ann Duffy on Rabbie Burns', *Daily Record*, 7 August 2011.

BBC News, 'Wales to get its own "poet laureate"', 26 February 2005, <http://news.bbc.co.uk/1/hi/wales/4300625.stm> (accessed 27 August 2016).

BBC News, 'Clarke named Wales' national poet', 31 March 2008, <http://news.bbc.co.uk/1/hi/wales/7323258.stm> (accessed 27 August 2016).

Belfast Telegraph, 'Meehan is new poetry professor', 14 September 2013.

Benton, Peter, 'Unweaving the rainbow: poetry teaching in the secondary school', *Oxford Review of Education*, 25.4 (1999), pp. 521–31.

Benton, Peter, 'The Conveyor Belt Curriculum? Poetry Teaching in the Secondary School II', *Oxford Review of Education*, 26.1 (2000), pp. 81–93.

Bertram, Vicki (ed.), *Kicking Daffodils: Twentieth-Century Women Poets* (Edinburgh: Edinburgh University Press, 1997).

Bertram, Vicki, 'Editorial: Contemporary Women Poets', *Feminist Review*, 62 (1999), pp. 1–5.

Bhabha, Homi K., *The Location of Culture* (London and New York: Routledge, 1994).

Billington, Michael, 'My Country: A Work in Progress review – Carol Ann Duffy tackles Brexit', *Guardian*, 12 March 2017.

Blake, J. V., *What Did the National Curriculum Do for Poetry? Pattern, Prescription and Contestation in the Poetry Selected for GCSE English Literature 1988–2018*, PhD thesis (University of Cambridge, 2020), <https://doi.org/10.17863/CAM.47726> (accessed 3 May 2021).

Boland, Eavan, *Outside History: Selected Poems 1980–1990* (New York: Norton, 1990).

Boland, Eavan, *Collected Poems* (Manchester: Carcanet, 1995).

Boland, Eavan, '"Gods make their own importance: the authority of the poet in our time" – The Ronald Duncan Lecture 1994', *PN Review*, 21.4 (1995), pp. 10–14.

Boland, Eavan, *Object Lessons: The Life of the Woman and the Poet in Our Time* (Manchester: Carcanet, 1995).

Boland, Eavan, 'Unfinished Business: The Communal Art of Paula Meehan', *An Sionnach: A Journal of Literature, Culture, and the Arts*, 5.1–2 (2009), pp. 17–24.

Boland, Eavan, *A Journey with Two Maps* (Manchester: Carcanet, 2011).

Boland, Eavan, 'A Woman Without a Country', *PN Review*, 41.2 (2014), p. 45.

Boland, Eavan, *A Woman without a Country* (Manchester: Carcanet, 2014).

Boland, Eavan, *Eavan Boland: A Poet's Dublin*, ed. Paula Meehan and Jody Allen Randolph (Manchester: Carcanet, 2014).

Boland, Eavan, 'Romantic readings: "To My Sister", by William Wordsworth', <https://wordsworth.org.uk/blog/2016/12/25/romantic-readings-to-my-sister-by-william-wordsworth/> (accessed 25 March 2020).

Boland, Eavan, *The Historians* (Manchester: Carcanet, 2020).

Boland, Rosita, 'Paula Meehan is named Ireland professor of poetry', *The Irish Times*, 14 September 2013.

Boyd, Brian, 'Hot Licks', *Irish Times*, 13 November 1992.

Boyd, S. J., 'The Voice of Revelation: Liz Lochhead and Monsters', in Robert Crawford and Anne Varty (eds), *The Edinburgh Companion to Liz Lochhead* (Edinburgh: Edinburgh University Press, 1993), pp. 38–56.

Broadus, Edmund Kemper, *The Laureateship: A study of the office of poet laureate in England, with some account of the poets* (Oxford: Clarendon Press, 1921).

Brown, Mark, 'Poets, palaces and butts of sherry: exhibition brings poets laureate to life', *Guardian*, 6 August 2014.

Bryant, Marsha, *Women's Poetry and Popular Culture* (London: Palgrave Macmillan, 2011).

Butler, Susan (ed.), *Common Ground: Poets in a Welsh Landscape* (Bridgend: Poetry Wales Press, 1985).

Carrell, Severin, 'Scotland stalls on new poet laureate', *Guardian*, 3 January 2011.

Carruthers, Gerard, 'Scotland, Britain and the Elsewhere of Poetry', in Natalie Pollard (ed.), *Don Paterson: Contemporary Critical Essays* (Edinburgh: Edinburgh University Press, 2014), pp. 85–97.

Childs, Tony, *Revise the NEAB Anthology for GCSE English Literature 2000/2001* (Oxford: Heinemann, 1999).

Clapp, Susannah, 'My Country: A Work in Progress review – a laudable but limp look at Brexit Britain', *Observer*, 19 March 2017.

Clarke, Gillian, *Snow on the Mountain* (Swansea: Christopher Davies, 1971).

Clarke, Gillian, *The Sundial* (Llandysul: Gomer Press, 1978).

Clarke, Gillian, 'Letter from a Far Country', *Poetry Wales*, 16.1 (1980), pp. 7–19.

Clarke, Gillian, *Letter from a Far Country* (Manchester: Carcanet, 1982).

Clarke, Gillian, 'A Musical Nation', *Poetry Review*, 72.2 (1982), pp. 48–51.

Clarke, Gillian, 'Beyond the Boundaries: A Symposium on Gender in Poetry', *Planet: The Welsh Internationalist*, 66 (1987/8), pp. 60–1.

Clarke, Gillian, *Letting in the Rumour* (Manchester: Carcanet, 1989).

Clarke, Gillian, *The King of Britain's Daughter* (Manchester: Carcanet, 1993).

Clarke, Gillian, 'Beginning with Bendigeidfran', in Jane Aaron et al. (eds), *Our Sisters' Land: The Changing Identities of Women in Wales* (Cardiff: University of Wales Press, 1994), pp. 286–93.

Clarke, Gillian, 'The Traders and the Troubadours', in R. Geralt Jones (ed.), *Towards the Millennium* (Newton, Powys: Gwisg Gregynog Ltd, 1995), p. 12.

Clarke, Gillian, 'The King of Britain's Daughter', in Tony Curtis (ed.), *How Poets Work* (Bridgend: Seren, 1996), pp. 122–36.

Clarke, Gillian, *Five Fields* (Manchester: Carcanet, 1998).

Clarke, Gillian, *Nine Green Gardens* (Llandysul: Gomer Press, 2000).

Clarke, Gillian, *Making Beds for the Dead* (Manchester: Carcanet, 2004).
Clarke, Gillian, *At the Source* (Manchester: Carcanet, 2008).
Clarke, Gillian, 'Mother Tongue', *South Wales Evening Post*, 1 April 2008.
Clarke, Gillian, *A Recipe for Water* (Manchester: Carcanet, 2009).
Clarke, Gillian, *Ice* (Manchester: Carcanet, 2012).
Clarke, Gillian, 'National Poet of Wales/Bardd Cenedlaethol Cymru, Report, April–October 2013-10-20', Literature Wales Archive.
Clarke, Gillian, 'National Poet of Wales/Bardd Genedlaethol Cymru. 1. Retrospective report: October 2014 – April 2015. 2. Forthcoming events and commissions for 2015', Literature Wales Archive.
Clarke, Gillian, *Zoology* (Manchester: Carcanet, 2017).
Clune, Jackie, 'Hearing Voices: Monologues and Revues', in Robert Crawford and Anne Varty (eds), *Liz Lochhead's Voices* (Edinburgh: Edinburgh University Press, 1993), pp. 75–92.
Coles, Jane, '"Every child's birthright"? Democratic entitlement and the role of canonical literature in the English National Curriculum', *Curriculum Journal*, 24.1 (2013), pp. 50–66.
Conboy, Katie, 'Revisionist Cartography: The Politics of Place in Boland and Heaney', in Kathryn Kirkpatrick (ed.), *Border Crossings: Irish Women Writers and National Identity* (Dublin: Wolfhound Press, 2000), pp. 190–203.
Conran, Anthony, 'Lynette Roberts: War Poet', *Anglo-Welsh Review*, 65 (1979), pp. 50–62.
Craig, Cairns, *Out of History: Narrative Paradigms in Scottish and English Culture* (Edinburgh: Polygon, 1996).
Crawford, Robert, *Devolving English Literature* (Oxford: Clarendon Press, 1992).
Crawford, Robert, *Identifying Poets: Self and Territory in Twentieth Century Poetry* (Edinburgh: Edinburgh University Press, 1993).
Crawford, Robert, 'On "Something I'm Not"', in Anne Varty (ed.), *The Edinburgh Companion to Liz Lochhead* (Edinburgh: Edinburgh University Press, 2013), pp. 15–18.
Crompton, Sarah, 'Review: *My Country: A Work in Progress* (Dorfman, National Theatre)', *What's on Stage*, 10 March 2017, <https://www.whatsonstage.com/london-theatre/reviews/my-country-a-work-in-progress-dorfman-national_43092.html> (accessed 17 December 2020).
Crown, Sarah, 'The Contenders', *Guardian*, 3 January 2011.
Crown, Sarah, 'Liz Lochhead', *Guardian*, 16 January 2016.
Cunningham, John, 'Animal rights campaigner', *Guardian*, 8 February 1990.
Curtis, Polly, 'Top exam board asks schools to destroy book containing knife poem', *Guardian*, 4 September 2008.

Daily Mirror, 'Carol Ann Duffy: "Poetry is in your everyday life"', 2 May 2009.

Dalby, Douglas, 'A Contest Honors Ireland's Poets and Past', *New York Times*, 12 March 2015.

Dawson, Emma, 'Re-visioning the National Curriculum at KS3 and 4 and its Stipulation to Teach Literature "From Different Cultures and Traditions"', *Changing English*, 16.2 (2009), pp. 193–201.

Denholm, Andrew, 'Teachers criticise limited list of Scottish exam texts', *Herald (Glasgow)*, 29 November 2012.

DfE and Welsh Office, *English in the National Curriculum* (London: HMSO, 1995).

Donovan, Katie, 'Poetry with a Purpose', *Irish Times*, 8 March 1993.

Donovan, Katie, 'Passion's Battles', *Irish Times*, 11 August 1994.

Dorgan, Theo, 'An Interview with Paula Meehan', *Colby Quarterly*, 28.4 (1992); pp. 265–9.

Doug, Roshan, 'The British schools' National Curriculum: English and the politics of teaching poetry from "different cultures and traditions"', *Journal of Curriculum Studies*, 43.4 (2011), pp. 439–56.

Dougary, Ginny, 'Poetry is the music of being human', *Times*, 1 October 2011.

Dowson, Jane, '"Older sisters are very sobering things": Contemporary Women Poets and the Female Affiliation Complex', *Feminist Review*, 62 (1999), pp. 6–20.

Dowson, Jane, *Carol Ann Duffy: Poet for Our Times* (London: Palgrave Macmillan, 2016).

Doyle, Martin, 'Brexit is aggressive and dangerously nostalgic', *Irish Times*, 29 March 2019.

Draper, Dave, Chris Sutcliffe, Imelda Pilgrim and Peter Thomas, *Carol Ann Duffy and Simon Armitage: Working with the Literature Anthology for AQA A 2004–6* (Oxford: Heinemann, 2004).

Draper, Dave, Chris Sutcliffe, Imelda Pilgrim and Peter Thomas, *Seamus Heaney and Gillian Clarke: Working with the Literature Anthology for AQA A 2004–6* (Oxford: Heinemann, 2004).

Duffy, Carol Ann, *Standing Female Nude* (London: Anvil Press, 1985).

Duffy, Carol Ann, *Selling Manhattan* (London: Anvil Press, 1987).

Duffy, Carol Ann, *The Other Country* (London: Anvil Press, 1990).

Duffy, Carol Ann, *Mean Time* (London: Anvil Press Poetry, 1993).

Duffy, Carol Ann, *The World's Wife* (London: Anvil Press, 1999).

Duffy, Carol Ann, *Feminine Gospels* (London: Picador, 2002).

Duffy, Carol Ann, *Rapture* (London: Picador, 2005).

Duffy, Carol Ann (ed.), *Answering Back: Living poets reply to the poetry of the past* (London: Picador, 2008).

Duffy, Carol Ann, 'Sisters in Poetry', *Guardian*, 2 May 2009.
Duffy, Carol Ann, 'Politics', *Guardian*, 13 June 2009.
Duffy, Carol Ann, 'The 12 Days of Christmas', *Daily Mirror*, 7 December 2009.
Duffy, Carol Ann, *The Bees* (London: Picador, 2011).
Duffy, Carol Ann, 'Poems for a wedding', *Guardian*, 23 April 2011.
Duffy, Carol Ann (ed.), *Jubilee Lines* (London: Faber and Faber, 2012).
Duffy, Carol Ann, 'Poetry: Permission not to be nice', *Guardian*, 3 November 2012.
Duffy, Carol Ann, *Ritual Lighting* (London: Picador, 2014).
Duffy, Carol Ann, 'September 2014', *Guardian*, 23 September 2014.
Duffy, Carol Ann, *Collected Poems* (London: Picador, 2015).
Duffy, Carol Ann, 'Poets' tour: "the UK has been torn in two like a bad poem"', 'Shore to Shore tour diary', *Guardian* blog, 24 June 2016, <https://www.theguardian.com/books/2016/jun/24/poets-on-tour-part-five-carol-ann-duffy> (accessed 3 May 2021).
Duffy, Carol Ann, 'Poets' tour: reaching the "unsure shore"', 'Shore to Shore tour diary', *Guardian* blog, 7 July 2016, <https://www.theguardian.com/books/2016/jul/07/poets-tour-reaching-the-unsure-shore> (accessed 3 May 2021).
Duffy, Carol Ann, *Sincerity* (London: Picador, 2018).
Duffy, Carol Ann, 'Poems to get us through', *Guardian*, 9 April 2020.
Duffy, Carol Ann and Rufus Norris, *My Country: A Work in Progress* (London: Faber and Faber, 2017).
Duffy, Carol Ann, 'Carol Ann Duffy's favourite poems', Pan Macmillan blog, 11 February 2021, <https://www.panmacmillan.com/blogs/literary/carol-ann-duffy-favourite-poems> (accessed 3 May 2021).
Dugdale, John, 'Robert Burns: was the beloved poet a "Weinsteinian sex pest"?', *Guardian*, 24 January 2018.
Dymoke, Sue, 'The Dead Hand of the Exam: The impact of the NEAB anthology on poetry teaching at GCSE', *Changing English*, 9.1 (2002), pp. 85–93.
Eaglestone, Robert, 'Cruel Nostalgia and the Memory of the Second World War', in Robert Eaglestone (ed.), *Brexit and Literature: Critical and Cultural Responses* (London: Routledge, 2018), pp. 92–104.
Elfin, Menna (ed.), *Trying the Line: A Volume of Tribute to Gillian Clarke* (Llandysul: Gomer Press, 1997).
Eliot, T. S., *The Sacred Wood: Essays on Poetry and Criticism* (London: Methuen and Co., 1920).
Elliott, Victoria, 'The treasure house of a nation? Literary heritage, curriculum and devolution in Scotland and England in the twenty-first century', *Curriculum Journal*, 25.2 (2014), pp. 282–300.

Elliott, Victoria, 'Gender and the contemporary educational canon in the UK', *International Journal of English Studies*, 17.2 (2017), pp. 45–62.

Ellison, Mike, 'Birth of the Muse', *Guardian*, 13 January 1994.

English, Shirley and Jack Malvern, 'Poetic justice for the free-thinking Scots', *Times*, 17 February 2004.

Entwistle, Alice, *Poetry, Geography, Gender: Women Rewriting Contemporary Wales* (Cardiff: University of Wales Press, 2013).

Flood, Alison, 'Carol Ann Duffy becomes first female poet laureate', *Guardian*, 1 May 2009.

Flood, Alison, 'Leeds academy unveils mural', *Guardian*, 21 November 2011.

Flood, Alison, 'Poet laureate writes sonnet for Danny Boyle's Armistice Day centenary events', *Guardian*, 22 October 2018.

Flood, Alison, 'Carol Ann Duffy leads British poets creating "living record" of coronavirus', *Guardian*, 20 April 2020.

Forbes, Peter, 'Winning lines', *Guardian*, 31 August 2002.

Fowler, Rebecca, 'New generation reclaims poetry', *Sunday Times*, 24 April 1994.

Galloway, Janice, 'Introduction', in *Meantime: Looking Forward to the Millenium – An Anthology of Women's Writing* (Edinburgh: Polygon, in association with Women 2000, 1991), pp. 1–8.

Gentleman, Amelia, 'Rufus Norris: "We are living in an age of extreme selfishness"', *Guardian*, 27 February 2017.

Ghosh, Ranjan (ed.), *Philosophy and Poetry: Continental Perspectives* (New York: Columbia University Press, 2019).

Gill, Jo, *Women's Poetry* (Edinburgh: Edinburgh University Press, 2016).

Gish, Nancy K., 'Shakespeare and the Invention of Language', in Anne Varty (ed.), *The Edinburgh Companion to Liz Lochhead* (Edinburgh: Edinburgh University Press), pp. 48–60.

Glaister, Lesley, 'Picture This', *Scottish Review of Books*, 10 August 2016.

Gonda, Caroline, 'An Other Country? Mapping Scottish/Lesbian/Writing', in Christopher Whyte (ed.), *Gendering the Nation: Studies in Modern Scottish Literature* (Edinburgh: Edinburgh University Press, 1995), pp. 1–24.

González, Carla Rodríguez, '"Scotland, Whit Like?" Coloured Voices in Historical Territories', in Meere Falck Borch, Eva Rask Knudsen, Martin Loer and Bruce Clunies Ross (eds), *Bodies and Voices: The Force-Field of Representation and Discourse in Colonial and Postcolonial Studies* (Amsterdam: Rodopi, 2008), pp. 363–77.

González-Arias, Luz Mar, '"Playing with the ghosts of words": An Interview with Paula Meehan', *Atlantis*, 22.1 (2000), pp. 187–204.

Goodson, Ivor F., '"Nations at risk" and "national curriculum": ideology and identity', *Journal of Education Policy*, 5.5 (1990), pp. 219–32.

Gordon, John, 'Sound[']s right: pupils' responses to heard poetry and the revised National Curriculum for English', *Curriculum Journal*, 20.2 (2009), pp. 161–75.

Goring, Rosemary, 'This is a woman's world', *Herald (Glasgow)*, 23 October 2004.

Goring, Rosemary, 'Makar Jackie Kay says Brexit vote could force her to quit Manchester home for Scotland', *Herald (Glasgow)*, 10 July 2016.

Gorman, Sophie, 'Spirit of Heaney fills room as poets gather', *Irish Independent*, 14 September 2013.

Greer, Germaine, *Slip-Shod Sibyls: Recognition, Rejection and the Woman Poet* (London: Penguin, [1995] 1996).

Gregson, Ian, *Contemporary Poetry and Postmodernism: Dialogue and Estrangement* (Bayswater: Macmillan, 1996).

Guardian, 'The female poets who have earned their laurels', 3 March 2014.

Guardian, 'Sometimes the world goes feral – 11 odes to Europe', 9 December 2019.

Hampson, Robert, 'Custodians and Active Citizens', in Jonathan Bate (ed.), *The Public Value of the Humanities* (London: Bloomsbury Academic, 2011), pp. 68–75.

Hardy, Barbara, 'Women Poets', *Poetry Wales*, 15.9 (1979), pp. 84–9.

Herald (Glasgow), 'Teachers slam SNP "diktat" over Scottish question in English exam', 10 June 2012.

Hoffenberg, Peter H., 'Landscape, Memory and the Australian War Experience', *Journal of Contemporary History*, 36.1 (2001), pp. 111–31.

Hulse, Michael, David Kennedy and David Morley (eds), *The New Poetry* (Newcastle: Bloodaxe Books, 1993).

Hurtley, Jacqueline, Rosa González, Inés Praga and Esther Aliaga, *Ireland in Writing: Interviews with Writers and Academics* (Amsterdam/Atlanta, GA: Rodopi, 1998).

Irish Daily Mail, 'Poet Meehan honoured with top accolade', 14 September 2013.

Jamie, Kathleen, 'Holding Fast – Truth and Change in Poetry', in W. N. Herbert and Matthew Hollis (eds), *Strong Words: Modern Poets on Modern Poetry* (Newcastle-upon-Tyne, 2000), pp. 277–81.

Jarvis, Matthew, 'Repositioning Wales: Poetry after the Second Flowering', in Daniel Williams (ed.), *Slanderous Tongues: Essays on Welsh Poetry in English 1970–2005* (Bridgend: Seren, 2010), pp. 21–59.

Johnston, Neil, 'Montague takes Chair of Poetry', *Belfast Telegraph*, 15 May 1998.

Kay, Jackie, *Other Lovers* (Newcastle: Bloodaxe, 1993).

Kay, Jackie, 'Poets on tour, part four: in and out with lettuce and lardy cake', 'Shore to Shore tour diary', *Guardian* blog, 23 June 2016, <https://www.theguardian.com/books/2016/jun/23/poets-tour-part-four-in-and-out-with-lettuce-and-lardy-bread> (accessed 3 May 2021).

Kearney, Maire, 'Broadcast News', *Irish Times*, 1 September 2001.

Kennedy, Maev, 'Carol Ann Duffy poem celebrates Dover's famous white cliffs', *Guardian*, 7 November 2012.

Kennedy, Maev and Severin Carrell, 'Liz Lochhead appointed as makar, Scotland's national poet', *Guardian*, 19 January 2011.

Kerrigan, John, 'Divided Kingdoms and the Local Epic: "Mercian Hymns" to "The King of Britain's Daughter"', *The Yale Journal of Criticism*, 13.1 (2000), pp. 3–21.

Kinnahan, Linda, *Lyric Interventions: Feminism, Experimental Poetry, and Contemporary Discourse* (Iowa City: University of Iowa Press, 2004).

Kirkpatrick, Kathryn (ed.), *Border Crossings: Irish Women Writers and National Identities* (Tuscaloosa, AL: University of Alabama Press, 2000).

Kirkpatrick, Kathryn, '"A Murmuration of Starlings in a Rowan Tree": Finding Gary Snyder in Paula Meehan's Eco-Political Poetics', *An Sionnach: A Journal of Literature, Culture, and the Arts*, 5.1 and 2 (2009), pp. 195–207.

Kirkpatrick, Kathryn, 'Between Country and City: Paula Meehan's Ecofeminist Poetics', in Christine Cusick (ed.), *Out of the Earth: Ecocritical Readings of Irish Texts* (Cork: Cork University Press, 2010), pp. 108–26.

Kirkpatrick, Kathryn, '*Geomantic* by Paula Meehan (review)', *New Hibernia Review*, 21.3 (2017), pp. 148–50.

Knittel, Janna and Paula Meehan, '"Nature Doesn't Stop at the Limits of the City": An Interview with Paula Meehan', *New Hibernia Review*, 20.1 (2016), pp. 77–86.

Lane, Harriet, 'I think, therefore iamb', *Observer*, 23 May 1999.

Lawrie, Campbell, 'How they created the NT's Brexit play *My Country*', *What's on Stage*, 10 March 2017, <https://www.whatsonstage.com/bath-theatre/news/how-they-created-the-nts-brexit-play-my-country_43103.html> (accessed 15 December 2020).

Lazebnik, Rob, 'Arise! Arise! The British Are . . . Acting!', *Wall Street Journal*, 23 March 2013.

Ledbury Poetry Critics, *The State of Poetry and Poetry Criticism*, 2020 Annual Report, <https://www.liverpool.ac.uk/media/livacuk/schoolofthearts/documents/english/State,of,Poetry,and,Poetry,Reviewing,2020,Ledbury,Critics,Report,-,final.pdf> (accessed 3 May 2021).

Light, Alison, 'Outside History? Stevie Smith, Women Poets and the National Voice', *English*, 43 (1994), pp. 237–59.

Lister, David, 'New generation of writers presents poetry in motion', *Independent*, 13 January 1994.
Lloyd, David T. (ed.), *The Urgency of Identity: Contemporary English Language Poetry from Wales* (Evanston, IL: Triquarterly Press, 1994).
Lochhead, Liz, *Dreaming Frankenstein and Collected Poems* (Edinburgh: Polygon, 1984).
Lochhead, Liz, *Islands* in *Dreaming Frankenstein and Collected Poems* (Edinburgh: Polygon Books, 1984).
Lochhead, Liz, *Memo for Spring* in *Dreaming Frankenstein and Collected Poems* (Edinburgh: Polygon Books, 1984).
Lochhead, Liz, *True Confessions and New Clichés* (Edinburgh: Polygon, 1985).
Lochhead, Liz, *Mary Queen of Scots Got Her Head Chopped Off & Dracula* (London: Penguin, 1989).
Lochhead, Liz, *Bagpipe Muzak* (London: Penguin, 1991).
Lochhead, Liz, *Britannia Rules* (Learning and Teaching Scotland, 2003).
Lochhead, Liz, *The Colour of Black and White* (Edinburgh: Polygon, 2003).
Lochhead, Liz, *A Choosing: Selected Poems* (Edinburgh: Polygon, 2011).
Lochhead, Liz, 'Opening the doors again', *Herald*, 2 July 2011.
Lochhead, Liz, 'Review of *The Bees*', *Guardian*, 4 November 2011.
Lochhead, Liz, 'My Hero Robert Burns', *Guardian*, 26 January 2013.
Lochhead, Liz, *Fugitive Colours* (Edinburgh: Polygon, 2016).
London Evening Standard, 'Ten years late, this lesbian icon is the right poet for the nation', 1 May 2009.
Longley, Edna, *From Cathleen to Anorexia: The Breakdown of Irelands* (Dublin: Attic Press, 1990).
MacAvock, Desmond, 'Poets and Painters at the Rubicon Gallery', *Irish Times*, 30 July 1992.
MacMonagle, Niall, 'Conference Preview', *Irish Times*, 26 June 1999.
Maguire, Sarah, 'Dilemmas and Developments: Eavan Boland Re-Examined', *Feminist Review*, 62 (1999), pp. 58–66.
Major, Nick, 'The SRB Interview: Carol Ann Duffy', *Scottish Review of Books*, 10 November 2018.
Manchester Metropolitan University Magazine, 'The Music of Being Human', <https://www2.mmu.ac.uk/metmagazine/story/index.php?id=10269> (accessed 20 February 2021).
Markham, E. A., *Love Poems* (Cambridge: Lobby Press, 1979).
Marks, Peter, *Literature of the 1990s: Endings and Beginnings* (Edinburgh: Edinburgh University Press, 2018).
Marsack, Robyn, 'On the National Poet's First Year', in Anne Varty (ed.), *The Edinburgh Companion to Liz Lochhead* (Edinburgh: Edinburgh University Press, 2013), pp. 9–13.

McClements, Freya, '"My passport's green": why was Seamus Heaney used in Northern Ireland branding?', *Irish Times*, 19 December 2020.

McCrum, Robert, 'The royal family doesn't need a poet', *Guardian*, 1 December 2008.

McCulloch, Margery Palmer, 'Women and Scottish Poetry, 1972–1999', *The Irish Review*, 28 (2001), pp. 58–74.

Mcfarlane, Mhairi, 'Knife crime and poetry', *Nottingham Evening Post*, 9 September 2008.

McGann, Jerome J., 'Laura (Riding) Jackson and the Literal Truth', *Critical Inquiry*, 18.3 (1992), pp. 454–73.

McGuckian, Medbh, 'Kepler 452B', *The Lonely Crowd*, issue 8, 11 April 2017, <https://thelonelycrowd.org/2017/11/04/kepler-452b-by-medbh-mcguckian/> (accessed 2 January 2021).

McMillan, Dorothy, 'Twentieth-century Poetry II: The Last Twenty-five Years', in Douglas Gifford and Dorothy McMillan (eds), *A History of Scottish Women's Writing* (Edinburgh: Edinburgh University Press, 1997), p. 549–78.

McMillan, Dorothy, 'Choices: Poems 1972–2011', in Anne Varty (ed.), *The Edinburgh Companion to Liz Lochhead* (Edinburgh: Edinburgh University Press, 2013), pp. 25–36.

Meehan, Paula, *Return and No Blame* (Dublin: Beaver Row Press, 1984).

Meehan, Paula, *Reading the Sky* (Dublin: Beaver Row Press, 1986).

Meehan, Paula, *The Man Who Was Marked by Winter* (Loughcrew: The Gallery Press, 1991).

Meehan, Paula, *Pillow Talk* (Loughcrew: The Gallery Press, 1994).

Meehan, Paula, *The Mysteries of the Home* (Newcastle: Bloodaxe, 1996).

Meehan, Paula, *Mrs Sweeney* in Siobhán Bourke (ed.), *Rough Magic: First Plays* (Dublin: New Island Books, 1999), pp. 393–464.

Meehan, Paula, *Cell: A Play in Two Parts for Four Actors and a Voice* (Dublin: New Island Books, 2000).

Meehan, Paula, *Dharmakaya* (Manchester: Carcanet, 2000).

Meehan, Paula, *Painting Rain* (Manchester: Carcanet, 2009).

Meehan, Paula, 'Poetry and the power of healing', *Irish Times*, 6 October 2009.

Meehan, Paula, 'Ireland Chair of Poetry: Report to the Trustees 2013–2014', Ireland Chair of Poetry Trust Archives.

Meehan, Paula, 'Ireland Chair of Poetry: Report to the Trustees 2014–2015', Ireland Chair of Poetry Trust Archives.

Meehan, Paula, 'My favourite W. B. Yeats poem', *Irish Times*, 10 June 2015.

Meehan, Paula, *Geomantic* (Dublin: Dedalus Press, 2016).

Meehan, Paula, *Imaginary Bonnets with Real Bees in Them: Writings from the Ireland Chair of Poetry* (Dublin: University College Dublin Press, 2016).

Michelis, Angelica and Antony Rowland (eds), *The Poetry of Carol Ann Duffy: 'Choosing Tough Words'* (Manchester: Manchester University Press, 2003).

Millar, Frank, 'Carol Ann Duffy becomes first female poet laureate of Britain', *Irish Times*, 2 May 2009.

Moi, Toril, 'I am not a woman writer', *Feminist Theory*, 9.3 (2008), pp. 264–7.

Moore, Matthew, 'Carol Ann Duffy is first woman Poet Laureate', *Telegraph*, 1 May 2009.

Moorhead, Joanna, 'Carol Ann Duffy: Poems are a form of texting', *Guardian*, 5 September 2011.

Morrissey, Sinéad, *Parallax* (Manchester: Carcanet, 2013).

Morrissey, Sinéad, *On Balance* (Manchester: Carcanet, 2017).

Mullen, Adrian, 'Carol Ann Duffy leads the way in Grasmere poetry festival', *Westmorland Gazette*, 23 March 2014.

Nicholson, Colin, 'Knucklebones of Irony', in Colin Nicholson, *Poem, Purpose and Place: Shaping Identity in Contemporary Scottish Verse* (Edinburgh: Polygon, 1992), pp. 203–23.

Nisbet, Robert, 'Poems for Radio', *Anglo-Welsh Review*, 65 (1979), p. 118.

O'Halloran, Eileen, Kelli Maloy and Paula Meehan, 'An Interview with Paula Meehan', *Contemporary Literature*, 43.1 (2002), pp. 1–27.

Olsen, Redell, 'Strategies of Critical Practice: Recent Writing on Experimental and Innovative Poetry by Women – A Review Essay', *Signs*, 33.2 (2008), pp. 371–87.

O'Reilly, Jacqueline, Julie Froud, Sukhdev Johal, Karel Williams, Chris Warhurst, Glenn Morgan, Christopher Grey, Geoffrey Wood, Mike Wright, Robert Boyer, Sabine Frerichs, Suvi Sankari, Akos Rona-Tas and Patrick Le Galés, 'Discussion Forum. Brexit: Understanding the socio-economic origins and consequences', *Socio-Economic Review*, 14.4 (2016), pp. 807–54.

Ostriker, Alicia, *Stealing the Language: The Emergence of Women's Poetry in America* (London: The Women's Press Ltd, 1987).

Ouseby, Jenny, 'GSCE exam poem was "glorifying" knife crime', *Leicester Mercury*, 13 September 2008.

Panecka, Ewa, *Literature and the Monarchy: The Traditional and the Modern Concept of the office of Poet Laureate of England* (Newcastle: Cambridge Scholars Publishing, 2014).

Parker, Andrew, Mary Russo, Doris Sommer and Patricia Yaeger (eds), *Nationalisms and Sexualities* (London: Routledge, 1992).

Peach, Linden, 'Wales and the Cultural Politics of Identity', in James Acheson and Romana Huk (eds), *Contemporary British Poetry: Essays in Theory and Criticism* (Albany: State University of New York Press, 1996), pp. 373–96.

Peach, Linden, 'Paper margins: the "outside" in poetry in the 1980s and 1990s', in Glenda Norquay and Gerry Smyth (eds), *Across the Margins: Cultural identity and change in the Atlantic Archipelago* (Manchester: Manchester University Press, 2002), pp. 101–16.

Poetry Wales, 6.1 (1970); 6.2 (1970); 6.3 (1970); 15.9 (1979); 16.1 (1980); 23.1 (1987); 23.2 (1987).

Powell, David, 'Poet to take on tenure as voice of Wales', *Daily Post (North Wales)*, 4 April 2008.

Preston, John, 'Carol Ann Duffy interview', *Telegraph*, 11 May 2010.

Price, Karen, 'New Calls for Wales to Have Poet Laureate', *Western Mail*, 4 October 2001.

Protherough, Robert and Peter King, *The Challenge of English in the National Curriculum* (London and New York: Routledge, 1995).

Quinn, Justin, 'Eavan Boland', in Gerald Dawe (ed.), *Cambridge Companion to Irish Poets* (Cambridge: Cambridge University Press, 2017), pp. 335–44.

Rahim, Sameer, 'Carol Ann Duffy wins Pen Pinter Prize', *Telegraph*, 13 July 2012.

Randolph, Jody Allen, 'The Body Politic: A Conversation with Paula Meehan', *An Sionnach: A Journal of Literature, Culture, and the Arts*, 5.1 and 2 (2009), pp. 239–71.

Randolph, Jody Allen, '*Painting Rain*: A Conversation with Paula Meehan', *PN Review*, 190 (2009), pp. 48–50.

Randolph, Jody Allen and Michael Schmidt (eds), 'A Celebration of Eavan Boland', *PN Review* 41.2 (2014), pp. 43–6.

Rees-Jones, Deryn, *Carol Ann Duffy* (Plymouth: Northcote House, 1999).

Rees-Jones, Deryn, 'The power of absence: Gillian Clarke in Conversation with Deryn Rees-Jones', *Planet: The Welsh Internationalist*, 144 (2001), pp. 55–60.

Rees-Jones, Deryn, 'A Dog's Chance: The Evolution of Contemporary Women's Poetry?', in Peter Robinson (ed.), *The Oxford Handbook of Contemporary British and Irish Poetry* (Oxford: Oxford University Press, 2013), pp. 152–70.

Reizbaum, Marilyn, 'Canonical Double-Cross: Scottish and Irish Women's Writing', in Karen R. Lawrence (ed.), *Decolonizing Tradition: New Voices of Twentieth-Century Literature Canons* (Urbana and Chicago: University of Illinois Press, 1992), pp. 165–90.

Rich, Adrienne, *Adrienne Rich's Poetry and Prose*, ed. Barbara Charlesworth Gelpi and Albert Gelpi (New York and London: W. W. Norton, 1975).
Richards, Julie, 'Poetry not just for the posh', *The Western Mail*, 14 April 2008.
Roberts, Alison, 'Hit parade of new poets to stop the music on Radio 1', *Times*, 13 January 1994.
Robins, Elizabeth, *Woman's Secret* (London: Garden City Press, 1905).
Rogers, Asha, 'Crossing "other cultures"? Reading Tatamkhulu Afrika's "Nothing's Changed" in the NEAB Anthology', *English in Education*, 49.1 (2015), pp. 80–93.
Ross, Peter, 'Interview with Carol Ann Duffy', *Scotsman*, 2 December 2012.
Rowland, Anthony, 'Love and Masculinity in the Poetry of Carol Ann Duffy', *English*, 50 (2001), pp. 199–217.
Royle, Trevor (ed.), *Jock Tamson's Bairns: Essays on a Scots Childhood* (London: Hamish Hamilton, 1977).
Rumens, Carol, 'A Huff of Rain', *Guardian*, 9 May 2009.
Rumens, Carol, 'Poem of the Week: Vocation by Carol Ann Duffy', *Guardian*, 3 June 2019.
Sampson, Fiona, *Lyric Cousins: Poetry and Musical Form* (Edinburgh: Edinburgh University Press, 2016).
Savage, Claire, 'Poets in the City', *Culture Northern Ireland.Org*, 15 May 2014, <https://www.culturenorthernireland.org/reviews/literature/poets-city> (accessed 3 May 2021).
Schmidt, Michael and Grevel Lindon (eds), *British Poetry since 1960* (Manchester: Carcanet, 1973).
Scotsman, 'Scots literature to be made compulsory part of school exams', 25 January 2012.
Scotsman, 'We're bigger than the referendum', 4 December 2014.
Scullion, Adrienne, 'A Woman's Voice', in Anne Varty (ed.), *Edinburgh Companion to Liz Lochhead* (Edinburgh: Edinburgh University Press, 2013), pp. 116–25.
Severin, Laura, *Poetry off the Page: twentieth-century British women poets in performance* (Aldershot: Ashgate, 2004).
Severin, Laura, 'Distant Resonances Contemporary Scottish Women Poets and African-American Music', *Mosaic: An Interdisciplinary Critical Journal*, 39.1 (2006), pp. 45–59.
Severin, Laura, '*The Colour of Black and White* and Scottish Identity', in Anne Varty (ed.), *The Edinburgh Companion to Liz Lochhead* (Edinburgh: Edinburgh University Press, 2013), pp. 36–47.
Shaw, Michael, 'Board ditches knife poem', *Times Educational Supplement*, 5 September 2008.

Simpson, A., 'National Curriculum Stifling Creativity – Poet Laureate', *Telegraph*, 5 May 2009.
Smith, Jordan, 'Review: Poetry Books', *The Antioch Review*, 68.1 (2010), p. 199.
Smith, Stan, 'The things that words give a name to: The "New Generation" poets and the politics of the hyperreal', *Critical Survey*, 8.3 (1996), pp. 306–22.
Smith, Stan, 'Suburbs of Dissent: Poetry on the Peripheries', *Southwest Review*, 86. 4 (2001), pp. 533–51.
Smith, Stan, *Poetry and Displacement* (Liverpool: Liverpool University Press, 2007).
Stevenson, Anne, 'Houses of Choice', *Poetry Review*, 70.3 (1980), pp. 57–9.
Stevenson, Anne, 'Review: Gillian Clarke, *Selected Poems* (Manchester: Carcanet, 1982)', *Powys Review* 17 (1985), p. 64.
Swift, Carolyn, 'Dance Strokes 11', *Irish Times*, 8 October 1992.
Swift, Carolyn, 'New Music, New Dance', *Irish Times*, 9 June 1994.
Swift, Carolyn, 'Fire in the Soul', *Irish Times*, 13 December 1995.
Taylor, Matthew, 'Scots appoint first poet laureate', *Guardian*, 17 February 2004.
Thomas, Gwyn, 'Dafydd ap Gwilym the Nature Poet', *Poetry Wales*, 8.4 (1973), pp. 28–33.
Thorpe, Adam, 'The candyfloss of attention', *Observer*, 5 June 1994.
Thorpe, Vanessa, 'Laureate puts political spin on 12 days of Christmas', *Guardian*, 6 December 2009.
Thurston, Michael, '"Writing at the Edge": Gillian Clarke's "Cofiant"', *Contemporary Literature*, 44.2 (2003), pp. 275–300.
Timbs, John, 'The First English Poet Laureate', *The Mirror of literature, amusement, and instruction*, 29 May 1830, 15 (430), pp. 367–8.
Trilling, Lionel, 'The Wordsworths', *The New Republic*, 12 August 1942.
Turner, Jenny, 'The blank verse generation', *Guardian*, 16 April 1994.
Varty, Anne, 'National Poets on Tour in June 2016: "Shore to Shore" and Brexit', *The Review of English Studies*, 70.293 (2019), pp. 135–57.
Villar-Argáiz, Pilar, '"Act Locally, Think Globally": Paula Meehan's Local Commitment and Global Consciousness', *An Sionnach: A Journal of Literature, Culture, and the Arts*, 5.1 and 2 (2009), pp. 180–93.
Villar-Argáiz, Pilar, 'The Enchantment of Myth in Paula Meehan's Poetry', *Journal of Irish Studies*, 24 (2009), pp. 91–100.
Viner, Katharine, 'Metre Maid', *Guardian*, 25 September 1999.
Wade, Mike, 'Resign call is bonkers, says Makar', *Times*, 1 December 2014.
Waldram, Hannah, 'Cardiff gets dedicated poem to mark completion of city's new museum', *Guardian*, 2 March 2011.

Warner, Marina, *Monuments and Maidens: The Allegory of the Female Form* (London: Weidenfeld and Nicholson, 1985).
Waters, Colin, 'The SRB Interview: Liz Lochhead', *Scottish Review of Books*, 12 November 2011.
Western Mail, 'Poets are really nice to each other; I think it's because we don't earn much', 26 October 2012.
Wexford People, 'Readings were a "celebration of poetry"', 10 March 2015.
White, Victoria, 'Trojan work for change', *Irish Times*, 1 June 1993.
Wilson, Rebecca E. and Gillean Somerville-Arjat (eds), *Sleeping with Monsters: Conversations with Scottish and Irish Women Poets* (Edinburgh: Polygon, 1990).
Winterson, Jeanette, 'A Return to Simple Pleasures', *Times*, 29 August 2009.
Winterson, Jeanette, 'On the poetry of Carol Ann Duffy – of course it's political', *Guardian*, 17 January 2015.
Woolf, Virginia, *Three Guineas* (London: Hogarth Press, 1938).
Wordsworth, Dorothy, *The Grasmere and Alfoxden Journals*, ed. Pamela Woof (Oxford: Oxford University Press, 2008).
Wroe, Nicholas, 'The great performer', *Guardian*, 26 May 2007.
Wroe, Nicholas, 'Carol Ann Duffy on five years as poet laureate', *Guardian*, 27 Sept 2014.
Yeats, W. B., *Collected Poems* (London: Macmillan, [1933, 2nd ed.] 1981).
Yun, Jihyun, 'The Power of Women's Laughter in Carol Ann Duffy's "The Laughter of Stafford Girls' High"', *Texas Studies in Literature and Language*, 61.3 (2019), pp. 291–310.

Websites

Arts Council Ireland, <http://www.artscouncil.ie/Initiatives/The-Ireland-Chair-of-Poetry-Trust/> (accessed 3 May 2021).
Belfast Agreement, 10 April 1998, <https://www.gov.uk/government/publications/the-belfast-agreement> (accessed 3 May 2021).
Clarke, Gillian, <http://www.gillianclarke.co.uk> (accessed 3 May 2021).
Ireland Chair of Poetry, <http://irelandchairofpoetry.org/> (accessed 3 May 2021).
Literature Wales, <https://www.literaturewales.org/our-projects/national-poet-wales/> (accessed 3 May 2021).
Manchester Metropolitan University: 'Write Where We Are Now', <https://www.mmu.ac.uk/write/> (accessed 3 May 2021).
National Gallery Scotland, <https://www.nationalgalleries.org> (accessed 3 May 2021).

National Theatre: *My Country*, <https://www.nationaltheatre.org.uk/shows/my-country-uk-tour> (accessed 3 May 2021).

National Theatre Scotland, <https://www.nationaltheatrescotland.com> (accessed 3 May 2021).

Poetry Foundation, <https://www.poetryfoundation.org> (accessed 3 May 2021).

Poetry Society, <https://poetrysociety.org.uk> (accessed 3 May 2021).

Royal Collection Trust, 'Poetry for the Palace', <https://www.rct.uk/collection/themes/exhibitions/poetry-for-the-palace/the-queens-gallery-palace-of-holyroodhouse> (accessed 3 May 2021).

Scottish Poetry Library, <https://www.scottishpoetrylibrary.org.uk> (accessed 3 May 2021).

Universal Teacher, <http://universalteacher.org.uk> (accessed 3 May 2021).

Wordsworth Trust, <https://wordsworth.org.uk/> (accessed 3 May 2021).

Index

Abbey Theatre, 86, 90–1
Abbott, Diane, 187–8
Aberfan disaster, 202–3
Act of Union 1536, 16
Act of Union 1707, 16
Act of Union 1801, 16
Adams, Sam, 37
Afshan, Suna, 209
Allen, Rachel, 209–10
Allnutt, Gillian, 147
Anglophone poetry
   Irish, 7, 9–10
   Scottish, 102
   Welsh, 60
The Anglo-Welsh Review, 35, 38, 41–3, 45–6, 50–1, 53–4
AQA Literature Anthology, 177–8, 180–1, 187
AQA Syllabus, 177–81, 183
Arcade, 53
Armistice Day centenary, 138
Armitage, Simon, 123, 139, 177, 179–80
Armour, Jean, 154
Arnold, Matthew, *On the Study of Celtic Literature*, 109
artists, 115–16
Arts Council of Northern Ireland, 20, 71–2
Arts Council of the Republic of Ireland/An Chomhairle Ealaíon, 20

Arts Council of Wales, 27, 53
Arvon Poetry Competition, 49
Auerbach, Nina, *Woman and Nation*, 4
Austin, Alfred, 16
'Aye Talks', 155

Bakhtin, M. M., 54–5
BAME critics, 210
bath magg, 209
Battle of New Ross, Wexford, 74
BBC, 27–8
   Burns' 250th celebrations, 155
   Radio 1, 124
   Radio 4, 12, 171
Beat Generation, 78
Belfast City Poet Laureate, 147, 203
Belfast Maze Prison, 76
Belfast Telegraph, 20–1
Benton, Peter, 174, 176
Bernard, Jay, 139
   Surge: Side A, 139
Berry, Emily, 209
Bertram, Vicki, 3, 144, 146
Betjeman, John, 17
Bhabha, Homi, 55
Bidgood, Ruth, 38–9, 47
   'Hymn to Sant Ffraed', 43
Bielski, Alison, 47
bilingualism, 27–8, 50–65, 168
Billington, Michael, 198

Black Lives Matter, 139, 210
Blair, Tony, 123
Blake, Julie, 173, 174–5, 180, 191n
Bloodaxe, 48, 92
Boland, Eavan
   'The Achill Woman', 9
   activism, 71–2
   aesthetic sensibility, 48–9
   'Anna Liffey', 10
   authority, 7–11, 126
   'Becoming an Irish Poet', 94
   edges, 210
   Irish poetry, 77
   'Letter to a Young Woman Poet', 144
   'Margin', 210
   and Meehan, 159
   Object Lessons: The Life of the Woman and the Poet in Our Time, 5, 93
   'Our Future Will Become the Past of Other Women', 4
   'outside history', 3–7
   'Paula Meehan: Being an Irish Poet', 94
   Selected Poems, 5
   'Statue 2016', 204–5
   United Nations, 73
   woman as metaphor of Ireland, 81–2
   A Woman Without a Country, 5
   women as object of poems, 79, 106
   women's exclusion from national identity, 156
   and Wordsworth, 150–1
Bolderston, Natalie Linh, 209
Bourdieu, P., 189
Boyd, Billy, 200–1
Boyd, S. J., 105
Boyle, Danny, 'Pages of the Sea' installation, 138
Brexit, 130, 194–207
Bridges, Robert, 16
Britannia, 194–207
'British' identity, 1, 11–12, 98
Broadus, Edmund Kemper, *The Laureateship. A study of the office of poet laureate in England, with some account of the poets*, 16

Brontë, Emily, 40
Brookes University, Oxford, 144
Brown, Adrienne, 92
Browning, Robert, 127, 128
Bryant, Marsha, 127, 128
Bryce, Colette, 209
Buddhism, 73, 78–80, 82, 89, 93–4
Burnavon Writers, Cookstown, 23
Burns, Robert, 144–66, 182
   'Mary Morison', 156–7
   'To a Mouse', 154–5

Calypso Productions, 86
Cameron, David, 197, 198
Capildeo, Vahni, 209
Carcanet, 35
The Cardiff, Story, 122
Carol Ann Duffy and Simon Armitage: Working with the Literature Anthology for AQA A 2004–2006, 179–80
Carruthers, Gerard, 157
Cathleen ni Houlihan, 6
Catholicism, 79–80, 127–8
Celtic Revival, 86
Celtic Twilight, 158, 159
censorship, 186–8
The Challenges of English in the National Curriculum, 182–3
Charles II, 16
Chaucer, Geoffrey, 16
Chuilleanáin, Eiléan Ní, 9, 81
Clapp, Susannah, 198
Clarke, Ella, 92
Clarke, Gillian, **35–70**
   appointment, 1–2, 27–8
   AQA Syllabus 2004–2011 (series 4), 177–81
   authority, 12, 126
   curriculum, 174–5
   and Duffy, 121–2
   EU, 205–6
   and Plath, 7
   poetry journals, 209
   shared platforms, 29–31
   'Shore to Shore' reading tour, 196

'For Students' (website), 176–7
Wales, 208
and Wordsworth, 146–7
and Yeats, 157–8
poems:
 'Beech Buds', 36–7
 'Border', 55
 'Buzzard', 46
 'Cofiant,' 53, 56–7, 64–5
 'Cordelia's Nothing', 57
 'Dyddgu Replies to Dafydd', 62
 'Fflam', 58
 'First Words', 58
 'The Fox', 36–7, 46
 'Glas y Dorlan', 58
 'Gleision/for the four miners killed at Gleision drift mine, 15 September 2011', 61
 'The King of Britain's Daughter', 57, 65
 'Letter from a Far Country', 65, 121, 146
 'Miracle on St David's Day', 146–7
 'Mother Tongue', 28
 'A Musical Nation', 62–3
 'Neighbours', 59–60
 'Nightride', 36–7
 'Not', 58
 'Otter', 58
 'Pigeon House Wood', 60–1
 'A Pocket Dictionary', 58, 59
 'Polar', 30
 'The Presence', 210–11
 'A Recipe for Water', 58–9
 'Running Away to the Sea – 1995', 170–1
 'Sailing', 36–7
 'Taliesin. *Frank Lloyd Wright 1867–1959*,' 63
 'Translation/after translating from Welsh, particularly a novel by Kate Roberts', 59–60
 'Voice of the Tribe', 58
 'The Water Diviner', 58–9, 61
 'Whoever They Were', 121–2
poetry collections:
 Five Fields, 59–60
 Ice, 61, 63
 The King of Britain's Daughter, 6, 157–8
 Letter from a Far Country, 35, 42–4, 50, 58–9, 64, 137
 Letting in the Rumour, 53, 56
 Nine Green Gardens, 60–1, 69n
 A Recipe for Water, 58–9
 Selected Poems, 63
 Snow on the Mountain, 35
 The Sundial, 35
Clarke, Kenneth, 173–4
Clarke, Owain, 43
Clifton, Harry, 21
Clune, Jackie, 105
Coleridge, Samuel Taylor, 148
 'Frost at Midnight', 148
 Lyrical Ballads, 145
Coles, Jane, 189
Collins, Bob, 21–2
colonialism, 19–20
'colour of the mind', 103–5
Combat Poverty Agency, 91
Commane, Jane, 210
Conboy, Kate, 94
Concern for Somalia, 90
Conran, Anthony, 41, 44
Cox, Brian, 182–3
Cox, Jo, 198
Craig, Cairns, 104
Crawford, Robert, 42, 54–6, 125, 183
Creative Scotland, 25
Cresswell, Mike, 186–7
Crompton, Sarah, 198
cultural consensus, 189–90
'cultural insider', 127–8
curriculum
 'covert curriculum', 172, 177–81
 GCSE, 172–7, 177
 and the national poets, 167–93
 poetry by women, 172–7, 182–9

Curriculum for Excellence 2010–11, 173
Curtis, Tony, 39
  How Poets Work, 57
cynghanedd, 62–3

Daily Mirror, 'Poetry Corner', 138
Davies, Gloria Evans, 47
Dawe, Gerald, *Cambridge Companion to Irish Poets*, 8, 9–10
Day-Lewis, Daniel, 17
Dearing Report, 173–4
Deeny, Sir Donnell, 20
Denholm, Andrew, 184
Department of Education (DfE), 173–4
devolution
  Britannia, 201
  curriculum, 172–3, 177, 181, 183–4
  'English Poet Laureate' and, 17–20
  language duality, 51–2
  laureateship, 2, 11–12, 24
  National Poet of Wales, 27
  past and present, 117
  Scotland, 103
Dharker, Imtiaz, 196
Dhomhnaill, Nuala Ní, 9, 21
Dickey, Susannah, 209
Dickinson, Emily, 40
diversity
  Britannia, 198
  Duffy, 139
  laureateship, 12
  of poetry, 210
  in Scotland, 102, 116, 195
divided self, 6–7, 64, 75–6, 85–6, 90
domestic themes
  Clarke, 36–8, 41–4, 47–8, 72, 121, 178
  Light, 8
  Lochhead, 170
  Meehan, 6, 75
  Wordsworth, Dorothy, 149
Donovan, Katie, 90
Dorothy Wordsworth Festival of Women's Poetry, 147

doubleness of voice, 55, 128–9
Dowson, Jane, 3, 19–20, 171, 176
Doyle, Se Merry, *Alive, Alive O: A Requiem for Dublin*, 93–4
Dryden, John, 16
Dube, Janet, 45
Dublin
  Ireland Chair of Poetry, 20–3
  'Kepler 452B', 205
  Meehan, 73–5, 86–7, 89–94, 159
  Snyder, 78–80
Dublin Theatre Festival, 90
Duffy, Carol Ann, **121–43**
  'Anonymous', 128, 133
  aphorisms and authority, 133–8
  appointment, 1
  AQA Syllabus 2004–2011 (series 4), 177–81
  boundaries of nation, 211
  'Britannia', 202–3
  curriculum, 174–5, 182, 182–9
  and Dorothy Wordsworth, 147–150
  'Englishness', 11–12
  and Kay, 195
  Lyric Interventions: Feminism, Experimental Poetry, and Contemporary Discourse, 127
  'mainstream extreme', 127
  and Meehan, 91
  My Country: A Walk in Progress in the words of people across the UK and Carol Ann Duffy, 197–200
  'people's poet', 26
  and Plath, 7
  'Poet for our Times', 127
  Poet Laureate, 15–20
  press interviews, 133–8
  references to past work, 132
  Robert Burns, 154
  Scottish poetry, 100
  shared platforms, 29–31
  'Shore to Shore' reading tour, 196–7, 201
  'torturing' of poetry, 176
  and Yeats, 158

poems:
  'Anon', 128–9
  'Apostle', 129, 133
  'Auden comes through at the seance', 130–1, 137
  'Blackbird', 132
  'Clerk of Hearts', 133
  'The Creation of Adam and Eve', 129
  'CXVI', 132
  'Dark School', 132
  'Demeter', 129
  'Dorothy Wordsworth's Christmas Birthday', 148–50
  'Education for Leisure', 127, 186–8
  'The Ex-Ministers', 132, 202, 203
  'A Formal Complaint', 131–2, 202
  'Give', 158
  'Gorilla', 132, 202
  'Head of English', 176
  'How Death Comes', 128
  'Io', 132
  'Little Red-Cap', 129
  'Mrs Schofield's GCSE', 30, 188–9
  'Once', 132
  'Originally', 182
  'Oval Map Sampler', 133
  'Politics', 131
  'Prayer', 126–7
  'Psychopath', 127
  'The Rain', 132
  'Rapture', 152–3
  'Scarecrow', 133
  'September 2014', 156
  'Sincerity', 133
  'Skirtful of Stones', 132
  'Sleeping Place (What He Said)', 132
  'Standing Female Nude', 106
  'Stone Love', 132
  'Sung', 156–7
  'Swearing In', 132, 202
  'The Thames, London 2012', 19
  'The Twelve Days of Christmas', 131
  'Two Small Poems of Desire', 153
  'Vocation', 132
  'The Way My Mother Speaks', 182
  'White Cliffs', 19–20
  'Whoever She Was', 121–2
  'Words, Wide Night', 127
  'The Wound in Time', 138
poetry collections:
  Answering Back: Living poets reply to the poetry of the past, 144–6, 152, 157, 162
  The Bees, 130, 132, 188–9
  Collected Poems, 19–20
  Feminine Gospels, 132, 171–2
  Jubilee Lines, 18–19, 209
  The Laughter of Stafford Girls High, 171–2, 175
  Mean Time, 124, 125, 126–7, 132
  The Other Country, 131, 132, 202
  Rapture, 132, 158
  Ritual Lighting, 130
  Sincerity, 128–33, 202
  Standing Female Nude, 6, 132, 137, 188
  The World's Wife, 123–4, 129, 132
Dugdale, Sasha, 209
Durcan, Paul, 21
Dymoke, Sue, 175–6

Eagleton, Terry, 126
Easter Rising 1916, 74, 76, 204
Eastern Washington University, 74, 78
education *see* curriculum; poems about school, 167–72
Education (National Curriculum) (Attainment Targets and Programmes of Study in English) (England) Order 2000, 177
Education Reform Act (1988), 172–3, 188
Educational Institute of Scotland, 183–4
Edward IV, 16
Elfin, Menna, 44, 58, 65
Eliot, T. S., 145
  'Tradition and the Individual Talent', 144
Elizabeth I, 16
Elliott, Tom, 23
Elliott, Victoria, 172, 173, 184–6
English lyric tradition, 62, 151–2
'Englishness', 11–12, 17–18, 182–3

Entwistle, Alice, 50, 57, 64, 157–8
environmentalism, 78–9
Equality Act 2010, 11
Eric Gregory Awards, 209
EU, 181, 205–6
Evans, Christine, 47–8
Evaristi, Marcella, 105

Fahey, Aisling, 30
Fallen Angel Theatre Company, 86
Farage, Nigel, 198
feminism
    Anglo-American feminism, 36, 103, 162
    Boland, 9, 144
    Clarke, 37–40, 44–5
    Duffy, 122, 129–30, 145, 171–2
    Lochhead, 103–10
    Meehan, 72, 86, 94
    Woolf, 4–5
    and Wordsworth, 151
Feminist Review, 3
Fenton, James, 122–3
Fermanagh Women's Aid Group, 23
Festival of Women's Poetry for Grasmere, 147
Fhrighil, Ní, 9
Finch, Peter, 27–8
first-person speaker, 132
Flanagan, Phil, 23
Forbes, Peter, 124, 125
Forward Prize, 123, 125
Fraser, Dame Antonia, 131

Gaelic language, 7, 9–10, 81, 102–3, 114, 156
Gallery Press, 92
Gardiner, Luke, 74
Gentleman, Amelia, 199
Gilbert and Gubar, 40
    The Madwoman in the Attic, 36
Gill, Jo, 126
Ginsberg, Alan
    'Howl', 78
    'Kaddish', 80

glàs, 102, 114
Glasgow School of Art, 104
Glasgow Tron Theatre, 107–8
Gomer Press, 35
Gonda, Caroline, 124
González, Carla Rodríguez, 104
Good Friday Agreement 1998, 21, 204
Goodson, Ivor, 181, 186
Gorsedd of the Bards, 65
Gove, Michael, 173, 185–6, 198
Granta, 124, 209–10
Greenlaw, Lavinia, 209
Greer, Germaine, 7
Gregory, Lady, 86
Gregson, Ian, 122
Grenfell Tower tragedy, 202–3
    anniversary, 139
Griffiths, Steve, 38–9
Guardian
    '11 Odes to Europe', 203
    Britannia, 198
    Burns, 156
    curriculum, 188–9
    Duffy, 18, 19–20, 182
    Lochhead, 117
    Makar, 24–5
    poems by women, 12
    Women of the World (WOW) Festival, 30
    Wordsworth, Dorothy, 148
Gulbenkian, 91
Gwilym, Dafydd ap, 62–3

Hampson, Robert, 11
Hardy, Barbara, 'Women's Poetry', 37–8, 39–40
Hartmann, Erich, 17
Hay-on-Wye Literary Festival, 'Squantums', 57
Heaney, Seamus, 20–2, 48, 177–9
    Nobel Prize for Literature, 20
    'When all the others were away at Mass', 82
Heinemann, 178–80
Henri, Adrian, 64

Henry, Brian, 9
Henry I, 16
Herald, 182, 184
Higgins, Michael D., 21, 23, 30
Higgins, Sabina, 23
Hill, Greg, 46
Hoffenberg, Peter, 16
Holland, Kevin Crossley, 121
Hopkins, Gerald Manley, 63
House of Commons Knife Crime Debate, 187
Howe, Sarah, 210
Hughes, Ted, 123, 208
Humphreys, Emry, 64

I Ching, 75, 78, 152
Independent, 173–4
interlinking, 116
International Women's Day, 90–1
Ireland, female images of, 6, 81–9
Ireland Chair of Poetry, 1, 20–3, 29, 71
Ireland Professor of Poetry, 12, 21, 73, 75, 92
The Irish Daily Mail, 92
Irish Famine, 76
Irish Free State, 16
Irish Gaelic poetry, 7, 9–10; *see also* Gaelic language
Irish Independent, 22
Irish poetic tradition, 7, 10
Irish Times, 22, 81, 90, 92, 123, 158–9, 175

Jama, Amina, 209
James VI of Scotland, 16
Jamie, Kathleen, 2
Jarvis, Matthew, 53, 70n
Jenkins, Mike, 47, 50
Johnson, B. S., 'Good News for Her Mother! *probably the Last Poem I shall Write about Her Daughter*', 37
Johnson, Boris, 198
Johnston, Fergus, 89–90
Jones, Sally Roberts, 47
Joseph, Jenny, 47–8

Kapil, Bhanu, *How to Wash a Heart*, 209
Kavanagh, Patrick, 92
Kave, John, 16
Kay, Jackie
  The Adoption Papers, 126
  'Black Bottom', 126
  and Brexit, 194–7
  curriculum, 182
  'Extinction', 196
  Lochhead and, 111–12
  Makar, 26–7
  'In My Country', 128
  The New Poetry, 126
  'Threshold', 26, 194–6, 200, 205
Kerrigan, John, 55
Kicking Daffodils, 144, 146
Kinnahan, Linda, 127
Kipling, Rudyard, 'If,' 157
Kirkpatrick, Kathryn, 6, 12, 73, 89, 103, 159
knife crime, 186–8

Lampeter Writers Group, 46–7
language duality, 50–65
Larkin, Philip, 10, 48, 124, 128
laureateship, 11–12, 15–34; *see also* national poets; Poet Laureate
Leaving Certificate, 173, 175
Ledbury Emerging Critics, 210
Ledbury Poetry Critics, 209
Leeds West Academy, 188
Leonard, Tom, 180–1
  'The nine o'clock news', 180
  'Unrelated Incidents', 180
Lewis, Gwyneth, 12, 27, 44, 50, 54, 72
Lewis, Saunders, 53
Light, Alison, 'Outside History? Stevie Smith, Women Poets and the National Voice', 8–9, 10–11
Literature Forum for Scotland, 23–4, 25
Literature Wales, 157
Liverpool Beats, 78, 137
Llewellyn-Williams, Hilary, 46
  The Tree Calendar, 46

Lochhead, Liz, **100–20**
  'Anon', 128–9
  Arvon Poetry Competition, 49
  Britannia Rules, 200–2, 205
  and Burns, 153–7
  curriculum, 174–5, 176, 180–1, 182–9, 183–5, 188–9
  Dorothy Wordsworth Festival of Women's Poetry, 147
  Dracula, 109
  Dreaming Frankenstein, 6, 101, 116, 137
  Frankenstein, 109
  'fugitive colours of the day', 211
  laureateship, 1–2
  Makar, 24–7
  'Makar Songs, Occassional [sic] and Performance Pieces Mainly', 114–15
  mapping Scotland, 100–11
  Poet Laureate, 123
  revue works, 105–8
  shared platforms, 29–31
  poems:
    'In Alan Davie's Paintings', 116
    'Almost Miss Scotland', 110–11
    'Another, Later, Song for That Same Dirty Diva', 116–17
    'Bagpipe Muzak, Glasgow 1990', 108
    'In the Beginning', 116
    'Black and White Allsorts', 111–12
    'In the Black and White Era', 111–12
    'Burns', 155
    'The Complete Alternative History of the World, Part One', 116
    'Connecting Cultures: for Commonwealth Day in Westminster Abbey, 2012', 115
    'Dirty Divas', 116–17
    'In the Dreamschool', 169
    'Fat Girl's Confession', 107
    'Favourite Place', 114
    'Five Berlin Poems', 116
    'From a Mouse', 154–5
    'Gentlemen Prefer Blondes', 107
    'Grace', 113–14
    'Hell for Poets', 101
    'How to Be the Perfect Romantic Poet', 150–1
    'Kidspoem/Bairnsang', 167–9, 170, 174, 188
    'Look at Us', 107
    'Love and Grief, Elegies and Promises', 114
    'Lucy's Diary', 116
    'In the Mid-Midwinter', 30
    'Mrs Abernethy: Burns the Hero', 154
    'My Hero Robert Burns', 156
    'Notes on the Inadequacy of a Sketch at Millport Cathedral, March 1970', 105
    'Open', 114–15, 194
    'Page Three Dollies', 107
    'Phyllis Marlowe: Only Diamonds Are Forever', 106–7
    'Poem for Other Poor Fools', 101–2
    'Poets Need Not', 114
    'In Praise of Old Vinyl', 114
    'A Protestant Girlhood', 168–9
    'Random', 129
    'Rapunzstilskin', 180
    'Revelation', 101
    'Scotch Mist (The Scotsport Song)', 107
    'Something I'm Not', 102
    'Spring 2010, and at His Desk by the Window is Eddie in a Red Shirt', 115
    'Storyteller', 109
    'The Suzanne Valadon Story (Rap)', 105–6
    'Usherette Scene', 107–8
    'Vymura: The Shade Card Poem', 107
    'Way Back in the Paleolithic', 115
    'What-I'm-Not-Song', 107, 116

'Year 2K email epistle to Carol Ann
  Duffy, Sister-poet & Friend of my
  Youth', 112
poetry collections:
  Bagpipe Muzak, 108–9, 110–11,
    113, 116
  A Choosing, 100
  The Colour of Black and White,
    104–5, 111–17
  Elizabeth, 200–2
  Fugitive Colours, 104, 111–17
  Good Things, 108
  The Grimm Sisters, 109
  Islands, 100, 102, 105
  *Mary Queen of Scots Got Her Head
    Chopped Off*, 103, 109–11
  Memo for Spring, 100–2, 105
  Perfect Days, 108
  Shanghaied, 200–2
  Sugar and Spite, 105–6
  True Confessions and New Cliches,
    108, 116
London Evening Standard, 123
London Laureate, 30
Longley, Edna, 9, 94
Longley, Michael, 21
Lovett, Ann, 82–3
Lutterworth College, 186–7
lyric 'I', 37, 43, 101–2, 111–13,
  133, 169
lyricism, 153–4, 158

Maastrict Treaty 1992, 205–6
Mabinogion, 157
McAuley, Jim, 74
McConnell, Jack, 24, 25
MacCraig, Norman, 182
McCrum, Robert, 12
MacDermott, Séan, 74
McGann, Jerome, 138
McGinty, Thom, 80
McGuckian, Medbh, 'Kepler 452B,' 205
McKenzie, Alan, 184
McLeish, Henry, 25
McMillan, Dorothy, 101, 182

McMillan, Ian, 111–12
MacMonagle, Niall, 175
  Poetry Now, 175
MacNeice, Louis, 'Bagpipe Music', 108–9
Maguire, Sarah, 5, 125
Makar, 1, 17, 23–7, 153–4, 183–5,
  194–6
Markham, E. A.
  'Cool (ii)', 41
  Love Poems, 41
Markievicz, Constance, 204–5
Marks, Peter, 125
Marsack, Robyn, 23–5
Masefield, John, 16
Mathias, Roland, 35, 46
Meehan, Paula, **71–99**
  creating distance, 73–7
  curriculum, 175
  Irish Professor of Poetry, 21–3
  laureateship, 1
  'margins moving to the centre', 11
  myth in poems, 159–60
  poetry of breath, 77–81
  shared platforms, 29–31
  and Wordsworth, 151–2
  and Yeats, 158–62
  poems:
    'The Apprentice', 159
    'Autobiography', 85–6
    'On Being Taken for a Turkish
      Woman', 93
    'Berlin Diary, 1991', 92–3
    'Buddleja' of 'The Lost Children of
      the Inner City', 87
    'Chameleon', 75
    'Death of a Field', 80–1, 211
    'Dialogue', 72
    'The Exact Moment I Became a
      Poet', 169–70
    'Folktale', 92
    'Hannah, Grandmother', 30
    'Home by Starlight', 84
    'Hunger Strike', 76
    'Imaginary Bonnets with Real Bees
      in Them', 88, 137–8, 160

Meehan, Paula, (*cont.*)
   'The Island', 160
   'Liadain's Dream of Cuirtheoir', 159
   'Literacy Class, South Inner City', 81
   'The Lost Children of the Inner City', 93–4
   'Molly Malone', 94
   'Mrs Sweeney', 91
   'Odds On', 78
   'The Other Woman', 85–6
   'The Pattern', 77
   'Pillow Talk', 82, 84–9
   'Planet Water', 152
   'Return and No Blame', 75, 77
   'The Road to Agios Kirkos', 133
   'She-Who-Walks-Among-The-People', 91
   'Southside Party', 78–9
   'The Standing Army', 92
   'The Statue of the Virgin at Granard Speaks', 77–8, 81–4, 88, 94
   'Well', 91–2
   'The Wounded Child', 89–90
  poetry collections:
   Cell, 82, 86–9
   Dharmakaya, 78, 80, 93, 169–70
   Geomantic, 73, 78, 160
   Imaginary Bonnets with Real Bees in Them, 22
   The Man Who Was Marked by Winter, 76–8, 81–4, 89, 91–2
   Mrs Sweeney, 91
   Mysteries of the Home, 6, 92
   Painting Rain, 78, 80–1
   Pillow Talk, 78, 84–6, 90, 91–3, 137
   Reading the Sky, 75–8
   Return and No Blame, 72, 74–5, 78–9, 159
Midland Review, Irish Women's Writing, 77
Miles, Kathy, *Metaphors*, 46
Millett, Kate, *Sexual Politics*, 36
Molière, *Tartuffe*, 109
Moloney, Aedin, 86
Montague, John, 20–1

Moore, Christy, 92
  'Folk Tale', 92
  Graffiti Tongue, 92
Moore, Marianne, 'Poetry', 137–8
Morgan, Edwin, 17, 24–5, 27
  'Open the Doors', 24, 26, 115, 194
Morris, Kadish, 209
Morrissey, Sinéad, 29–30, 34n, 203–5
  '1801', 147
  On Balance, 204
  'The Mayfly', 204
  'The Millihelen', 204, 205
  Parallax, 147
Motion, Andrew, 12, 17, 18, 27, 122–3, 125, 176
Moules, Sue, 46
Muldoon, Paul, 17
Muses, 39–40, 132, 150, 158, 159, 171, 188
My Country: A Walk in Progress in the words of people across the UK and Carol Ann Duffy, 197–200, 202, 203, 205

Nasmyth, Alexander, 155
The Nation, 176
National Grades, 173, 182–9
national identity, 2
  Clarke, 56–8
  curriculum, 181–3, 186
  Duffy, 17
  laureateship, 24
  Scotland's masculinised, 109
  Welsh, 50–65
  women and, 3–13
National Poet of Scotland, 12
National Poet of Wales, 1–2, 12, 17, 23–4, 27–8, 58, 208
National Poetry Competition, 121
National Poetry Prize, 121
national poets
  and the national curriculum, 167–93
  shared platforms, 29–31
  see also laureateship; Poet Laureate
National Portrait Gallery, Edinburgh, 155

National Theatre, London, 197–200
National Theatre of Scotland, 'Dear Scotland' project, 155
National Trust, 19
nature, 78–84, 90–1, 150–3, 158, 161–2
New Cross Massacre 1981, 139
New Generation poets, 124–7, 139
New Music, New Dance Festival, 92
The New Poetry, 125–6
Newmann, John, 23
Newmann, Kate, 23
Nichols, Grace, 151
  'Spring', 146
Nicholson, Colin, 109
Nine Arches Press, 210
Nisbet, Robert, 42
Norris, Rufus, 197–200
North Wales *Daily Post*, 2
Northern Examination and Assessment Board (NEAB), 180
Northern Examination and Assessment Board (NEAB) Anthology, 175–6
Northern Ireland
  Boland, 9
  and Brexit, 203–5
  curriculum, 172–3, 177
  'Englishness', 19
  Ireland Chair of Poetry, 20–1
  laureateship, 16
  Meehan, 23
  Morrissey, 30–1, 34n
  My Country: A Walk in Progress in the words of people across the UK and Carol Ann Duffy, 197, 203–5
Northern Ireland Assembly, 23
Nottingham Evening Post, 187, 188

O'Brien, Sean, 124
Observer, 198
O'Driscoll, Mary, 92
Olsen, Redell, 127
Olympic Theatre, Dublin, 90
Orbach, Susie, *Fat is a Feminist Issue*, 107
Ostriker, Alicia, 6, 64, 128

'othering', 170, 180, 199
'outside history', 3–7
Owens, Philip, 59

Pan Macmillan blog, 158
Parker, Andrew, 4
Parmar, Sandeep, 210
Paterson, Don, 123, 125
  'A Private Bottling', 49
Patten, John, 173–4
Pavilion Press, 209
Peach, Linden, 63–4, 122
Pen Pinter Prize, 131
The Penguin Book of Contemporary British Poetry, 125, 178
'people's poet', 18, 26
People's Republic of China, 23
performance, 100–20
Planet: The Welsh Internationalist, 'Symposium on Gender in Poetry,' 48–9
Plath, Sylvia, 7, 38, 40, 44, 48
  'The Disquieting Muses', 40
PN Review, 209
Poet Laureate, 1–2, 15–20, 122–4, 138–9, 208; *see also* laureateship; national poets
'Poet Laureate and National Poet' event, 157
poetic sensibility, 48–9
poetic traditions, 126–9
poetry
  across boundaries, 71–99
  in conversation with other poets, 144–66
  as 'public speech', 71
  as a way of telling truth, 137–8
Poetry Aloud, 175
Poetry Birmingham Literary Journal, 209
Poetry Book Society, 49, 139
Poetry by Heart, 176
'Poetry for the Palace' exhibition 2014, 15–16, 17
Poetry Ireland, 209
poetry journals, 209

'Poetry Live!', 29
Poetry London, 209
poetry publishers, 209–10
Poetry Review, 41, 44, 53, 62–3, 124, 209
Poetry Society, 16, 121, 124–5, 138–9
Poetry Wales, 35, 36, 40–1, 50, 54, 62
   'Criticism in Wales', 37–40
   'A Garland for Dafydd ap Gwilym', 62
   poetry by women, 37–40
   'Symposium: Is There a Women's Poetry?', 47–8
Poole, Richard, 54
'postmodern provinicials', 122–3
Project Arts Centre, Dublin, 92
Project@the Mint, 91
Pugh, Sheenagh, 47

Queen's Diamond Jubilee, 18–19, 209
Queen's Gold Medal for Poetry, 117
Queen's University Belfast, 20, 22–3
Quilligan, Fiona, 89–90
Quinn, Justin, 'Eavan Boland,' 8, 9–11

radio, 43
   Radio 1, 124
   Radio 4, 12, 171
Raine, Craig, 122–3
Randolph, Jody Allen, 72, 78, 81
rap, 105–8, 116
Raw, Stephen, 188
Red Hot Shoes, 107–8
Redmond, Siobhan, 113
Rees-Jones, Deryn, 209
Reizbaum, Marilyn, 104, 109
Republic of Ireland
   and Brexit, 204–5
   and Empire, 74
RHA Gallagher Gallery, 89–90
Rhys, Jean, *Good Morning, Midnight*, 42
Rich, Adrienne, 40
   'When We Dead Awaken: Writing as Revision', 162
Robathan, Andrew, 186–7
Robert Burns Birthplace Museum, Alloway, Ayrshire, 153

Roberts, Lynette, as 'war poet', 41–2, 44
Roberts, Sally, 'A Waste of Heroes', 43
Robins, Elizabeth, *Woman's Secret*, 5
Robinson, Mary, 90–3
Romantic poets, 127, 137, 150–2, 158, 159
Rona-Tas, Akos, 195
Rosen, Michael, 187
Rough Magic, 91
Rowland, Anthony, 153
Rowling, J. K., 197
Royal Family, 18–19
Royal Incorporation of Architects in Scotland, 113–14
Royal Irish Academy, 73
Royal Lyceum Theatre, Edinburgh, 109, 200–2
RP (Received Pronunciation), 180–1
RTE, 'A Poem for Ireland', 82
RTE1, *Alive, Alive O: A Requiem for Dublin*, 93–4
Rubato Ballet, 89–90
Rubicon Galley, Dublin, 'Balance and Imbalance', 89
Rumens, Carol, 58, 132
Russell, Michael, 183–4, 185

Sabah, Naush, 209
Salmond, Alex, 24, 25
Sampson, Fiona, 126–7, 128
Samuel Beckett Centre, 92
San Francisco Six Gallery, 78
Scannell, Vernon, 121
Schofield, Pat, 186–7
school, poems about, 167–72
Scotland
   devolution, 103
   diversity in, 102, 116, 195
   likened to woman, 109–10
   masculinised national identity, 109
   as a place of work, 103
Scotland Act 1978, 103
Scots language, 153–6; *see also* Gaelic language

Scots Makar *see* Makar
Scottish Conservatives, 183–4
Scottish culture, 184–5
Scottish independence, 183–4
  referendum, 130, 155–6, 184–5
  'Yes' campaign, 155
Scottish National Party (SNP), 103, 182–9
Scottish Parliament, 114–15, 194
Scottish Poetry Library, 23–4, 25, 129, 156, 176, 182
  'Living Voices' project, 26
Scottish Qualifications Authority (SQA), 176, 182–9
Scottish Review of Books, 145
Scottish Secondary Teachers Association, 184
Scottish Studies, 184–5
Scottish Studies Working Group, 27, 182, 183
Scottish Whisky Industry, 27
Scottishness, 103–4, 153–4
Scullion, Adrienne, 108
Seamus Heaney and Gillian Clarke: Working with the Literature Anthology for AQA A 2004–2006, 178–9
Severin, Laura, 105
Sexton, Anne, 38
sexuality, 123–4
Shakespeare, William, 128, 132, 188
  All's Well That Ends Well, 132
  King Lear, 188
shape-changing, 88–9, 132
Shuttle, Penelope, 49
sincerity, 129–33
Smart, Christopher, 'Jubilato Agno', 80
Smith, Jordan, 80
Smith, Liz, 183, 185
Smith, Stan, 125, 126
Smith, Stevie, 10
Snyder, Gary, 73, 77–81, 83, 89, 161
  'The Berry Feast', 78
  Native American traditions, 85
  Regarding Wave, 78
  Turtle Island, 79

'What You Should Know to Be a Poet', 78, 161
'Who owns the land?', 79
'the space between', 56–7
Spenser, Edmund, *The Faerie Queene*, 16
Der Spiegel, 188
Sprackland, Martha, 209
Stephens, Meic, 38, 62
Stevenson, Anne, 44, 49, 63
Strauss, Peter, 187
Sturgeon, Nicola, 194
'suburbia', 9–11
Sunday Times, 124
Swainson, Bill, 124–5

T. S. Eliot Prize, 209
The Táin, 85–6
Taliesin, 63
Ted Hughes Award for New Work in Poetry, 138–9
Tennyson, Alfred Lord, 16
TES, 186–7
Thatcher government, 131–2, 181
Thomas, Gwyn, 27, 58
Thorpe, Adam, 126
Thurston, Michael, 56, 63–4
Timbs, John, *The Mirror of Literature, Amusement and Instruction*, 16
The Times, 1
Times Literary Supplement, 93
'torturing' of poetry, 176–7
translation, 59–61
  glas, 60–1, 69n
Traverse Theatre, Edinburgh, 105, 109
Trinity College Dublin, 20, 23, 74
Tripp, John, 38–9
Trump, Donald, 130, 132, 198, 202

UK Poet Laureate, 12
Ulster Cycle, 85
Union of the Crown 1603, 16
University College Dublin, 20, 23, 74

Vallance, E., 172
Vernon, J. J., 92

Villar-Argáiz, Pilar, 72, 160
Viner, Katherine, 122–3

Wales
　daffodils, 146–7
　voice of the tribe, 50–65
Wall Street Journal, 16–17
war poetry, 41–4
Ward, J. P., 53
Warner, Marina, 5
Warner, Val, 47
Watt, Roseanne, 209
Welsh Academi, 27–8, 58
Welsh language, 50–65
Welsh national identity, 50–65
Western Mail, 28
Whelan, Mariah, 209
Winterson, Jeanette, 123, 147
Woman's Hour, 12
women and nation, 3–7
women in poetry, 5–6, 37–8, 79, 101–102, 106
　female images of Ireland, 6, 81–2
　Scotland likened to, 109–10
Women of the World (WOW) Festival, 29–31, 34n
Women's Aid, 90–1
'women's poetry'
　in the 1980s, 44–50
　aesthetics over politics, 44–5
　authority, 7–13
　national poets, 35–70
　women's suffrage, 3–4, 5
Woolf, Virginia, 3–7, 4–5
Wordsworth, Dorothy, 147–50
Wordsworth, William, 144–66
　'The Daffodils', 146–7, 153
　Lyrical Ballads, 145, 149
　'To My Sister', 150–1
　'Nature', 152
　The Prelude, 149, 152
　'Tintern Abbey', 152
　'Westminster Bridge', 149
The Wordsworth Trust, 147
Writers in Prison Foundation, 86
Writers Union of Wales, 45–6

Y Genhinen, 51–2
Yeats, W. B., 144–66
　2015 celebrations, 30–1
　'Among School Children', 159
　Autobiographies, 161
　Cathleen ni Houlihan, 6
　Celtic Revival, 86
　class politics, 159–60
　'Easter 1916', 158–9
　'The Lake Isle of Innisfree', 160
　'The Song of Wandering Aengus', 158
Yeats Festival, 157
Yeoman, Iain, 173
Yun, Jihyun, 171

EU representative:
Easy Access System Europe
Mustamäe tee 50, 10621 Tallinn, Estonia
Gpsr.requests@easproject.com

www.ingramcontent.com/pod-product-compliance
Lightning Source LLC
Chambersburg PA
CBHW070345240426
43671CB00013BA/2405